After the Asian Crises

After the Asian Crises

Perspectives on Global Politics and Economics

Edited by

Maria Weber
Affiliated Professor of International Relations and Comparative Politics
Bocconi University
Milan, Italy

Foreword by Franco Bruni

in association with
ISTITUTO PER GLI STUDI DI
POLITICA INTERNAZIONALE

First published in Great Britain 2000 by
MACMILLAN PRESS LTD
Houndmills, Basingstoke, Hampshire RG21 6XS and London
Companies and representatives throughout the world

A catalogue record for this book is available from the British Library.

ISBN 0–333–77762–X

First published in the United States of America 2000 by
ST. MARTIN'S PRESS, INC.,
Scholarly and Reference Division,
175 Fifth Avenue, New York, N.Y. 10010

ISBN 0–312–23046–X

Library of Congress Cataloging-in-Publication Data
After the Asian crises : perspectives on global politics and economics / edited by
Maria Weber.
p. cm.
Includes bibliographical references and index.
ISBN 0–312–23046–X
1. Asia—Politics and government—1945– 2. Financial crises—Asia.
I. Weber, Maria, 1951–

DS35.2 A37   1999
327.5—dc21
99–049751

10   9   8   7   6   5   4   3   2   1
09 08 07 06 05 04 03 02 01 00

Printed and bound in Great Britain by
Antony Rowe Ltd, Chippenham, Wiltshire

Contents

List of Tables   vii

List of Figures   viii

Foreword   ix

List of Abbreviations   xi

Notes on the Contributors   xiii

Editor's Introduction   xvi

Part I: Area Studies   1

1   Great China: Towards the Year 2000
    Renzo Cavalieri and Maria Weber   3

2   The Crisis in Northeast Asia: the Cases of Japan and
    South Korea
    Corrado Molteni   28

3   Southeast Asia Facing Economic, Political and Social Crisis
    Benedetta Trivellato   50

4   Central Asia: The Illusion of a World Order
    Valeria Fiorani Piacentini and Gianluca Pastori   70

5   At the Foot of the Himalayas: India from the 'Hindu
    Equilibrium' to an Asian Regional Power?
    Paolo Panico and Gianni Vaggi   96

Part II: International Issues   117

6   Facing the Environmental Problems in Changing Asia
    Maria Julia Trombetta   119

7   Security Implications of the Asian Crises
    Marta Dassù and Stefano Silvestri   139

8   Coping with the Dragon: Western Relations with China
    Filippo Andreatta   158

9   The Wobbly Triangle: Europe, Asia and the US after the
     Asian Crisis
     Vinod K. Aggarwal   173

10 Conclusions
     A   The Economics of the Asian Crises: Roles and Myths
     Fabrizio Galimberti   199
     B   After the Asian Crises: Open Issues
     Maria Weber   206

Index   211

List of Tables

1.1 China's economic indicators   4
2.1 Classification of loans of Japan's 17 major banks   31
2.2 Comparative data of the two nationalized banks   34
3.1 SEA countries: real GDP growth   67
3.2 Indonesia: economic indicators   67
3.3 Thailand: economic indicators   67
3.4 Malaysia: economic indicators   68
4.1 Central Asia Republics' GDP   83
4.2 Russia's share of Central Asian trade   85
4.3 Central Asia Republics' net FDI as a percentage of GDP   87
4.4 China's share of trade with Katakhstan and Kyrgyzstan   89
5.1 The three big countries of South Asia   97
5.2 The largest Indian states: the main social and economic indicators   103
9.1 Exports patterns pre- and post-Asian crisis   185
9.2 Gross private long-term debt flows to developing Asia   186
9.3 Post-Asian crisis institutional trends in trade and finance   188

List of Figures

1.1 Scenarios for China 2020   22
9.1 The institutional bargaining problem   174
9.2 Country exports by region   177
9.3 The old trading order   183
9.4 Which trading order?   187

Foreword

This book is the result of a project organized by Milan's Institute for International Political Studies (ISPI). ISPI's research activities are framed into sections corresponding to political and economic regions of the global world. Asia occupies a peculiarly important place in this framework. This research has been preceded and will be followed by other projects, monitoring the developments of an area that we deem strategically crucial for our understanding of international relations. Each of ISPI's project is under the responsibility of a co-ordinator and it involves a network of contributors located in Italy and abroad, assisted by a group of young research fellows at the Institute. Maria Weber has been responsible for the Asia project this year: we owe her our deep thanks for a rich and timely work.

International political studies at ISPI are characterized by a special emphasis on economic issues. We look at the evolving pattern of international relations with an interdisciplinary approach and a strong attention to their implications for business decisions and economic policies. From this point of view the discussion of Asia's crises offers a rare opportunity to see political and strategic factors interacting with economic problems. I have also been impressed by how naturally the analysis of what looked like a short-term, speculative, financial crisis, developed into a study of long-term structural features and of the subtleties of polity in a highly diversified region. In fact, it seems to me instructive that recent and current events in Asia challenge superficial views of globalization in two respects. First, they prove how complex and rapidly changing is the relationship between market developments and the underlying political, social, institutional and cultural determinants of international relations. It is this evolving relationship that can suddenly turn miracles into disasters. Second, they show how precarious is the road that claims to quickly lead to 'globalism', that is to a rather homogeneous and standardized world, starting from a 'clash of civilizations'. From the latter perspective the interest of the research collected in this book is that it tries to encompass different cases such as those of Central Asia, India, China, the Southeast, Japan, and to conduct a parallel analysis of numerous crises.

Some of the contributions to this research dare to trace possible scenarios for the near and longer term future of economic and political systems of Asia, and of its relations with Europe and America. Obviously, 'pessimist' as well as 'optimist' scenarios are described. From a European point of view I strongly hope that optimist scenarios will come true, in the shortest possible time. But I also think that a reformed and recovered Asia will issue a new strong challenge to the European political, social and economic model. Asia's accelerated process of growth and global integration has been for several years a mixed blessing for the West. If at least part of Asia succeeds in discovering a more solid and reliable road to economic growth and international integration, we should be prepared to enjoy the benefits of its energetic, co-operative contribution to global progress. But we should also get ready and be flexible enough to make the difficult adjustments required by the new ambitions of a competitor that would have gained valuable experience by overcoming complex and acute crises.

Franco Bruni
Director, Scientific Committee, ISPI

List of Abbreviations

ADB	Asian Development Bank
APEC	Asia-Pacific Economic Cooperation
ARF	ASEAN Regional Forum
ASEAN	Association of South East Asian Nations
ASEM	Asia Europe Meeting
ASOEN	ASEAN Senior Officials on the Environment
ASEP	ASEAN Environment Programme
BJP	(Hindu Nationalist) Bharatiya Janata Party (India)
BL	Basic Law (Hong Kong SAR)
BPA	Bilateral Payment Arrangement
CA	Central Asia
CCP	Chinese Communist Party
CIS	Commonwealth of Independent States
CTE	Committee on Trade and Environment
EA	East Asia
EFTA	European Free Trade Area
EIA	Environmental Impact Assessment
EMS	Environmental Management Standard
EU	European Union
FDI	Foreign Direct Investment
GATT	General Agreement on Tariffs and Trade
GDP	Gross Domestic Product
GEF	Global Environmental Facility
GMD	Guomindang
HKMA	Hong Kong Monetary Authority
IDB	Inter-American Development Bank
IMF	International Monetary Fund
ISO	International Organization for Standardization
LAFTA	Latin American Free Trade Area
LDP	Liberal Democratic Party (Japan)
Legco	Legislative Council (Hong Kong)
MEA	Multilateral Environmental Agreement
MITI	Ministry of International Trade and Industry (Japan)
NAFTA	North American Free Trade Area
NATO	North Atlantic Treaty Organization
NEA	North East Asia

NGO   Non-Governmental Organization
NPC   National People's Congress (China)
NTBs   Non-tariff Barriers
ODA   Official Development Assistance
OPEC   Organization of Petroleum Exporting Countries
OSCE   Organization for Security and Cooperation in Europe
PDP   Progressive-Democratic Party (Taiwan)
PRC   People's Republic of China
RMB   renminbi
SA   South Asia
SAARC   South Asian Association for Regional Cooperation
SAPTA   South Asia Preferential Trading Agreement
SAR   Special Administrative Region (Hong Kong)
SEA   South East Asia
SEPA   State Environmental Protection Administration
SEZ   Special Economic Zones
SOE   State Owned Enterprises
SU   Soviet Union
TABD   Transatlantic Business Dialogue
TAFTA   Transatlantic Free Trade Agreement
TDP   Telugu Desam Party
TEP   Transatlantic Economic Partnership
TFAP   Trade Facilitation Action Plan
TVE   Township and Village Enterprises
UN   United Nations
UNCED   UN Conference on Environment and Development
UNDP   UN Development Programme
UNEP   UN Environment Programme
UNIDO   UN Industrial Development Organization
USSR   Union of Soviet Socialist Republics
VERs   Voluntary Export Restraints
WTO   World Trade Organization

Notes on the Contributors

Vinod K. Aggarwal is Professor of Political Science, affiliated Professor at the Haas School of Business, and Director of the Berkeley APEC Study Center at the University of California at Berkeley. He is also editor-in-chief of the journal *Business and Politics*.

Filippo Andreatta teaches Advanced Theory of International Relations at the Faculty of Political Science of the University of Bologna at Forli.

Franco Bruni directs the Scientific Committee of ISPI and is a member of its Executive Board. He is Director of the Department of Economics of Bocconi University, President of the Société Universitaire Européenne de Recherches Financières and member of the European Shadow Financial Regulatory Committee.

Renzo Cavalieri is Assistant Professor of Comparative Law in the University of Pavia and counsel of the law firm Pavia & Ansaldo. His research focuses mainly on the developments of Chinese and South-East Asian political and legal systems.

Marta Dassù is the Director of the Centre for International Political Studies (CeSPI). She is the editor of *Pax Pacifica? Il futuro della sicurezza asiatica e le nuove responsabilità dell'Europa* (The future of Asian security. Europe's new responsibilities, 1996), and of the forthcoming book *La Cina e la crisi asiatica* (China and the Asian Crisis, 1999).

Fabrizio Galimberti is chief economic writer for *IL SOLE-24 ORE*. Formerly at the OECD Department of Economics in Paris, economic advisor to the minister of the Treasury in Rome, and chief economist at Fiat, he is author of numerous books, the most recent (with Luca Paolazzi and Claudia Galimberti): *Il volo del calabrone: a brief history of the Italian economy in the 20ᵗʰ century*.

Corrado Molteni is associate Professor of Japanese studies at the State University of Milano and affiliated Professor of Comparative Economic

Systems at Bocconi University, he gained a Ph.D in Social Studies from Hitotsubashi University in Japan.

Paolo Panico teaches economics of the firm at the University of Bergamo, Italy, comparative economics (post-graduate programme) at Bocconi University, Milan, and he co-operates with the Institute of Social and Economic Studies on South East Asia (ISESAO) of the same University.

Gianluca Pastori is working on his Ph.D at Cagliari University, and collaborates with the Department of Political Science of the Catholic University of Milan. He drafted, in 1998, *L'embargo e le altre misure economiche come mezzo di gestione e soluzione delle crisi. Riflessioni e considerazioni*, a research paper on behalf of the Military Centre for Strategic Studies (*Ce.Mi.S.S.*), Rome.

Valeria Fiorani Piacentini is Professor of History and Institution of the Muslim Countries at the Catholic University of Milan. Her publications include: *Il pensiero militare nel mondo musulmano* (Military thought in the Muslim World), 1996, and *La disintegrazione dell'impero sovietico: Problemi di sicurezza regionale e collettiva in Asia Centale* (The Disintegration of the Soviet Empire: Problems of Regional and Collective Security in Central Asia), 1995, and numerous essays on Central Asian history, and political and strategic issues, published both in Italy and on abroad.

Stefano Silvestri is the Vice President of the Istituto Affari Internazionali and international editorialist of the *IL SOLE-24-ORE*. He has written extensively on international and European security issues.

Benedetta Trivellato, graduate in Economics at Bocconi University, is researcher on East Asia at ISPI. Her research interests include international trade, regional integration, international economics and security. She has been awarded recently an ASEAN-EU Research Grant by the Consortium of the European Studies Program to analyze the impact of the Asian crisis on regional co-operation in Southeast Asia.

Maria Julia Trombetta graduated in 'Discipline Economiche e Sociali' from Bocconi University and continued her research on environmental issues and international relations at ISPI. Her interests include international environmental politics, environmental security and regime theory.

Gianni Vaggi is Professor of History of Political Economy at the University of Pavia. He is the Director of the Centre for the Co-operation with Developing Countries of the University of Pavia. His previous publications are *From the debt crisis to sustainable development* in 1993 and *The economics of Francois Quesnay* in 1987.

Maria Weber is affiliated Professor of International Relations and Comparative Politics at Bocconi University in Milan. She teaches comparative economics (post-graduate programme) at Bocconi University and comparative economics at Free University of Castellanza (LIUC). She is research leader at the Institute of East Asian Studies, Bocconi University and she is the co-ordinator of the research on Asia at ISPI. She has written extensively on China and Asia. Her most recent book *Vele verso la Cina* (Sails toward China, 1996) won the Booz-Allen & Hamilton – Financial Times Awards, 1996.

Editor's Introduction

Asia is a vast and multiform geographical entity where different civilizations meet and often clash – Western, Confucian, Japanese, Islamic and Induist[1]. This already complex scenario has been aggravated since the summer of 1997 by a financial crisis that has brought to light all the hidden problems of the so-called 'Asian development model'[2]. In particular, the crisis highlights some gaps in the role Asian governments have faced in the management of the economic miracle. It also portends important changes for relations among other powers in the global system, both from a political and economic standpoint.

The Asian crisis began in Thailand, drawing in Malaysia, the Philippines and Indonesia, and then Singapore and Hong Kong. The crisis has also caused an economic breakdown in South Korea. Japan, although able to cope with financial turmoil because of vast reserves, has been obliged to start structural reforms to adjust its economic management model. China, which has so far remained relatively undamaged, now faces major repercussions on its investment and trade flows. The East Asian region is entering a new phase that will lead to an experiment to cope with an overproduction crisis and stagnant markets. South Asia, on the other hand, which remained immune from the Asian contagion thanks to the relative isolation of the Indian and Pakistani economies, is experiencing high levels of tension because of the nuclear tests that made the world fear a nuclear war. Central Asia, still more or less closely linked to the area of the rouble, even after the dissolution of the Soviet Union and the declaration of independence of the former Soviet Republics in 1991, is facing serious challenges depending more on the crisis of the Russian rouble, rather than on the East Asian contagion.

The relentless process of globalization that characterizes the world economy makes national economies increasingly interdependent. The chain effects of the Asian crisis are not confined only to a regional economic context. Besides leading to shifting competitive positions in a number of countries, the Asian crises seem to be strong enough to put into question geopolitical and strategic equilibria that formed after the end of the cold war. In its recent history, Asia has not produced security strategies of its own, having been dominated by colonial powers, and then by the juxtaposition of the superpowers. It is difficult to predict medium-term scenarios for the evolution of Asia with any certainty,[3] as the end of the bipolar system has changed the global geopolitical equilibria and created a particularly fluid and dynamic situation in Asia as well. Some alternative analytical perspectives can be considered. The theories of the 'return to the future' (based on the so-called 'realistic approach') underline how the end of the cold war could restart conflicts which had been previously in hibernation, creating a real 'security dilemma'.

The analysis in the volume is divided into two parts. The first portion includes area studies of the main Asian countries during the crisis, beginning with China, Japan and Southeast Asia, followed by South Asia and Central Asia. The second part focuses on international variables, including environmental, political and regional issues.

In the first chapter, Maria Weber and Renzo Cavalieri analyze possible scenarios for the development of a Greater China, questioning whether the development of 'Chinese regional hegemony' is possible through the progressive integration of China, Hong Kong and Taiwan. They first discuss the risks China faces from the Asian financial contagion and show how the crisis has left the country largely unaffected. In real terms, the economy has fared well, and the predicted official outlook for 1998 is good: 7.8 per cent GDP growth, positive growth of industrial production. Moreover, at the time of writing, the *renminbi* has maintained its value. Nevertheless, China has many of the same structural problems as South Korea, Thailand, and Indonesia: bank-dominated financial systems, weak central bank regulation, poor supervision of commercial banks, excessive lending and a large build-up of non-performing loans. The analysis of Zhu Rongji's Reform Program describes the reform's main steps (state owned enterprizes and banking system reforms, as well as government streamlining) and the problems faced by the Chinese government in implementing them. The second part of the chapter examines the effects of the gradual weakening of central power in China at three different territorial levels: in the ordinary provinces, in the large western autonomous regions (Xinjiang and Tibet), and in the special administrative regions (Hong Kong and Macao). The authors present four possible scenarios for the future of China. As for now, optimistic scenarios are more likely to be achieved, but the outcome of the current situation will strongly depend on possible changes in the political and economic equilibria of the region.

In Chapter Two, Corrado Molteni analyzes the crisis in Northeast Asia. Japan and South Korea – the powerful economic engines that used to push and pull the Asian economies – have been severely hit by the crisis affecting the region. Growth rates have fallen, the basis of their financial systems have been shaken and well-established economic institutions like the Japanese keiretsu and the Korean chaebols have to restructure, downsize and change time-honoured customs and practices. The author highlights some of the issues raised by the crisis and the future prospects of both economies, focusing particularly on Japan as the main economy and market of the region, but also the socio-economic model that has inspired many of the reforms and the policies of Asian countries. Japan is in the midst of a recession despite extremely low interest rates, a supplementary budget for additional public works and a special income tax reduction. Concerning the economic policy agenda, Molteni points out the limited effects of monetary and fiscal measures, calling for a faster and more aggressive restructuring of the financial system. On the issue of structural reforms, Molteni concludes that once again a pragmatic approach will prevail. Reforms are and will be introduced to reduce the government's intervention in the marketplace and, at the same time, develop the capital and labour markets. Even 'sacred' institutions such as the lifetime employment system and cross-shareholdings are gradually but surely changing. However, Japan is and will develop its own solutions, retaining some of its distinctive features that are the real source of its strength and dynamism. With respect to the future role in the international arena, the government and the majority of Japanese continue to support the strategic alliance with the US. However, dissatisfaction with American policies is also growing and the country leadership might opt for a more assertive role as a leader in Asia. In such a case, it will be at the helm of a group of Asian nations that will not necessarily include China. Its attempts to develop particularly strong ties with ASEAN provide a clear indication of what are its strategic priorities and goals in the region. On the other hand, it might try to strengthen its ties with the EU in its attempt to reduce dependence on the US.

Chapter Three, by Benedetta Trivellato, highlights the outbreak, the evolution and major implications of the crisis in Southeast Asia. The first part summarizes the main steps through which the crisis broke out and developed in the years 1997–98. The second part of her chapter analyzes the economic and political effects of this evolution, starting from the countries that have been most damaged: Indonesia, Thailand and Malaysia. The former two countries have been forced to turn to the IMF for financial support, while Malaysia has introduced restrictive policy measures that have contributed to leading the economy into recession. Yet the actual political and economic situation remains very different in the three countries. From an economic perspective, Indonesia and

Thailand are suffering the most, while Malaysia is enjoying a breathing space provided by currency controls imposed in September 1998. From the point of view of political and social stability, Indonesia and Malaysia present the most worrying threats. Singapore and the Philippines, very different from each other both economically and politically, enjoy the feature of having been relatively less affected by the crisis, but they nonetheless are feeling its impact on slowing investment flows and financial business. Decreasing trade and investment flows have hit also Vietnam, Laos, Cambodia and Myanmar, which is particularly damaging, given these countries' reliance on foreign capital for economic development. The last part of the chapter evaluates the role played by the most important regional association, ASEAN, in dealing with the consequences of the economic and political crises, and efforts to organize an effective regional and co-operative response. The lack of such a response raises a series of questions relating to the effectiveness of some of ASEAN's basic principles as well as the association's ability to overcome the challenges posed by the Asian crisis.

Chapter Four, written by Valeria Piacentini Fiorani and Gianluca Pastori on Central Asia, give us an analytical description of the main actors of the region, identifying two main groups. The first group is composed of the countries which are commonly named as Central Asia (Kazakistan, Uzbekstan, Tagikstan, Turkmenistan, Kyrgyzstan) and which are products of the Soviet Union disintegration. These states are characterized by a series of common problems and have a special relationship with Russia. The second group is composed of countries like Russia, Afghanistan and Iran, which generally share borders with one or more countries of the former group, and interact with them in a manner that determines the framework for the entire regional context. The authors highlight the fact that Central Asian countries' foreign policies are often ambiguous, due to their needs to find elsewhere the support that was previously given them by Moscow. Economic ties with Russia and the West are then described, pointing out that things have not changed so much since the fall of the Soviet Union. FDI's role in the region is also analyzed: FDI has contributed to the region's development, but deep differences remain among countries. The regional co-operation issue is considered at the end of the chapter: the likelihood for Central Asian countries to play an active role in Asia is very low, leaving Russia with the leading position.

In Chapter Five on South Asia, Paolo Panico and Gianni Vaggi explore some of the social and economic features of the main South Asian economies: India, Bangladesh and Pakistan. Economic growth is lower than in the rest of Asia and even if investments are not particularly low with regard to other developing countries, their economies are still relatively closed to foreign trade. Since 1989 the economies of South Asia have suffered from collapse of the Soviet Union and the crisis of Eastern European economies with which they had considerable trade relations. India is by far the biggest country in South Asia and the only one which can possibly lead a process of regional economic integration. Indian GDP growth rate is estimated to be around 5 per cent, but India needs no less than 7 per cent to reduce its share of world poverty, which is now 25 per cent. As overcapacity is one of the main reasons for the economy's slowdown, significant private investment is unlikely to be forthcoming. This is mainly due to a lack of appropriate infrastructure, which in turn prevents private investment activity. Uncertainties in economic policies, coupled with recent nuclear tests, led to a downgrading of India's sovereignty rating, causing an increase in the cost of external borrowing and further restrictions in the access of Indian firms to foreign capital. The chapter also considers the role of India within regional co-operation frameworks. The main regional institution, the SAARC, cannot be seen as a significant regional player. Controversies with Pakistan, Bangladesh and Sri Lanka hinder deeper economic co-operation. Nevertheless, as India remains the core of the region's political scene, its role has to be re-defined in the post-cold war era: India is already getting closer to ASEAN's interests, without ignoring that the US and the EU remain its main trading partners and investors.

The second part of the volume opens with an analysis of environmental issues. Chapter Six, by Maria Julia Trombetta, highlights the role of ecological issues in geopolitical and geoeconomic equilibria. A first group of problems relates to security issues: even if environmental issues cannot be directly taken into account as the main cause for conflicts, they can worsen interstate relationships due to their impact on the competition for resources, flows of refugees, diminishing growth rates and political instability. A second group of problems concerns the connections between international environmental policies and the globalization of the economy: should we expect a harmonization of standards or environmental dumping? The author describes the current situation in Asia, with specific reference to each region. Economic and security effects of the situation are then analyzed – in particular the influence of environmental problems on foreign policies and on the international position of different countries.

In Chapter Seven, Marta Dassù and Stefano Silvestri describe the main security issues in Asia before the outbreak of the crisis: Russia's decline and the rise of Central Asia, China's emerging power, the reunification of the two Koreas, the limits of Japanese power, and growing tensions in the Indian sub-continent. International relations within the area are also considered – in particular the role of Asian regionalism and changing US strategy in Asia. The US position is then considered in the context of the 'imperfect Asian triangle', which also comprises China and Japan. Possible scenarios for the future are presented. The likelihood of a continent-wide war is low, while local conflicts due to social and political tensions caused by the crisis are more likely. It is particularly difficult in this context to build a multilateral security system because of the weaknesses of local regional institutions. The only conclusion to be drawn is that the situation remains unstable and threatening.

Chapter Eight, by Filippo Andreatta, compares the East Asian subsystem with Europe. In Europe, systemic stability is unprecedently high, while high volatility still persists in the East Asian region. Europe today resembles a unipolar configuration, compromised within a single coalition rather than a set of competing blocs of allied countries. By contrast, the system in Asia is more genuinely multipolar as alignments between the great powers in the region are quite fluid and flexible. In the second section of this chapter, a closer look at the Western (especially US) relations with China as the future major power in the region puts today's issues into perspective. Relations with the West are analyzed by means of a four-stage model, with special attention to the post-Tienanmen Square massacre's period. Problems related to China's access to the WTO and to political tensions with Taiwan are also considered. Andreatta proposes three possible scenarios, 'democratic', 'liberal' and 'realist', which cover the range of opinions on the future role of China, and then goes on to assess their strengths and weaknesses, as well as their potential political implications.

In Chapter Nine Vinod K. Aggarwal examines the changing strategic relationship among Europe, Asia and the US, with a focus on institutional forms of co-operation in the economic arena. He begins with an analysis linking governance structures and economic interactions, the driving factors that account for institutional development and change, and consideration of how institutions might be reconciled. In the second section, he discusses the three major trends in organizing the global economy – globalism, regionalism and sectoralism – and provides a stylized empirical discussion of how these regions' economic relationships and institutional arrangements have varied prior to the Asian crisis. The third section of his chapter then turns to an examination of scenarios for possible new economic and institutional patterns after the Asian crisis. With respect to trade trends, the author shows how falling exports to Asia and a rise in imports from this region will pose a critical challenge for the liberal trading system. From an institutional perspective, he demonstrates the strong negative effects and spillovers from the crisis that have undermined transregional arrangements such as APEC and ASEM. Ironically, as he notes, the need to cope with financial problems enhances the position of the WTO; yet at the same time trade problems raise the spectre of unilateral trade measures. He concludes by arguing that additional efforts are needed to increase collaboration between the Bretton Woods institutions and the World Trade Organization.

I would like to thank my friends and colleagues, Vinod Aggarwal, Renzo Cavalieri, Corrado Molteni and Benedetta Trivellato, for their comments and assistance. Thanks also go to Franco Bruni, Director of ISPI Scientific Committee, who strongly supported me in this research project.

Notes

1. S.P. Huntington, *The Clash of Civilizations and the Remaking of World Order*, (New York: Simon and Shuster, 1996).
2. World Bank, *The East Asian Miracle*, (Oxford University Press, 1993).
3. The boundaries themselves of the Asian region are definable with difficulty because they go past the national ones: for example, a huge part of a European country such as Russia extends into Asia even though it is not an Asian country in itself.

Part I
Area Studies

1
Great China: Towards the Year 2000

*Renzo Cavalieri and Maria Weber**

1.1 The Chinese economic miracle

Chinese economic growth is characterized by a complex morphology: on the one hand the average yearly growth rate is extremely high (an average of 9 per cent over the last ten years) while, on the other hand, there are wide regional imbalances and the government has been unable to tackle the reform of the state sector head on. The benefits of economic growth can clearly be seen in all the macroeconomic data: in 1978, 270 million Chinese lived below the poverty line; today the number of people living below this line has fallen sharply to about 60 million. The lower levels of poverty have had an immediate effect on life expectancy, which rose from 64 years of age in 1975 to 69 years in 1995. Growth forecasts were high until the advent of the Asian crisis. Today many wonder what repercussions the Asian financial crisis will have.

Officially, the Asian crisis has only marginally affected China. The *renminbi* (RMB) is not convertible for capital account transactions. Chinese savers concerned about the viability of China's financial institutions cannot legally convert their RMB deposits and purchase foreign currency-denominated financial assets. The absence of capital account convertibility also means that speculators have no way of acting on their suspicion that the RMB is overvalued and likely to depreciate. Foreign investment flows continued to grow in 1997, only falling in 1998. At least one third of foreign investment flows originate from Hong Kong, Taiwan, Japan, Korea and the ASEAN countries – and these are bound to diminish in the near future. As far as the trade flows are concerned, since the mid-nineties China has recorded hitherto unknown surpluses – US$ 16.7 billion in 1995, US$ 12.3 in 1996 and US$ 40.3 billion in 1997.

Table 1.1   China's economic indicators (% real change, unless otherwise indicated)

	1996 (a)	1997 (a)	1998 (a)	1999 (b)
Real GDP growth	9.6	8.8	8.0	6.6
Consumer price inflation (av)	8.3	2.8	−0.6	4.0
Exports	2.3	20.2	5.1	0.7
Investment Rate (as a % of GDP)	33.5	32.9	34.5	35.0
Current account balance	0.9	3.2	3.3	4.5
Reserves excl. Gold (US$ bn)	107.0	142.8	n.a.	n.a.
Exchange rate (av; RMB: US$)	8.3	8.3	8.3	8.9

Notes: (a) Official data and estimates; (b) IMF forecasts.
Source: IMF (1998).

At the end of 1997 Chinese exports had grown by 18 per cent compared to the preceding year and foreign currency reserves were still sufficient to finance a whole year of imports. However, in the first six months of 1998 the figure had decreased to 8 per cent. This partly depends on the fact that one third of Chinese exports are traditionally directed toward neighbouring countries – 15 per cent to Japan, 11 per cent to Taiwan, 7 per cent to the ASEAN countries and 5 per cent to Korea.

As a consequence of the reduction in exports, the Chinese government has sought to diversify its export markets' and foreign investments' strategy, no longer concentrating on the Asian markets, but on European and US partners, as well as Africa and Latin America.

The Asian crisis has not involved China directly, but it is having a direct impact on its economy, also because of the declining competitivity of Chinese products in an area of the world in which most countries have been compelled to make sizeable devaluations. Furthermore, China is very vulnerable because it suffers from the same structural problems as South Korea, Thailand and Indonesia. First of all, China's banking system is poorly regulated, not at all transparent and the Central Bank is very weak as far as supervizing commercial banks. The banking system suffers from many bad debts, or potentially so. Between 1978 and 1997 outstanding credits soared from RMB 190 billion to RMB 7.5 trillion, doubling as percentage of GDP (from 53 per cent in 1978 to 100 per cent in 1997)[1]. This was mainly the result of lending to the loss-making state owned enterprises (SOEs) sector, whose credit at the end of 1995 exceeded the balance by 500 per cent. Many SOEs are insolvent and the banking system does not have the means to recover its debts. A further indicator of China's weakness is the residential property speculation, also financed to excess by the banking system. Overproduction in many sectors – typically the automobile, beer production, chemicals and synthetic fibres sectors – is another weak point of the Chinese economy.

Besides these Chinese weaknesses, one must also bear in mind that at the moment the Hong Kong economy is in full recession and many commentators have questioned its ability to come out quickly. Towards the end of 1998, the real growth rate in the SAR shrank well beyond expectations – 3 per cent, reaching as low as –7 per cent at the end of 1998. Domestic demand shrank rapidly and private consumption fell by 5 per cent, partly as a consequence of a rise in unemployment, at its highest level for 15 years. The recession in Hong Kong is mainly due to the high degree of openness of the economy, which has made it vulnerable to the impact of the Asian crisis. Stagnation in the Asian markets has led to a sharp decrease in exports (-4 per cent in the second quarter of 1998), especially towards China and Japan (*Far Eastern Economic Review*, 27 August 1998).

In June 1998 the Hong Kong SAR government, fully aware of the seriousness of the current recession, announced a series of measures to stimulate the economy. At the end of August the Hong Kong Monetary Authority (HKMA), which *de facto* has the role of Central Bank, decided to respond to an increase in bank interest rates and to the progressive fall of stock exchange indices by directly intervening in the stock market itself. This decision was initially criticized very harshly by the main international financial dealers who feared that such an intervention would question Hong Kong's credibility as a regional financial centre. In particular, the direct intervention of the HKMA gave rise to the following hypothesis: 'after 15 months under the same territorial sovereignty, the economies of China and Hong Kong seem to be moving in opposite directions: China is actively working on dismantling the state owned enterprise system, whilst Hong Kong is working on building public boundaries in the private sector' (*Financial Times*, 1 September 1998). In fact, what international observers fear is that underlying the intervention of the HKMA is Beijing's determination to influence Hong Kong's traditional free market philosophy.

1.2 Zhu Rongji's reform programme

Premier Zhu Rongji has perfectly understood the risks facing the Chinese economy and on more than one occasion he has focused attention on the need to reform the banking system and the SOEs. At the plenary meeting of the 9th NPC (March 1998), Zhu reiterated that China must solve the SOEs issue within three years by speeding up the partial privatization programme and closing bankrupt enterprises.[2] The primary objective of the new government is to reform the SOEs.[3] This is expected to be completed relatively smoothly by the year 2000. Most SOEs are in the red, even those equipped with the latest technology. SOEs tend to lose money through the transfer of profits to loss-making departments and divisions and they tend to be overstaffed. Party cadres in charge of such enterprises and employees with lifetime tenures all have vested interests in perpetuating the state sector. The eventual success of economic reforms under way in China will depend mainly on revitalising these 'socialist relics'. In fact, although state enterprises' share of industrial output has shrunk since reforms began (48 per cent today, nearly 80 per cent in the late 1970s) (Weber, 1998) and – according to government statistics – one third of them were loss-making at the end of 1995, these firms still constitute the single most important sector in the national economy and claim the lion's share of investment resources. We need only consider that 484 of China's 500 biggest companies are SOEs. State-owned enterprises employ 108 000 million people, which means a substantial proportion of the urban industrial work force (70 per cent of workers in the industrial sector). As of this year, state enterprises will no longer provide free housing to their employees, who will instead be able to obtain mortgages to buy a house.

By the year 2000, Zhu Rongji intends to complete the reform of the financial sector, which he himself initiated when he was Governor of the Central Bank (CB). The reorganization of the CB should proceed on a regional basis, thus reducing political interference and increasing the decision-making autonomy. The Prime Minister has very much insisted that the CB should have greater supervisory and regulatory powers, promising that more control through the People's CB will mean more independence for the trading banks. However, it is not clear how determined Zhu is to pursue obtaining full convertibility of the *renminbi*.

Other reforms announced by Zhu concern the political apparatus, the construction industry – which should create a property market – welfare – which seek to introduce a leaner welfare system supported by private insurance – and the reform of fiscal system. The bureaucratic structure is to be slashed, laying off half the civil servants and reassigning them new jobs. Restructuring of central government was to be completed by 1998 and it will take three years to resettle officials displaced as a result of streamlining. All these objectives are not easy to achieve, given that they were already on the agenda of the preceding government. Any reform programme must confront certain facts – above all the risk of social tensions fuelled by rising unemployment (inevitable in the case of the SOEs), a phenomenon which was unheard of in the pre-reform era. According to official figures, by the end of 1998 the number of laid-off workers who had not been re-employed stood at 15 million, up by 4 million from 1997 (*Far Eastern Economic Review*, 14 January 1999). To this one might add that every year about 30 million young people enter the labour market, which is unable to absorb them.

1.3 Regionalism, autonomy and political democracy in post-reform China

Since the beginning of the reform process, Deng's government decided to decentralize to the localities, and particularly to the provinces (*sheng*, each of which is as large as a European state), vast normative and administrative functions, to allow economic growth to take place with different speeds and characteristics. As a result, the gap grew between the wealthier and the more backward areas of the country, between the cities and the rural areas, and between the coastal areas and the interior, and over the years the seeds of a many-speed China matured. There was a 'red' China located in the north and west of the country, which was poor and still dominated by a state-owned economy, a 'white' China located in the south, which was rich, capitalist and open to the outside world, and a 'pink' China located in the central coastal regions, which was not wealthy as yet, but well placed on the road to growth. Meanwhile, liberalization of the markets for goods, services, capital and labour boosted diversification of production and led to swift growth in interregional trade. Political and economic competition among provinces and between these and the centre intensified and this particularism spilled over into worrying cases of 'localism', such as the setting up of arbitrary barriers to interprovincial trade, bureaucratic obstructionism and judicial hostility towards non-locals and the flouting of laws and orders issued by the central authorities.

Toward the mid-eighties central government's ability to co-ordinate and control the periphery had reached its lowest point in the history of the PRC. In fact, prior to the reforms, it was the Party that guaranteed the unity of the State, by means of the usual instruments used in socialist systems – from democratic centralism to ideology, from self-discipline to the mechanism of the *nomenklatura* – guaranteed by the state ownership of the means of production and economic planning. Following reforms and socio-economic differentiation, however, the mechanisms of socialist centralism – which were put in the hands of a new ruling class based on economic and political might, on personal relationships (*guanxi*) and on corruption – not only began to lose their effectiveness, but also became instruments with which powerful local bureaucrats could violate, circumvent or not apply the rules imposed by the centre, making the burgeoning socialist market economy murky and preventing the spread of the rule of law. The principles of the party's guiding role, in particular, formed the pillars of the *rule of politics* against the gradual growth of the *rule of law* and – paradoxically – of localism against efforts to maintain national unity and cohesion.

In the meantime, other threats to China's unity lurked on the horizon. First of all, the political framework of the large autonomous regions on the borders of the country (Xinjiang, Tibet, and Inner Mongolia) had completely changed: social diversification and the relaxation of physical and ideological controls had polarized the contradictions existing between the Han majority and the national minorities living in the country, causing the spread of pro-independence ideas and movements in these regions and surging tension and permanent instability. This was all the more worrying in view of the break-up of the USSR and the rise of Islamic fundamentalism.

Second, the signing in 1984 of the Sino-British Joint Declaration launched the reunification process of Hong Kong with China: the Chinese government committed itself to absorbing the British colony while fully respecting its autonomy, thereby accepting the co-existence of two completely different socio-economic models within the same national system. This commitment, which was important in itself but could also serve as a model for any future rapprochement with Taiwan, was to imply a complication and a new risk factor in Beijing's relations with its periphery. The grave economic, political and social crisis at the end of the eighties which led to the crackdown at Tiananmen Square in 1989, forced the central government to reconsider the decentralization policy it had adopted in the first decade of reform. Much of the blame for the ensuing economic chaos was attributed to the localities, particularly the provinces which were accused of using their new powers improperly. The broad sweep of the differentiated growth strategy was not abandoned, but efforts were made to reduce inequalities and curb, where possible, the risks – such as recentralizing some public functions under the control of central organs, reducing the privileges granted to the most developed areas and restricting the worst excesses of localism. Without, however, slowing down economic growth and burdening the state with the enormous social costs of modernization.

The development and implementation of this new balanced policy, however, are encountering countless obstacles due to strong opposition by groups whose interests are threatened by the change and the uncertainty of the central authorities, who although seeking to smooth the pace of development of the country, also fear they might harm the most advanced – and the most competitive at international level – areas now that the crisis in Southeast Asia is hitting them hard. It is only natural for the government and the central organs of the CCP to appear ineffective on these issues. There is a debate and perhaps even a clash inside the party between those who favour decentralization and further autonomy and the more decidedly centralist-minded, for whom national cohesion can only be maintained by keeping or restoring central control over the localities and repressing secessionist tendencies.

Here the debate on regionalism naturally entwines with the need for further democratization of Chinese politics. In fact, quite apart from the government's position, it is the very institutional order of the PRC – which is still founded on Leninist dogma in stark contrast with the pluralism of contemporary Chinese society – that seems inappropriate to tackling the centrifugal forces engendered by reforms, while the need for a new political project that could embrace Hong Kong and – in future – Taiwan into the national political fabric becomes all the more pressing. For such a project to be effective in running China in the year 2000, it will not only have to provide a wide amount of autonomy, especially to those areas which, for economic, social or cultural reasons must be considered 'different' from China in its strict sense, but above all, it will have to find the right way to give localities – and to other lobby groups – a fair say in shaping national policies and laws.

1.4 Institutional issues between the centre and the periphery

1.4.1 Autonomy and participation

Under the Chinese Constitution, the provincial and major municipal congresses have the power to promulgate laws appropriate to the socio-economic specificities. The five autonomous regions (Tibet, Xinjiang, Mongolia, Guangxi-Zhuang, Ningxia-Hui) enjoy a particular form of autonomy as do the 'special economic zones' (SEZ), that is those territorial areas which were created in the southern provinces in the eighties to attract foreign investment and to apply the boldest reforms.

Over the years local legislation has extensively filled the space assigned to it, thereby diversifying the legal framework in the various provinces. In many cases these laws have been the model used for nation-wide reforms. But what kind of autonomy do these laws express? More to the point, are they truly an expression of local autonomy, or are they experiments in reform planned by the centre and conducted at local level? One key to answering these questions is to consider the power of the provincial congresses, which have not only promulgated many new laws, but have also taken to 'defending' local interests as well as challenging central policies and government candidates. This is the result of geographical differentiation and the multiplication of socio-economic interests, as well as the introduction of more liberal electoral legislation than under Mao, which, while retaining the CCP's crucial role in selecting candidates and in overseeing the work of deputies, nevertheless allows voters a greater say in the choice of candidates and therefore requires those elected to take appropriate account of the interests of those who have voted for them.

The Chinese government has made amazing efforts to gradually introduce representative democratic systems, especially at the village level. The *Organic Law of Villagers Committee* was approved on 24 November 1987, but became realistically operative in 1992, when 20 provinces, municipalities and regions were requested to vote. The law on village elections guarantees the secrecy of the vote and the plurality of the nominations, thus ensuring a minimum of two candidates for every seat. By recognizing the legitimacy of the interest groups, the government has agreed, in the last few years, to a growing competitivity between the different groups. In May 1994, for the first time, a commission of the International Republican Institute was invited to observe the regularity of the voting operations in some villages of the Fujian province and, in March 1997, a delegation of the Carter Center observed the electoral process in other villages situated in the Fujian and the Hebei provinces. The international observers witnessed the regularity of election procedures and the very enthusiastic participation of voters: the majority of the Assemblies elected resulted in being realistically pluralistic. Even though there are these very important novelties, one must not forget that Beijing has not wanted to make any sort of concession as far as human rights are concerned and that the political control of the CCP on the civil society is still extremely strong.

Despite the innovative importance of this trend – used only for the minor territorial organizations – so far dissent from local institutions is only tolerated as a form of pressure on central authorities. The establishment of alternative political movements capable of coalescing local interests is banned and power still continues to be wielded by a modernized form of *nomenklatura*. In actual fact, local autonomy is neither sufficiently spontaneous nor sufficiently free to give the local entities a say or as a mouthpiece for letting off steam, and local congresses, therefore, continue to be essentially the, sometimes unwilling, executors of decisions by central leaders of the CCP. Even if at the Central level there is no room for democratic and frank confrontation between the interests of the centre and those of the localities. In a process which in many ways is similar to the one taking place in the local congresses, the NPC and its Standing Committee also have a greater say in policy and legislation at national level. The congress, which until a few years ago was a mere executor of decisions taken by the party and the government, has recently shown signs of dissatisfaction with this role and a consistent, politically significant minority of members have begun to express a certain amount of dissent. At present we are by no means witnessing an open conflict between the most important state institution and the CCP, yet – to provide just one symbolic example – a two thirds majority needed to modify the Constitution may not be so easy to achieve. In short, given the declining cohesion of the Communist party and its poor ability to sufficiently reflect the interests of the various social components in the country, given the constant invocation by the leadership of the *rule of law* and the separation of State and Party, it is increasingly accepted that the right place for political debate is no longer the Central Committee or the Politburo, but state institutions, particularly the NPC. For these institutions to perform this role actively, however, forces capable of independently representing the interests of social groups will have to come together and find expression. Thus, even though very little has changed in recent years, new forces have begun to appear in the NPC. These include provincial parliamentary groups, which exercize the important function of co-ordinating deputies. They are not parties, but these and other lobby groups have the potential to become actual political subjects in the near future.

1.4.2 The signs of contradiction

Like the congresses, local governments also play an important role in the complex negotiations with the centre and with society. They strive to protect local interests and reconcile their various expressions. Where possible, this is done by avoiding clashes with the state and party hierarchies, but at times, due to the absence of a mature democratic forum, there may inevitably be more or less open clashes with other local administrations or opposition to Beijing's will and, therefore, to the law. The obstacles to the implementation of the government's recentralization policy which was adopted at the beginning of the nineties are the most obvious example of this attitude, as well as the change in the balance of power between the centre and the periphery and the political clout acquired by the local administrations. Of particular significance, for example, has been the opposition of the Guangdong government – and in its wake, of other provinces – to the adoption of the most drastic measures of financial restructuring after Tiananmen.

This is not the place to examine the myriad ways in which – thanks to the commixture of interests between members of the local governments, party's cadres and entrepreneurs and the survival of the 'rule of politics' approach – the local administrations have contrived to elude or obstruct the implementation of unfavourable central laws or policies, to divert resources or hide information from the centre, and to guard their prerogatives even beyond the limits of legality. Many foreign entrepreneurs, to give just one example, have experienced the lack of collaboration between central and local authorities. For instance, frequently the provincial committees for foreign investment will suggest that investors split or phase larger, more expensive projects so as to avoid having to refer the projects to the central authorities for approval.

In any case it is the judiciary (which in China is considered *de facto* a public administration like any other) which has experienced the worst effects of localism and the contradiction between Marxist–Leninist dogma and the new social pluralism. In the present Chinese legal system judges continue not to be guaranteed their independence, while the courts are still controlled by the respective people's congress and CCP organs, and judicial procedures are subject to external influence. Furthermore, the judiciary for all its requirements is directly dependent on the public administration and the Party, while judges earn meagre salaries, leaving them at risk – at the very least – to undue influence from the network of social relations (*guanxi*). Until a few years ago, these characteristics of the Chinese legal system still formed part of a relatively homogeneous political, economic and social context, in which the role of the Party and the State was unquestioned and pivotal. Today the situation has changed and the lack of independence of the judiciary from the political has profound and harmful effects on the efficiency of the legal system as a whole. This phenomenon has particularly grave consequences on regionalist tendencies: even senior members of the Chinese judiciary have recognized the problem of local governments interfering in the activity of the people's courts under their control and have condemned the protectionism accorded by many judges to local interests.

Thus, the servile nature of the judiciary – which is, it should not be forgotten, one of the organizational cornerstones of Leninism – amounts not only to a dangerous rejection of the demand for certainty, or at least for predictable rules, expressed by the different social components, above all by businesses, but also constitutes a factor constantly undermining the principle of national unity.

1.5 The autonomous areas question and the protection of the national minorities

The points already mentioned about the difficulties in relations between Beijing and the provinces takes on a different hue in the case of the autonomous regions. Here the contradictions are generated by socio-economic diversification as well as those due to the uneasy relations between the Han and the non-Han populations and those related to the strategic position of these regions, most of which lie on China's western and north-western borders. As we shall shortly see, these contradictions are particularly evident in two of the five autonomous Chinese regions, Xinjiang and Tibet, where clandestine political and even paramilitary groups operate. These groups have been responsible for demonstrations and riots ever since the start of reforms, and even on a number of occasions acts of terrorism, systematically followed by bloody repression by the Chinese authorities.

These events have been triggered by many factors, and an analysis is beyond the scope of this work. It is certainly true to say that even in such cases, relations between the centre and the periphery in China have been sucked into the whirlwind of reforms. Relaxation of the centre's grip over the economy and social organization, together with the greater personal freedom and independence – thanks also to China's open policy – has made the growth of organized dissent possible. It is very hard to question the PRC's legitimacy over its autonomous regions. The same cannot be said of the government's promises to provide greater autonomy to its minorities ever since the first version of the PRC constitution in 1954.

The Constitution of 1982 and the law on regional autonomies of 1984 re-established the position of the first constitution, restoring the minorities' right to retain their identity and granting the autonomous regions and other minor autonomous bodies a range of administrative and legislative powers, which on paper appear to be wide ranging. Local government bodies, for example, are allowed, within legal limits, to run their regional economy and finances, not to mention education and science, and even public order, provided these are compatible with national military requirements. In practice so far, however, Beijing's intention does not appear to be to respect or guarantee the specificity of these areas, nor to allow full-scale autonomy, but on the contrary, it seems bent on bringing them in line with the national standard, by encouraging Han Chinese to migrate to the regions inhabited by the minorities, and controlling the key levers of economic and political power so as to gradually replace local cultures and languages with the dominant one. Meanwhile, the autonomous regions are struggling to keep pace with economic development, and as the gap with the rich eastern zones widens, the more willing the locals are to listen to calls for secessionism.

Central government appears to have become aware of this danger for some time now and has tried to reduce inequalities, promising to invest more in the interior and offering a range of incentives. These instruments are only palliatives. However, the government is averse to the idea that the Tibetans, the Uighur, the Mongols, the Zhuang or the other national minorities, should enjoy the right to manage their own socio-economic growth. Likewise, very few representatives of the minorities are involved in national policy choices. Apart from some rare token figure, the entire top-flight leadership of party and state is of Han origin.

Xinjiang

The region of Xinjiang is huge and scarcely populated by different ethnic groups (60 per cent of which are not Han, and made up mostly by Uighur Muslim Turks, as well as Kazakhs and Hui), and is the region which causes the greatest concern to the Chinese leaders. Alongside the usual problems between the locals and Han, which have been exacerbated in this particular case by a strong Uighur (and partly Kazakh) independence movement, Xinjiang is also the scene of the worrying spread of Islamic fundamentalism, which is rife among all the main minorities and even attracts the Uighur and Kazakh cadres of the CCP. The Pan-Turk independence movements began to make their voice heard in 1990 – at the time that the USSR was disintegrating – through riots and clashes, which were kept secret by official sources. In the last two years pro-independence groups have been responsible for setting off bombs in Urumqi, the region's capital and even in Beijing, killing and injuring a number of people. Our knowledge of these groups is extremely vague, both due to the scarcity of information available, and because of the patronage-dominated and clan-like nature of Xinjiang society. Their international support and bases are mainly in Tajikistan and in Turkey, but some groups are linked to the Talibans in Afghanistan.

If, moreover, we consider the fact that in the last few years Xinjiang's economy has become closely intertwined with some of the former Soviet Asian republics and that both legal and illegal cross-border trade has grown exponentially, it seems clear that the regional question cannot be considered a domestic affair. The region's oil deposits and other strategic raw materials (uranium) found in the region have led to this question taking on greater international significance. This wealth, only a very small part of which has been exploited, represents a fundamental resource for China to satiate its energy needs, and has also caught the interest of Western and Japanese multinationals. Until a few years ago, Beijing banned all foreigners from exploring, drilling and distributing onshore oil and natural gas. Since 1993 these restrictions have been curtailed and a number of Western companies have been working together with Chinese firms to map out the region's energy reserves. So far, the Chinese authorities have conceded little in terms of exploration rights, but the situation is rapidly changing, and there is every likelihood that the region will allow further investments of foreign capital and technology.

To maintain Xinjiang's stability, as Beijing is well aware, it is necessary, though not enough, to adopt an economic policy that takes greater account of its needs and is capable of exploiting its potential better. If this does not occur, tensions between the Chinese majority and the local minority population are bound to grow. But even if the region's socio-economic conditions were to improve, there still remains the political conundrum of how to deal with that section of the population that is increasingly susceptible to the calls of religious fundamentalism and less inclined to tolerate Han rule. And on this issue the Communist leadership appears to be far from united.

Tibet

In many respects, the problems of Tibet are similar to those of Xinjiang. Here too, there is a major problem of co-operation between the Han and the non-Han populations; here too economic growth has been slow to take off. Pro-independence movements are strong and equally harsh is the repression by the authorities; here too events have major international implications. However, Tibet's situation is radically different from that of Xinjiang. First and foremost in cultural and religious terms. Second, in economic terms, since Tibet does not possess the huge resources and/or potential for growth as Xinjiang. Third, in political terms, given that Tibet, unlike Xinjiang, has a government in exile – led by the Dalai Lama in Dharamsala – which a large section of Tibetans still regard as legitimate. Finally, the nature of international support in favour of anti-Chinese movements in the two regions is radically different. In the case of Tibet this means little more than the solidarity of international public opinion. Xinjiang, in contrast, is a fundamental piece in the Great Game being played out in Central Asia.

The Dalai Lama's attitude towards Beijing is extremely cautious. The political aim of the Tibetan leader increasingly appears to be to reach an agreement with the Chinese government, thereby ensuring the survival of Tibetan culture. Achieving such an agreement is more urgent than ever – if it does not come, Tibetan civilization is destined to die out or, in any case, to be integrated into the dominant Han culture, barring, of course, a traumatic but equally improbable 'national liberation'. The bases on which to negotiate an agreement still appear to be quite open. At a theoretical level, the two positions are very distant: the exiled Tibetan government seeks political independence for Tibet (that is for the autonomous region of the same name) and the freedom to secede for those parts of the Tibetan nation dispersed in China's other western provinces (Qinghai, Xinjiang, Yunnan, Sichuan, and so on). The people's government, on the other hand, provides daily proof – through the use of the police to repress secessionists, as well as encouraging Hans to settle in Tibet and controlling funding from the centre – that it intends to concede as little autonomy as possible. In practice, the obstacles are a little less marked. The Tibetans have toned down their demands for independence into a more realistic, vociferous call for autonomy for a political Tibet. This could be modelled on the one currently enjoyed by Hong Kong – that is complete autonomy in the running of its internal affairs, a basic law to protect citizens' rights, and a democratically elected regional governor. For its part, in exchange for the recognition of Chinese sovereignty by Tibetan religious leaders, Beijing has provided some signs of its willingness to give greater consideration to protecting the Tibetans' linguistic and cultural identity, and distributing more fairly between Hans and Tibetans the main posts in the region and in the local CCP, and perhaps even rethinking its immigration policy.

The road to reconciliation, however, is still littered with various obstacles, and not only on the part of the Chinese. Despite general international approval for the Dalai Lama's readiness to talk, radical pro-independence groups strongly oppose it, as they consider that no agreement can be possible with the Chinese occupiers. Street clashes continue to occur, with occasional flare ups such as the one on Christmas Day in 1996, when a bomb was set off in front of a government building in Lhasa, wounding five people.

1.6 The other Chinas: Hong Kong and Taiwan

1.6.1 The reversion of Hong Kong

From a political viewpoint, China's management of Hong Kong, after one year, appears to be an overall success, although it may be too early to judge, following the winds of crises that hit East Asia in the months immediately after its reversion. The doomsayers forecasts of restrictions on citizens' freedoms and rights have proved unfounded and Hong Kong's social system has comfortably withstood the transition. On the other hand, it was highly unlikely that Beijing would behave so ineptly as to immediately upset the fragile equilibrium in Hong Kong, not to mention a good deal of its own international credibility. The effects of re-unification can only be assessed in the medium to long term. In actual fact, the solution adopted in its relations with Hong Kong is a new and extremely challenging path for Beijing. The Basic Law (BL) of the SAR, which was promulgated by the NPC in 1990 under Article 31 of the PRC Constitution but actually came into force on 1 July 1997, upon re-unification, provides that the former British colony will retain its present socio-economic and legal system for at least 50 years.

Many have expressed their doubts as to whether Beijing intends or is capable of respecting the autonomy granted on paper to Hong Kong fearing, on the contrary, that Chinese rule would lead, in the long term, to authoritarian control of the former colony and a gradual decline in the independence of the judiciary. These would both inevitably presage restrictions on citizens' rights and in the loss of confidence and credibility of its legal system, which are so important to Hong Kong if it is to retain its financial supremacy over the other competing cities in the area. The first point of concern is related to the autonomy of the (regional) legislature of Hong Kong. On the one hand, there is concern about Beijing's willingness to continue the task of democratizing the region's institutions initiated by Patten and to respect its commitment to gradually introduce direct elections to the Legislative Council (Legco), and, on the other hand, its ability to avoid interfering with the autonomy granted to the special region.

The BL provides the SAR with a 'high degree of autonomy' in all matters, except those concerning affairs of the state – particularly foreign affairs and defence – and/or relations between the region and the state. On paper, the legislative powers of the Legco are, therefore, quite wide-ranging, even more so than in many federal constitutions. Nevertheless, the BL provides the Standing Committee of the NPC with an enviable means of control, by granting it the power to refer to the Legco any local legislation felt to be incompatible with the BL, as well as provide a correct interpretation of those sections of the BL on matters that are attributed to the centre (such as 'public order'). The extent to which the Committee makes use of this instrument will reflect the level of autonomy actually granted to the Hong Kong legislative body.

Another major factor of uncertainty is the independence of the judiciary, which, although formally guaranteed by the BL, appears in reality to expose the cultural abyss that separates Hong Kong from the rest of China on this issue. The differences between the two systems could not be greater. In *common law* the independence of the judiciary is a tried and tested practice, reinforced by a legal tradition that requires judges to be impartial and rewards their professionalism by means of a commensurate social status and salary. In China, however, as has been already stated, the judiciary is institutionally subordinated to political goals.

Many are concerned about the destiny of the SAR's judiciary and fear that the political pressure to which the judges are subject may end up undermining one of the keystones on which Hong Kong's juridical credibility is founded. So far this danger has not materialized, and the judiciary has been able to reassure the world of its independence and dignity on a number of occasions. The Hong Kong model of *common law* – which has already made itself felt in legislation and legal practice in China – could also demonstrate how the efficiency of a legal system depends on a fair balance between powers and respect for the law.

1.6.2 Taiwan's rapprochement and its possible implications

After half-a-century of hostilities between the PRC and Taiwan, for some years now the conditions appear to be right for dialogue to begin once again between the two sides of the Straits. Yet little political progress seems to have been made. One factor, which is particularly hampering rapprochement between the two, is the democratization process taking place in Taiwan. Since the mid-eighties and particularly since Lee Teng-hui came to power, the Nationalist party (*guomindang*, GMD) has been working to democratize its institutions and those of the state. Martial law was revoked in 1987 and in the following years political parties and opposition groups were allowed to form, while police control over the opposition was curbed. The first democratic parliamentary elections were held in 1992. Since 1996, the president and vice-president – the two highest posts in the country, have been elected directly.

This process is of fundamental importance for the political history of East Asia since, for the first time, part of China has put representative democracy into practice and is freely choosing its rulers. Taiwan could become an innovative model of enormous importance for the People's Republic, and this is a further threat to the CCP and a challenge to its ideological roots. While the presidential elections have confirmed Lee's and the GMD's popularity, local elections held later showed that support was far from unanimous or unconditional and that in future it could be won by other political groups. The most worrying of these for the government party is the opposition Progressive – Democratic Party (PDP), which represents that key minority of Taiwanese who believe the time has come to be bold and proclaim independence – not only *de facto*, but also *de jure* – from Communist China. While the PDP may eventually come to power, this will probably not be at the next presidential elections in the year 2000. The danger of losing political control over Taiwan and seeing the island's secession turn *de facto* into a declaration of independence is undoubtedly one of the factors behind Beijing's slight from a policy of hostility towards one of slightly greater dialogue.

At the start of 1998, after three years of ostracism, Jiang Zemin himself proposed to Taipei that talks on normalizing relations between the two should begin. Beijing has proposed to extend the principle of 'one country, two systems', already experimented with Hong Kong. Under the system, Taiwan would enjoy wide-ranging autonomy, and would have its own legislative, executive and judiciary bodies as well as its own armed forces, and would retain its own political and economic system, but would have to recognize the sovereignty of the PRC and submit to its rule. Some have even suggested renaming the PRC, should such a reunification occur, – perhaps calling it simply 'China' – and modifying its flag and symbols, even courting the idea that the Chinese state could be restructured.

There is certainly a very long way to go, particularly now that Taiwan has become a fully-fledged democracy with the presence of political groups that no longer cherish the ideal of Chinese national unity (one wonders, particularly, what would happen once Taiwan were reunited with China, and the PDP were to win elections and the electors vote for secession). Hong Kong's re-unification is bound to fundamentally influence Beijing's future relations with Taipei. If Beijing is unable to administer its SAR and maintain its prosperity, this would finally break the link that joins Taiwan to the mother-country and push it towards independence, while, on the contrary, successful ties with the future authorities of Hong Kong and with the Taiwanese institutions operating in the former British colony could assuage any remaining fears and provide talks with key momentum. The rapprochement between the two Chinas would be a fundamental step in the restoration of Chinese national unity. Even more so than in the case of Hong Kong, the special administrative region of Taiwan could be a key model in any eventual democratization of China.

1.7 Time for a change

The contradictions generated by reforms in relations between the centre and the localities are some of the most apparent symptoms of the present and potential deficiencies of the Chinese Leninist system. They also act as a stimulus to urgently look for new political solutions that acknowledge China's diversification into a constellation of conflicting interests and permit these to be efficiently balanced. It is not only a question – albeit important – of extending or respecting more strictly the autonomy granted by the constitution and by law to the localities. As Chinese society becomes more complex and diverse, and new economic, political, social and cultural forces grow, as the rule of law acquires a central role in regulating social relations and the arbitrariness of the bureaucracy diminishes, so the need rises for democratic, transparent, more legitimate and, above all, more efficient institutions in order to achieve the equilibrium necessary to retain national unity.

The Chinese authorities are well aware of this problem, and are planning partial reforms. Even now, the fact that the NPC's dignity is gradually being restored and that direct democratic elections are more widespread and free than before is of great importance. While these developments are slow and painful, they could result in the birth of a new political culture. On the other hand, at present the PRC's rulers are unwilling to countenance a true multi-party model. Apart from the more or less clandestine opposition groups – which have been severely suppressed and which, in any case, have been unable to develop a viable alternative political project, the only parties that are recognized are the eight 'democratic parties' which are controlled by a special section of the Central Committee of the CCP and unable to express independent opinions. Following the long freeze that followed Tiananmen, things have started to move recently and some dissidents have tried (in vain) to set up small opposition groups, but the government continues to view such attempts with great hostility. Yet the government has not shown disdain for dialogue with economic research units and other independent think tanks and there is no ruling out that sooner or later a measure of freedom of political association will be granted.

The problem is when. The gradualness of the process taking place is worrying because the absence of an institutional mouthpiece for local interests transform them automatically into obstacles to the efficient functioning of the institutional apparatus and in some areas have generated dangerous secessionist tendencies. The times of the three-speed China are over. Today the task of the Chinese government is to keep united and co-ordinate the many different Chinas, whose coexistence is becoming more and more complex. And there is every reason to believe that the CCP will only be able to continue ruling the country as long as it can rise to this challenge of complexity and pluralism.

1.8 Some scenarios for China

China seems most likely to continue consolidating the horizontal or fragmented authoritarianism model (Weber, 1997), which is the most appropriate one for the consolidation of economic reforms, with a gradual extension of the decision-making base. Should this model hold sway in the coming years, it can be reasonably assumed that the forum for political participation will be extended and opened up to emerging social actors. Such a context would encourage an enlargement of the decision-making base to those political groups that accept the 'guiding role of the CCP' and are willing to contribute towards economic reforms.

What are the most likely political scenarios for China? There is every reason to believe that the scenarios for the coming decades will be built on the consolidation of economic reforms and on political stability. Four possible scenarios can be constructed for the future development of China, two of which focus on domestic issues and two on the PRC's external relations (see Figure 1.1).

	Positive outcomes	**Negative outcomes**
Focus on:		
Domestic issues	'Miracle' will continue	Authoritarian change
International issues	China's regional hegemony	Winds of war

Figure 1.1   Scenarios for China 2020

1.8.1 The Chinese miracle continues

The first scenario envisages that the Chinese leadership will succeed in controlling the tensions sparked by rapid economic growth while acting to sustain it. In his opening address as Prime Minister, Zhu Rongji assured that economic growth would be maintained at around 8 per cent for 1998 and 7 per cent in the following two years. The government, in response to the Asian crisis and the decline in Chinese exports at the beginning of 1998, partially modified its economic policy by trying to attract the more investment from Europe and the US and diversifying both the areas of destination of exports and the type of products. The fall in exports, due to a slump in demand for commodities from the Asian countries, could force the Chinese government into devaluing the RMB. The loss of competitivity of Chinese products and the growing internal unemployment, due to the reform of the state enterprises, could lead to the Chinese currency being devalued by at least 15 per cent. But international political pressure has, until now, held at bay calls to devalue and forced repeated official declarations to the contrary. Devaluation could trigger off further depreciations in the region and, even more importantly, threaten China's newly found hegemony in Asia as well as obstruct China's efforts to join the WTO.

According to this scenario, China is poised to become the next economic superpower, as has been suggested more than once by the World Bank (1997). Furthermore, China will be able to get away with pragmatic political reforms, without much attention to real democracy, through the creation of a series of structures which formally represent civil society. As we have observed, China is slowly moving in this direction, with the recent introduction of local elections, in villages and townships, and with a more assertive NPC. In other words the Chinese leadership seems willing to concede some formal powers to the localities as long as they do not question the central authority of Beijing and of the CCP.

In this scenario, China would become a 'horizontal type authoritarian political system' or an *'Asian-style* democracy' like Singapore, where one hegemonic party holds power and occupies all political ground, but accepts the political collaboration of all those who accept its supremacy and wish to co-operate in building society. In other words a political system in which pragmatism prevails, sustained by economic growth which allows the distribution of resources to the population, distracting it from making demands for real democracy. The reversion of Hong Kong will continue smoothly, under the BL.

1.8.2 China's regional hegemony

The second scenario is based on the international consequences of the economic miracle: it envisages China becoming increasingly integrated with the rest of the world, gradually complying with WTO rules and establishing relative hegemony within the Asian region, also thanks to the network of *overseas Chinese*. Clinton's long trip to China in July 1998 is the most tangible testimony of the importance that the US and the American business community attach to the Middle Kingdom. The trip enabled China to normalize its relations with Washington and even a little more. The US has recognized the need to involve Beijing constructively in managing Asia's problems and, more generally, in managing the international situation. Beijing thus reconfirmed its importance in managing the Asian crisis, and its willingness to accept the pivotal role played by the US in the management of Asia's financial problems. At a diplomatic level, Beijing has obtained some immediate benefits from the Asian crisis in as much as the crisis offered the Chinese leadership a great opportunity to reinforce its regional role and to offer itself as one of the terms of reference to fill the vacuum created on the international scene following the end of the cold war. Through its decision to pay a specific price (non-devaluation) in exchange for considerable political and diplomatic advantages, China has solved this dilemma very astutely. One should bear in mind that one of the advantages, from the Chinese point of view, of the end of the cold war has been greater regional ramifications for its foreign policy. More specifically, one can say that the rise of China as a global power will reflect first of all its central positioning in the Asian equilibrium. The appointment of a diplomat with an Asian background (Tang Jiaxun, former ambassador to Japan) as the new Foreign Minister is quite indicative of the government's scale of priorities. In this scenario all territorial disputes between China and its neighbours will slowly be smoothed over and the question of Taiwan will be solved diplomatically through a formula based on the one already used for Hong Kong of 'one country two systems'.

The third and fourth scenarios are less optimistic. Both cases envisage China being unable to sustain economic growth thereby triggering social and political tensions.

1.8.3 The risk of an authoritarian change

In the third scenario the Chinese miracle is in danger of running out of steam. The reform of the SOEs generates further social tensions. Indeed the government has also promised to tackle the long-standing problem of the SOEs, by accelerating the programme of partial privatization. The restructuring of the 500 biggest SOEs should be completed by 1999, while all the others are expected to be transformed into employee-owned collectives, or else declared bankrupt. The reform of the SOEs will inevitably result in unemployment – an estimated 70 million more jobless in a country that already has problems offering work to 30 million young people entering the labour market every year. In this scenario, growing social and political unrest would provide the more conservative elements in the CCP with the justification to seize power, supported by part of the Army and usher in the return of an oligarchic and totalitarian system. We must always consider the fact that, while a degree of critical discussion has been tolerated in the nineties, President Jiang Zemin recently reminded the world that: 'Any factor of instability, as soon as it appears, shall be resolutely nipped in the bud' (CCP Conference, 23 December 1998). Thus the crackdown of the China Democracy Party can be seen as a typical indicator of the CCP's intolerance of any kind of democracy.

1.8.4 Winds of war

In the fourth scenario, China, after failing to maintain growth, would be unable to join the WTO, or respect the international agreements on nuclear testing and would adopt a potentially aggressive stance towards its neighbours. This would fan the 'winds of war' in the region triggering territorial disputes in Central Asia, in the Gulf of Tonchino and with Taiwan. Up until today, China has had various territorial disputes with its neighbours. The greatest source of tension remains the Spratly archipelago, 30 islands in the South China Sea, whose sovereignty is contested by six Asian countries: China, Taiwan, Malaysia, Vietnam, the Philippines and Brunei, each of which have historical/geographic claims on part or all of the islands. The tensions which have been generated around the problem of these islands, mainly as a consequence of the discovery of considerable oil deposits, contain *in nuce* many problematics around which the debates on the stability of the region turn. These range from the discussions about territorial waters to those on the exploitation of natural resources, to economic rivalry. Even Japan has claims on the Spratly islands, because it had occupied them in 1939, even though it lost them after its defeat at the end of World War II. Today China, which controls eight of the 30 islands that form the archipelago, seems to want to play a role of strength. Ancient, mostly dormant, territorial disputes are also present along the 7000 km border with the former Soviet Union, involving both the three former Soviet republics of Turkmenistan, Kirghizistan and Kazakistan, and Russia. An agreement recently signed with Russia has defused tensions, while dialogue with the three former soviet republics in Central Asia seems to have been established, also thanks to their past trade links recalling the caravans that followed the 'silk road'. Innumerable political reasons justify China's commercial interest in Central Asia. Most of all the strong resurgence of Islam and the pro-independence movement in the north-western regions (Xinjiang, Qinghai, Gansu and Ningxia), where the politically strongest and greatest concentration of Muslims are to be found – about 20 million people, a little less than 2 per cent of the entire Chinese population.

The Chinese government has always been sensitive to the issue of the reunification of the country. While the pursuit of reunification has not created any problems in the case of Hong Kong, as it probably will not in 1999 in the case of Macao, the same thing certainly cannot be said about Taiwan. As we have seen, relations between China and Taiwan are in fact more delicate and problematic, not only because since 1949 both the government of Taipei and that of Beijing have claimed to be the only legitimate representatives of the whole of China, but because – as we have seen – in Taiwan there are more and more supporters of national independence. Since 1949, Taiwan has been considered a province of the PRC by Beijing. Relations with Taiwan have improved markedly although both Beijing and Taipei still claim to be the sole legitimate government of China. While political integration may be as far away as ever, the integration of the two economies continues apace. There are no reliable data on Taiwanese investments in China. Different figures are provided by different sources. Sources in Hong Kong put the value of contracts signed by Taiwanese businessmen on the mainland at between US$ 10.5 billion and US$ 20.4 billion by the end of 1992 up to 1997 (*China Perspectives*, May–June 1998). Japanese sources have estimated US$ 15 billion for the same period and more recently, the American and Taiwanese press have mentioned a figure of over US\$ 20 billion invested by 25 000 firms.

The economic integration between Taiwan and China is so deep that it makes the hypothesis of an armed conflict very unrealistic and certainly rather 'inconvenient'. The recent trip to China by Koo Chen-fu, the Taiwan's chief negotiator with Beijing, which reopened the path to a diplomatic solution, should be interpreted in the light of the above. Personally we are convinced that the pragmatism typical of the Chinese will prevail once again and that the winds of war will remain a fear of the Western observers.

As always when one talks of possible scenarios it is difficult to foresee what will really happen: as things stand at the moment, many signals make the optimistic scenarios more likely. But also within the optimistic scenarios there may be hidden unforeseen consequences: for example, an ever more integrated China in the international context is certainly the best guarantee for security in the region even if a strong and powerful big China could upset the already complex equilibrium between Japan, China and the countries of Southeast Asia.

Notes

* Maria Weber wrote sections 1, 2 and 8 of this chapter, while Renzo Cavalieri wrote sections 3 to 7.
1. A more detailed analysis of the risk that Asian crisis will affect China is in: Lardy (1998), and in 'Will China be next?', special report *The Economist*, 20 October 1998.
2. A bankruptcy law has existed in China since 1988, but until now has been used very rarely.
3. The reform of the state owned enterprises was meant to begin in 1995. On the SOEs reform projects see also: Weber (1998).

References

Bell, N.W., H.E. Kohr and K. Kockhar, 'China at the Threshold of Market Economy', International Monetary Fund, occasional paper 107, September (1993).

Cabestan, J.P., *Le système politique de la Chine populaire*, (Paris: PUF 1994).

Cabestan, J.P., *Taiwan Chine populaire: l'impossible réunification*, (Paris: IFRI 1995).

Ferdinand, P., 'Xinjiang: Relations with China and Abroad', in D. Goodman, G. Segal (eds), *China Deconstructs; politics, trade and regionalism*, (London: Routledge, 1994), p. 271.

Goodman, D.S.G. and G. Segal, *China Deconstructs. Politics, Trade and Regionalism*, (London: Routledge, 1994).

IMF, *World Economic Outlook and International Capital Markets*, 2 December 1998.

Jordan, A., 'Lost in Translation: Two Legal Cultures, the Common Law Judiciary and the Basic Law of the Hong Kong Special Administrative Region', *Cornell International Law Journal*, XXX, No. 2 (1997), p. 335

Lardy, N.R., *China in the World Economy*, Institute for International Economics, (1994).

Lardy, N.R., 'China and the Asian Financial Contagion', *Foreign Affairs*, August (1998).

Lasserre, P. and H. Schütte, *Strategies for Asia Pacific*, (London: Macmillan, 1995).

Lawrence, S., 'Democracy, Chinese Style', *The Australian Journal of Chinese Affairs*, XXXII (1994), p. 33.

Jinshan, Li, 'The NPC System and Its Evolution: From Nomenklatura to Selectorate', *Issues and Studies*, XXXIV (1998), p. 1.

Melis, G., ' Le autonomie regionali nella Cina contemporanea', *Mondo Cinese*, XV No. 4 (1987), p. 3.

O'Brian, K.J., 'Implementing Political Reform in China's Villages', *The Australian Journal of Chinese Affairs*, XXXII (1994), p. 61.

Scot Tanner, M., 'How a Bill Becomes a Law in China: Stages and Processes in Lawmaking', *China Quarterly*, No. 141 (1995), p. 39.

Tisdell, C., *Economic Development in the Context of China*, (New York: St. Martin's Press, 1993).

Weber, M., *Vele verso la Cina*, (Milano: Edizioni Olivares, 1996).

Weber, M., 'China: an evaluation of political risk', in S. Dzever and J. Jaussaud (eds), *Perspectives on Economic integration and Business Strategy in the Asia Pacific Region*, (London: Macmillan, 1997).

Weber, M., 'China in Transition', *World Affairs, The Journal of International Issues*, 2 (1998).

World Bank, *The East Asia Miracle*, Washington D.C. (1994).

World Bank, *China 2020*, Washington D.C. (1997).

Yabuki, S., *China's New Political Economy*, (Boulder: Westview Press, 1995).

Yang Dali, L., 'Reform and the Restructuring of Central-Local Relations', in D. Goodman and G. Segal (eds), *China Deconstructs; politics, trade and regionalism*, (London: Routledge, 1994), p. 59.

Zhu Ding, Zhong, 'Mainland China's New Dilemma: Decentralization and Central–Local Conflicts in Economic Management', *Issues and Studies*, XXXI (1995), p. 19.

Zweig, D., 'Internationalising China's countryside: the political economy of exports from rural industry', *The China Quarterly*, 128, December (1991), 716–41.

2
The Crisis in Northeast Asia: the Cases of Japan and South Korea

Corrado Molteni

Japan and South Korea, the powerful economic engines that used to push and pull the Asian economies, have been severely hit by the crisis affecting the region. Growth rates have fallen, the basis of their financial systems are shaken and well-established economic institutions like the Japanese *keiretsu* and the Korean *chaebols* have to restructure, downsize and change time-honoured customs and practices.

The crisis has also cast a shadow on the socio-economic model of both countries. What used to be considered a successful Asian model of market economy which could be transferred and transplanted in other countries and in other regions, is now looked upon as an inefficient system that has to be radically changed and reformed. For many economists and commentators both countries should adopt models and standards that more often than not coincide with those prevailing in the Anglo-Saxon economies. Is this the path that Japan and South Korea will follow? The chapter seeks to highlight some of the issues raised by the crisis and the future prospects of both economies, focusing particularly on Japan as the main economy and market of the region, but also the socio-economic model that has inspired many of the reforms and the policies of Asian countries.

2.1 Japan's economic and financial crisis: the future of the Japanese model and its role in the Asian region

Today Japan is in the midst of the most severe and protracted economic crisis of the post-war period. But it is not simply the scale and the length of the current economic difficulties that differs from past crises. First, the nature of this crisis is different as it does not originate from external shocks such as the oil price hikes of the 1970s or the depreciation of the dollar in the middle of the 1980s. This time Japan's economic woes are in large part the products of domestic factors, particularly the critical conditions of its financial institutions crippled by the huge amount of non-performing loans produced by the collapse of the speculative bubble of the 1980s. The country is also paying the price of the government's reluctance to act faster and in a more decisive way in order to solve the problems of the financial sector. The same government is responsible for the very untimely decision taken in the spring of 1997 to raise the consumption tax rate at a moment when the economy was still very weak, thus causing the economic downturn to become even more firmly entrenched.

Second, the scope of this crisis is different from previous ones. In past recessions the manufacturing system had to adjust to external shocks that threatened its competitiveness in the international markets, but the financial system and the other institutions remained strong and stable. This time, however, not only the financial and the manufacturing systems are facing enormous difficulties, but the crisis is also casting doubts on the validity and the efficacy of some of the most consolidated economic, political and social institutions of the country. Japan's position and role in the world is also openly questioned and debated both at home and abroad. As its economy is shrinking and its institutions under fire, the country's image has greatly changed. Gone are the days when Professor Ezra F. Vogel could write a book entitled *Japan as Number One. Lessons for America* (Vogel, 1979). The Japan of today is rather portrayed as a country which is deeply shaken, confused and uncertain about its economy, institutions and even its social and moral values.

But is Japan really so weak and fragile? The prevailing mood, at the end of the twentieth century is so grim and negative that many observers, both Japanese and foreigners, tend to forget or disregard Japan's strengths and potential. Not only does Japan have a huge current account surplus, but its citizens continue to be among the thriftiest in the world and ultimately are the only ones whose savings can finance America's ballooning trade deficit. Also the manufacturing sector's technological and innovation capabilities remain strong and intact. The Asian crisis has indeed deepened the economic difficulties, but it is also providing an opportunity for Japanese investors to strengthen their control over many companies and joint ventures in SEA, whose weaker local partners are in deep troubles. Japan could thus again surprise many observers and it might not take too long before some of the discredited institutions of today regain their reputation.

This does not imply that Japan's institutions and policies will remain unchanged. New ideas and powerful forces have been unleashed by the crisis and the demand for change and reforms is so strong that it cannot be disregarded. But what direction will reforms take? Will Japan adopt the Anglo-Saxon model of free labour and capital markets, as the Clinton administration and many American and Japanese economists do advocate? Or will it develop its own solutions? What are these solutions like and who is proposing them? And how could domestic changes affect Japan's role in Asia and the world after the crisis? Will Japan remain a loyal ally of the US or will it follow an independent course as a more assertive Asian leader? These are the questions addressed in the following pages. As opinions reflect, but also influence and shape reality, the attention is focused on both aspects: the debate among Japanese academics, opinion makers and policymakers but also the reforms that have been already introduced. However, before discussing future developments and scenarios, the current economic conditions, the causes of the crisis and the impacts of the policies are analyzed.

2.1.1 The current economic conditions and the crisis of the banking sector

Since the increase of the consumption tax rate in the spring of 1997 Japan's economic conditions have continued to deteriorate. Currently the country is in the midst of a severe economic recession due to the contraction of domestic demand. In particular, corporate sector fixed investment and housing investment have been decreasing significantly, while private consumption has not yet shown signs of recovery. Consumer confidence may weaken even further despite the special income tax reduction. The only positive factor remains the controversial increase of net exports (exports–imports), although the appreciation of the yen since early autumn 1998 may reduce the contribution of external demand. Against this background, production has been reduced substantially, corporate profits and employee income continue to decrease,[1] and the unemployment rate remains at a high level (4.4 per cent in November 1998), while the ratio of job offers to applications has recorded an historical low. Reflecting the continued expansion in the output gap, wholesale prices remain on a downward trend, while consumer prices are also declining (Bank of Japan, 1998a).

What is the main culprit of this unprecedented economic downturn? As mentioned above, the triggering factor was the untimely decision to raise the consumption tax rate. However, this fact alone does not explain

Table 2.1 Classification of loans of Japan's 17 major banks (as of March 1998 in billion yen)

Category 1 (loans that are classified as healthy)	344 708.5
Category 2 (loans that require monitoring)	43 781.2
Category 3 (loans difficult to recover)	5 342.6
Category 4 (loans that are irrecoverable)	375.6
TOTAL	394 207.9

Source: Financial Supervisory Agency.

the depth and the length of the recession. For Paul Krugman the problem lies in the level of aggregate demand that is inadequate to employ the country's productive capacity. Or, in other words, in the fact that 'at full employment Japanese savings would exceed Japanese investment by more than the country's current account surplus'. In Krugman's opinion, what is needed is therefore 'some kind of deeply unconventional response' such as negative real interest rates to be achieved through 'managed inflation' (Krugman, 1998). For many Japanese economists and policymakers, and also for the author of this chapter, Japan is obviously confronting a textbook case of the liquidity trap, but the main cause of the current economic recession is rather to be found in the weakness of the financial system and the consequent credit crunch. To quote Masaru Hayami, the Governor of the Bank of Japan, 'the disturbances in the financial system caused the declining trend to become firmly established' (Bank of Japan, 1998b). Sakakibara Eisuke, the influential and outspoken Vice Minister for International Affairs Finance at the Ministry of Finance (MOF), shares this view. In a sharp criticism of Krugmans' view, he points out that 'a very severe credit crunch is now taking place ... In this kind of situation not only bad loans but also good loans can be withdrawn.' And concludes by saying that 'aggressive recapitalisation of banks is the first, and necessary, step to stimulate the aggregate demand and to reflate the economy' (Sakakibara, 1998).

Indeed, as shown by the successive failures of several financial institutions since the fall of 1997 and by the large amount of bad loans held by the major banks (see Table 2.1), the Japanese financial sector is in a very bad shape and is facing a serious systemic risk since the problem is widespread and is not limited to a few, poorly managed institutions. In this context, banks and other financial institutions remain extremely cautious and reluctant to take an active lending stance. Institutions plagued with balance-sheet problems prefer to use any additional resources to write off non-performing assets rather than to extend new loans. Thus, firms, especially the small and medium sized ones, continue to face a severe environment in terms of both funds availability and fund-raising costs. In other words it is the credit crunch that severely affects the prospects of a rapid recovery.

This large amount of non-performing assets and the consequent credit crunch are the most visible outcome of the excesses of the second half of the 1980s, the years of Japan's economic bubble. At that time firms and individuals borrowed extensively to finance both fixed investment and the purchase of shares and real estate. In practice, individuals and firms received loans from banks and other financial institutions against the deposit of collateral as guarantee (land is normally used as collateral in Japan); the funds were then invested in land and stocks that were used again as overvalued collateral to obtain further loans. Thus a vicious circle was generated that lasted until the Bank of Japan decided to tighten monetary policy and raise interest rates.

With the collapse of the bubble, the values of the financial and real estate assets drastically depreciated, but remained on the banks and firms' books at their original values, giving rise to a large gap between assets and liabilities. Firms and financial institutions thus found and find it difficult to venture into new business or extend new loans due to the severe contraction of their capital base (Bank of Japan, 1998b).

But how did it happen that the Japanese bank managers, well known in the past for their prudent, conservative lending attitude, have so poorly performed? What caused the change in their consolidated customs and behaviours? Two possible explanations have been proposed. According to the first one, the extremely easy monetary policy of the late 1980s and the abrupt tightening of the same policy in the early 1990s produced the wide price fluctuations and in the end the non-performing loans problem. However, according to a different interpretation, the real cause was the ineffective regulatory framework developed in post-war Japan under the leadership and the guidance of the Ministry of Finance. According to Professor Akiyoshi Horiuchi of Tokyo University, the Ministry protected depositors and other investors from losses associated to bank failures (in fact until recently no bank was allowed to fail), but did not implement prudential regulations to prevent the moral hazard on the part of bank management. The fragility of the system did not surface during the high-growth period, because the regulations restricting competition provided, on the one hand, protection for the less competitive institutions and, on the other hand, guaranteed conspicuous rents for the stronger and better managed banks and other financial institutions. Moreover, the existence of rents induced bank managers to refrain from excessive risk-taking. This mechanism, known as the 'convoy system',[2] ceased to operate effectively in the 1980s, when a gradual but steady process of liberalization and deregulation of the Japanese financial system changed the rules of the game. In the new environment firms became more autonomous and independent from the banks, issuing corporate bonds and tapping new financing sources both in Japan and in foreign markets. On the other hand, banks were forced to extend aggressively their credit to new customers and to enter new, more risky and less familiar fields of activities. The easy monetary policy of the second half of the 1980s just provided additional, cheap fuel. Then, when the bubble collapsed, the Ministry of Finance and the Bank of Japan found themselves lacking a suitable and effective system for monitoring the banks and for dealing with the bad loans problem. According to this interpretation the liberalization of a protected, well-cushioned financial system lacking the expertise and the competence to operate in a competitive and uncertain environment were the ultimate cause of the bad loans problem and also the reason why the country has taken so much time to realize and tackle the problem (Horiuchi, 1997). This was also due to the unwillingness to admit and take responsibility for past failures and to the political instability and the weaknesses of the governments that have ruled Japan since 1992, when a series of scandals and political infighting have ended the era of the Liberal Democratic Party (LDP) supremacy.

The Asian crisis has then further aggravated the problems, giving rise to a vicious cycle that starts with a weak Japan reducing the changes of a rapid economic recovery in SEA and NEA that, in turn, negatively affect Japan. Recently however the Obuchi government has begun to act in a more resolute and decisive way. A new and, hopefully, more effective system of monitoring and supervision of the financial institutions is being reorganized with the establishment of the Financial Supervisory Agency under the Financial Revitalization Committee, an independent body within the Prime Minister Office but jointly responsible with the Ministry of Finance for the solution of the problem of ailing financial institutions. In October 1998 the Diet approved two

Table 2.2 Comparative data of the two nationalized banks

	Nippon Credit Bank	**Long-Term Credit Bank of Japan**
Date nationalized	13 December 1998	23 October 1998
Amount of bad loans	¥ 3.75 trillion	¥ 2.02 trillion
Liabilities in excess of assets (including latent losses)	¥ 274.7 billion	¥ 340 billion
Shareholders' equity	¥ 467.1 billion	¥ 512.4 billion

Source: Nihon Keizai Shinbun 1996.

bills for banks' 'revitalization' and recapitalization providing more than 60 trillion yen of public funds. Japan's major banks have indeed begun the preparations required to tap the government's fund, although the amount of the requests and the speed of the procedures seem to be less than impressive.[3] Thus, the timing and the actual size of the recapitalisation programme might require a more decisive and effective intervention by the government that will force the banks to comply.

The change in the government's attitude is more evident in the response towards the failure of two long-term credit institutions that have been recently nationalized. As shown in Table 2.2, the Long Term Credit Bank of Japan and the Nippon Credit Bank with liabilities in excess of assets for more than 340 and 270 billion yen, have been 'temporarily' nationalized by the government in October and December 1998. There are, however, major differences in the timing and the way the two banks were nationalized. In the case of the Long-Term Credit Bank of Japan the government hesitated and wavered on whether to save or to liquidate it, while bureaucrats and politicians argued that the bank was too big to fail. In the case of the nationalization of the Nippon Credit Bank the newly established Financial Supervision Agency alone took the decision to close the bank on the basis of the results of its own inspection of the bank. This rapid and decisive action, taken against the will of the bank's managers, indicates that the Agency is determined to play an active role in the restructuring of the banking system and is going to act swiftly and in an aggressive way.

The Financial Revitalisation Law and the nationalization of the Nippon Credit Bank could indeed represent the turning point in the restructuring process. Moreover, as pointed out by Japanese and foreign observers, these two decisive moves could mark the end of the traditional Japanese convoy system and open the way to the implementation of the structural, market-oriented reforms, that have been advocated for a long time, but so far only timidly adopted and implemented.

The government has also taken some bold action in trying to expand domestic demand and thus promote economic recovery. In November the Obuchi government approved the largest ever economic stimulus package including a 17.9 trillion yen public works programme and tax cuts of 6 trillion yen. In the recently announced budget draft for fiscal year 1999 (1 April 1999–31 March 2000), general spending is set at 81.86 trillion yen, an increase of 5.4 per cent from the previous year and the highest growth rate in the last 20 years. However, as pointed out by many economists, the governments still indulge excessively in financing outdated projects such as railways and highways in peripheral regions.[4] This policy is certainly very effective from a political point of view (powerful interest groups supporting the LDP will be among its main beneficiaries), but its efficacy is doubtful, particularly in the medium, long-term period. At this point the spending policy will result in a conspicuous budget deficit (central and local governments budget deficits combined will account for 10 per cent of GDP) that will have to be financed with the issue of government bonds. To cover the loss in revenues (due to tax cuts, but also and foremost due to declining corporate profits and family income) the government is actually planning to issue 31.05 trillion yen of government bonds in 1999, a 99.6 per cent rise from the previous year!

This huge burden left to future generations might even have a negative impact on economic recovery. The planned large issuance of bonds is already pushing up interest rates and this in turn will reduce investment and consumption. Moreover, higher interest rates also mean lower prices and capital losses for bondholders. Institutional investors will be particularly affected. According to a research by Merrill Lynch Japan, Japan's 18 major banks had combined latent profits of about 600 billion yen in their bond portfolios at the end of September 1998 (*Nikkei Weekly*, 28 December 1998). A surge in interest rates and the consequent decline in bond prices would erase these profits that will not be compensated by higher income through increased yields: a negative scenario that could delay the solution of the bad loans problems. From this perspective it seems that instead of an aggressive spending policy, the government should strive to reduce public expenditures and the tax burden and, as discussed below, concentrate on structural and institutional reforms.

2.1.2 The issue of structural reforms (the end of the Japanese model?)

The current crisis has also given new impetus to the debate on the Japanese socio-economic model and the need of structural reforms. Academics, columnists, business leaders, politicians and high-ranking bureaucrats are currently engaged in a wide-ranging discussion on the radical reforms that, according to many, are needed to change Japan's socio-economic structures.

This debate has been going on for a long time, although for many decades these issues were mainly of academic interest and did not seriously concern the public opinion and the country's policymakers. The question whether Japan is different from other countries and whether it should or it should not reform itself became a major, sensitive political issue in the 1980s, following Japan's emergence as an economic power that was challenging the American supremacy. The debate, however, was conducted mainly by a group of American scholars, who have come to be known as the 'revisionists'.[5] They argued that the Japanese economy follows a set of principles and rules that are profoundly different from those of other capitalist countries and from the American model, in particular. Far-reaching governmental intervention through administrative guidance, closed enterprize groups and underdeveloped, inefficient capital and labour markets are the distinctive ingredients of the Japanese model, that in the revisionists' opinion made Japan so different and, as a result, an unfair player in the international marketplace that had to be differently treated. The Japanese reaction was to deny the Japanese distinctiveness and to argue that the Japanese economy was operating within the neo-classical framework (see Miwa, 1995).

However, unlike in the 1980s, the debate is now first of all a debate among Japanese and for the Japanese. It is an impressively lively and vigorous debate, having direct implications on the political agenda and the policymaking. It covers a wide range of aspects but the main concern, the focus of attention are the state role in the marketplace, the power and the competence of the bureaucracy in a democratic society, the function of the capital markets and the system of corporate governance, the labour market and the model of human resource management and, of course, Japan's role in world affairs. Conflicting views and opinions have been published and aired in an attempt to influence the mind of the people and the course of events. What kind of solution will emerge we do not know, but it is possible to identify the main currents of thought that, for the intellectual stature of their proponents or for the strength of their ideas, seem to have a wider audience and a stronger power of influence. Specifically, in the flood of articles, papers and books on the issue of what and how to reform, the different positions and approaches can be regrouped in four major groups: liberal reformers, cultural relativists, traditionalists or nationalists and marxists.

The first one is represented by the thinking of liberal reformers. Like the revisionists, they are convinced that major structural faults in the Japanese socio-economic system are negatively affecting the performance and the future prospects of the country. Consequently, they advocate the adoption of a policy of far-reaching, sweeping reforms that should promote deregulation, increase competition and reduce the power and the influence of the bureaucracy. These reforms should remove many of the distinctive features of the Japanese economic system, and make Japan more similar to the other advanced industrialized countries. This view is indeed the mainstream one and is widely shared by many economists, business leaders and also by influential politicians.

A particularly strong advocate of reforms is Professor Iwao Nakatani, an economist at Hitotsubashi University and a prolific writer, who published a book *The Historical Turning Point of the Japanese Economy* (Nakatani, 1996). According to Nakatani, this point had been reached because the institutions that sustained the post-war high growth have become worn out and need to be radically reformed. In particular, he points out four elements of the Japanese economic system that are rapidly becoming obsolete. These four elements are: (1) the close relations binding the public administration and the private sector; (2) the so-called main bank system, the pillar of Japan's post-war financial system; (3) the employment system based on lifetime employment and seniority, 'now almost lifeless'; and (4) the vertical *keiretsu* in the consumer electronics and motor vehicle sectors, which have started to crumble, following the transfer abroad of production facilities.

For Nakatani all these elements have played an important, positive role in the past, when Japan was trying to catch up with the industrialised countries of the West, but today they are becoming a handicap, an obstacle to further economic development. For example, the main bank, besides providing funds to the growing, strategic sectors of the economy, in the past played an important role as the monitoring agent of a Japanese corporate system where shareholders' rights are quite neglected. Today, however, the importance of the main bank system has substantially declined, following the process of financial deregulation and the shift from indirect to direct financing. He argues, therefore, that there is an urgent need to develop a more efficient capital market or new institutional arrangements that can channel funds to innovative sectors and enterprises.

As for the too intimate relations between government and the private enterprises, Nakatani agrees that these effectively supported Japan's post-war economic development, but he also maintains that now they are more of a burden hampering economic activities. To overcome the problems of what he calls 'systemic' or 'institutional fatigue', he proposes an agenda for reforms aimed at deregulating the system, making it more transparent, innovation oriented and less egalitarian. Specifically, in an article published in the *Nihon Keizai Shinbun* (Nakatani, 1995), he mentions four points. The first one is the substitution of the traditional industrial policies with a more rigorous and effective competition policy. The second is the reform of the severance pay system in order to enhance labour mobility and the development of an efficient labour market. The third point is the already mentioned reform of the financial system, while the fourth one is the readjustment of the policymaking system, so as to reduce the discretionary power of the bureaucracy and to replace it with a new class of competent and, first of all, more assertive political leaders. This last proposal is obviously welcomed by many politicians who, like Ichiroo Ozawa, have been campaigning for a strengthening of the functions and power of the Prime Minister and the Cabinet (Ozawa 1993). It also fits in with the programme of administrative reforms sponsored by the press, and the *Yomiuri Shinbun* in particular, Japan's largest newspaper (1996).

However, more than in the political world, the views of liberal economists have found support and consensus within the Japanese business community. Indeed, the content of the *Keidanren's Vision for 2020* (Keidanren, 1996) is in various respects largely consistent with the assumptions and the prescriptions of this current of thought. It shares, first of all, the same view that the 'political, economic and social system that have brought Japan's prosperity to date are reaching an impasse in various respects, with a resulting loss of vitality and orientation in every sector of society.' For this powerful organization too, 'if Japan chooses to remain idle and fails to reform itself, it will be left behind in the global progress'. As for the main causes of 'Japan's stature shrinking in the world', the Keidanren's document points out 'a variety of constraints, notably government regulations and a bureaucratic habit of trying to manage the marketplace'. However, it also mentions 'the erosion of the sense of social solidarity and responsibility due to the spread of egocentric attitudes, a disregard of morals, and a loss of national identity'. This second part of the argument is unlikely to appear in the writings of liberal economists, but it is certainly a matter of concern for managers who have been used to enjoying the advantages of an orderly and trust-based society.

Concerning the reforms to be adopted, Keidanren proposes a ten-item list (the so-called Action 21 Programme) that, once again, is very much in line with the thinking of neo-classical economists. The list includes in fact the following items.

1) A thorough overhaul of government regulations. In this respect, according to Keidanren, 'entrance and new facilities restrictions . . . must be totally abolished by the year 2000 and . . . with very few exceptions, all economic regulations must be abolished by 2010'.
2) The promotion of administrative, fiscal and tax reforms to realize a transparent, small and efficient government. This should follow two principles: the transfer of power from the bureaucracy to the private sector and decentralization.
3) The deregulation of the labour market to improve labour mobility and the diffusion of a remuneration system based only on individual achievement.
4) The creation of an efficient and transparent financial and capital market, in principle free from regulations.
5) The promotion of the yen's globalization.

This is a very liberal programme unlikely to have been adopted in the past, when the corporate sector was much more dependent on 'the banks and the economic bureaucracy that functioned as a general staff behind the battlefield in the total war called high economic growth' (Sakakibara and Noguchi 1977). It is a programme that clearly shows that change in corporate thinking which begun in the 1980s, but which became particularly evident in the early 1990s. Since then, the business community has become the strongest advocate of reforms. This assertive attitude of the business community reflects a more fundamental shift in the structure of economic and political power in Japan. The corporate sector is in fact no longer so dependent on the support of the state as it used to be in the past. It believes that deregulation, more than government intervention, can help Japan to overcome the present difficulties. It is a corporate sector that has grown up and is confident. To use Keidanren's words, 'if Japan has to regain its identity and sense of direction, its business community must take the lead in suggesting the path the country needs to follow' (Keidanren 1996). Thus it is not a surprise that the strongest and most articulated challenge to the ideas of liberal reformists is coming from a high-ranking bureaucrat at the Ministry of Finance, the most powerful institution in the Japanese government.

Eisuke Sakakibara, the already quoted Vice Minister of Finance for International Affairs, is indeed the foremost critic of neo-classical economists and a leading figure in the cultural relativists camp. This second current of thought follows a more relativistic approach, which denies the existence of a universal model and tends to emphasize the positive features of the Japanese form of capitalism. Those who share this way of thinking do not deny the need for change, but tend to be more conservative and critical when it comes to the issue of domestic reforms concerning the fabric of society and the political set-up.

For Sakakibara, an outstanding personality who has followed a unique career path through various institutions in the strongly vertically organized Japanese society,[6] there is no such thing as an economic system having universal and normative values transcending time and space, but a variety of economic systems. He argues that the Japanese system is a completely legitimate alternative to Western (Anglo-Saxon)-style capitalism. In his words, 'Japan has developed a somewhat unique model during the past sixty odd years and established what might be called a *non-capitalistic market economy* with a pluralistic political regime' (Sakakibara, 1993). What makes the Japanese model different is basically what Sakakibara calls the 'employee sovereignty', that has replaced traditional capitalistic 'shareholders sovereignty'. He has actually borrowed this concept of 'employee sovereignty' from Hiroyuki Itami of Hitotsubashi University.[7] For Sakakibara the managers at the top of a Japanese company do no longer work for the shareholders, but for the benefit of the organisation's employees (Sakakibara 1993).

Moreover, opinion-makers like Sakakibara do not only believe in the legitimacy of a Japanese model, but also share a common view that its merits largely overcome the weaknesses. In their view, the greatest advantages of this arrangement are a higher degree of participation, motivation, and co-operation on the part of the employees, as well as the long-term outlook and a more efficient use of information on the part of the managers. Sakakibara is also an outspoken defender of the Japanese state and its role. In detailed, comparative research on advanced industrial countries he points out how the Japanese government is small and lean when compared with the bureaucracies of Western countries, US included (Sakakibara, 1995).[8] In another essay he criticizes the diffused 'bureaucrat bashing', although he does agree on the need for removing barriers among departments and strengthening the co-ordinating functions of the Prime Minister Office (Sakakibara, 1996). For Sakakibara the Japanese system should be more understood and appreciated, first of all by the Japanese themselves. In his opinion, 'calls for reform lacking a clear awareness of Japan's systemic realities have only led to a subservient Japanese pandering to US and European demands. . . . And precisely this lack of awareness is the main cause of the present difficulties and stagnation'. His conclusion is that unless the Japanese do not understand the reason behind their economic successes, 'they will find themselves in a perpetual catch-up syndrome' (Sakakibara, 1993).

In *Farewell to Progressivism* (1996), Sakakibara strongly argues against the majority of the 'reformers', who would like to Americanize Japan, and concludes by saying that 'the Japanese should grope for a new paradigm, if they do not agree with the principles and the ideas of the neo-conservative revolution'. However, which are the basic assumptions of this new paradigm it is not so clear, and this is the weakest point in his argument, although it cannot be denied that in today's Japan his view, although a minority one, is the most serious challenge to the mainstream one.

Like Sakakibara, the nationalists, the third current of thought, resent American influence and pressure, but first of all emphasize the importance of traditional values. Intellectuals like Nishibe Susumu, Eto Jun and Iida Tsuneo and the novelist and former parliamentarian Shintaro Ishihara are among the leading figures. Their influence is quite limited. However, the recession, the political uncertainties and, foremost, the actual or perceived foreign interference in Japan's domestic affairs, is making the nationalist message convincing and attractive for a growing number of Japanese.

The fourth and last current of thought is the marxist one. Although still powerful in the academia, the marxist school had lost ground since the 1970s. The current crisis has provided new ammunitions for their criticism of what they see as an oligopolistic, state-controlled Japanese capitalism. However, the marxist school does not seem to be able to provide viable and practical solutions. It is more a critical voice that, so far, has not been able to influence the policymaking.

Which current of thought will shape the future course of Japan? Will it be that of the reform-minded liberal economists like Nakatani, or that of the champions of the Japanese-type market economy? Will Japan and its policymakers continue to look West, or will they look more inside Japan for ideas and solutions of the current economic and social woes?

As happened in the past, Japan seems to have adopted a pragmatic approach that combines innovative and traditional elements. Competition will be introduced in those sectors of the economy that have been protected so far excessively under the 'convoy system'. Gradually but surely, even 'sacred' institutions such as the lifetime employment system are changing. Some companies are gradually shifting to an open, year-round recruiting system. Others are finding it advantageous to hire experienced workers, especially retired ones willing to work as temporary employees. Keidanren suggests the adoption of a system of in-house recruiting to provide ambitious employees with more career opportunities (Keidanren 1996). All this does not mean, however, that Japan will develop a labour market like the American one, but rather that the level of in-house competition will be further increased. Thus, in the future too top positions in Japan's large corporation will continue to be occupied by managers who have spent their career within the same company, but the survival rate will be lower and the competition tougher.

The system of corporate governance is also changing, as shown by the rapid weakening of cross-shareholdings. Will this imply the emergence of an open and developed capital market, where it will be possible to sell and acquire corporations like in the US? It is doubtful. The final outcome is more likely to be a system centred on financial holding companies, which has been forbidden in Japan but has recently been authorized.

The major reforms concern the public administration and the financial system. As for the first aspect, there are plans to streamline the bureaucracy, privatize government functions and reorganize the state machinery. The Economic Strategy Council, a key government's advisory council lead by Hirotaro Higuchi, the Keidanren's Vice President, has just published an interim report that calls for a revision of bureaucratic power, including a drastic reduction (more than 20 per cent in ten years) of the number of civil servants (see *Nikkei Weekly*, 28 December 1998). Obviously such plans will meet strong opposition from the concerned parties, but the impression is that the bureaucracy is on the defensive and will not be able to turn the tide. Indeed, even part of the bureaucracy, particularly in the powerful MITI, recognizes the need for reforms, and not only because by so doing they hope to chart them in the most desired direction.

As for the financial system, the government is going ahead with structural reforms known as the Japanese Big Bang that should establish a more competition-driven, open and transparent system with the goal of transforming the Tokyo market in an international financial market comparable to those of New York and London. To this end, several laws have been already approved that liberalize and deregulate the securities and financial markets, including the deregulation of foreign exchange transactions, of brokerage commissions and the removal of barriers between the different intermediaries.

Thus, reforms are and will be introduced. However, differences and peculiarities in the economic systems are not going to disappear. And this is particularly true for a country like Japan. It will, to some degree at least, follow the path of Western countries, but it will also retain its distinctive features that in many cases are the real source of its strength and dynamism.

2.1.3 Conclusion: Japan's international role

To summarize, let us briefly consider what will be the effect of the current crisis and debate on Japan's position in Asia and the world. According to Chalmers Johnson, the renown East Asian scholar and the author of *MITI and the Japanese Miracle*, in 'East Asia the prevailing trend is a tendency to cling to the old Cold War system in which the US provide the structure of military security while the various nations within this system seek to expand their economic capabilities' (Johnson, 1997). This is indeed the preferred option for many Japanese. The approval of the new guidelines on Japan–US defence co-operation in September 1998 has also confirmed the government's and the country's support for the alliance with the US.

Past and more recent developments, however, have certainly reduced the sense of security provided by the special partnership bounding the two countries. The more frequent and escalating trade disputes with the US, the American handling of the Asian crisis and the continuous attempts to instruct the Japanese on how to behave and how to run their economy are becoming too annoying and difficult to swallow even for the patient Japanese. The perception that the US is paying more attention to China than to their country, a perception strongly reinforced by the visit to China of President Clinton, contributes to the doubts on the American commitment and support. It is then not surprising that important sectors of the country's leading institutions and opinion makers have started to prepare the ground for a strategic disengagement from the US in favour of an attempt to acquire the leadership in Asia. Even the government itself has taken a more assertive, autonomous stance on international issues, indicating that it will not so readily follow the US, always and in any case. This was evident during

Jiang Zemin's historical visit to Japan and in the attempts to launch various initiatives aimed at solving the resurgence of a financial crisis. In particular, Japan's call for the creation of a 100 billion yen Asian Monetary Fund – an idea rejected by the US and the IMF – and the recent proposal by Finance Minister Miyazawa for controls on currency and short-term capital flows indicates that Japan has its own solutions and agenda.

These developments reflect the growing Japanese and Asian dissatisfaction with American policies and high-handed attempts to impose them on the Asian nations. A sentiment that is growing even stronger now that Asia is facing unprecedented economic woes and hardships. Indeed, there is a common thread between the ideas of the Malaysian Prime Minister Mahatir and the positions of many Japanese leaders advocating a more independent and assertive Japan. Does this pro-Asian, anti-American position mean that Japan will be able co-operate with China to the possible disadvantage of the US? Indeed the arguments in favour of a co-operation between the two Asian powers are plentiful, but it cannot be ignored that an influential government official as former ambassador Hisahiko Okazaki wrote recently in the house organ of the Japanese Ministry of Foreign Affairs that 'China will never be truly close to Japan even in the future.' (Johnson, 1997)

If Japan does try to play a leading role in Asia, it will be at the helm of a group of Asian nations that will not necessarily include China. It's attempts to develop particularly strong ties with ASEAN provides a clear indication of what are it's strategic priorities and goals in the region. Japan might not clash with China over who will be supreme in Asia, as scholars like Samuel Huntington seem to suggest (Huntington, 1993). Yet it will not seek either to enhance the Chinese chances to become a leading nation in the region. On the other hand, it might try to strengthen its ties with the EU in its attempt to reduce the dependence on the US and to assert itself as a leading Asian nation.

2.2 South Korea: the crisis and the future prospects[9]

The crisis in Korea exploded in the second half of 1997, but its origins can be found in the early months of 1995, when the government decided to maintain its policy of a strong won. With the aim of controlling inflation and minimizing exchange rate volatility, a virtually fixed nominal exchange rate against the dollar was thus maintained for over a decade until the currency was allowed to float freely in December 1997. The Japanese and the Chinese currency depreciation, from

1995 and 1994 respectively, further aggravated the Korean position. As a result, in 1997 the Korean currency was overvalued by 10 to 20 per cent. This, combined with a slowdown in the global demand and the collapse in the prices of semiconductors, led to a significant deceleration of export growth and a deterioration of the current account (a record deficit of US$ 23.7 billion was registered in 1996). The slowdown placed strong financial pressure on the *chaebols,* Korean large conglomerates, which needed high economic growth to maintain their high debt levels, including a high level of foreign debt (average debt-equity ratio was more than 500 per cent for the 30 largest conglomerates at the end of 1997).[10] The failure of Hanbo, a steel company, in January 1997 and particularly that of Kia, the eighth largest *chaebol,* in July signalled the beginning of the crisis. Foreign lenders' attitude and confidence in Korea changed and a massive capital flight occurred. After October 1997 Korean debtors faced increased difficulty in rolling over their short-term debts with international banks. On 21 November 1997, the new Deputy Prime Minister, Mr Lim, announced that the government had requested the IMF's support for an economic stabilization and reform programme.

The Korean crisis thus started as a financial and currency crisis. However, as in other Asian countries, underlying the high level of external and domestic debt were a number of structural weaknesses. In particular, the delay in introducing reforms, following the liberalization of the economy from the early 1990s. In the financial sector, a regulatory and supervisory framework was not developed. At the same time, banks and other financial institutions did not fully develop their own credit and risk assessment capabilities but, under the government's influence and pressure, continued to provide funds to the heavily indebted *chaebols*. Excessive investment in several industrial sectors also generated a substantial production overcapacity.

2.2.1 The restructuring programme

The key elements of the IMF-supported programme (which was approved on 4 December 1997) can be grouped under three broad headings: exchange market stabilization; financial restructuring; and structural reforms. At the heart of the programme are financial and corporate sector restructuring and the adoption of measures to increase the efficiency of the labour market. Corporate sector restructuring is particularly critical and controversial as it implies a drastic change of the structural features of the Korean economy. The government is urging the *chaebols* to reduce excessive diversification and to concentrate on core- business. However, shareholders resistance to break up the *chae-bols* and opposition from organized labour make the task particularly difficult. Only under heavy pressure from President Kim Dae-jung, the five biggest conglomerates have agreed in principle to downsize and reorganize themselves in what has come to be called the Big Deal (*Nikkei Weekly*, 21 December 1998). The first step has been a shift from a focus on size to one on profitability. But observers remain sceptical.

As for the employment system, which in Korea has been character-ized by a virtual lifetime employment, the government and the man-agement have recognized the necessity of easing restrictions on layoffs to support financial and corporate restructuring, but face strong resistance from labour unions.[11] After tripartite consultative talks be-tween labour, business and government, the Labour Standard Act was amended in March 1998, to establish conditions and procedures for layoffs. On the other hand, reforms were introduced to strengthen the unemployment insurance system, including retraining and job creation.

Foreign participation in the economy is also seen as a critical element. The goal is to eliminate all controls and restrictions by the year 2000 and several restrictions on foreign investment, including land owner-ship, have been already eliminated. Restrictions on foreign borrowing have also been reduced substantially.

2.2.2 Future prospects

Will the country be successful in its restructuring efforts? And what will remain of its famous state-led economic model? Will Korea also turn into a 'true' market economy? Indeed, important changes have been introduced in the government–market relationship. The policy of investment co-ordination has been abandoned. Even the model of selec-tive industrial policy has been dismantled (Ha-Joon, 1998). However, this does not mean that Korea will fully adopt the recipes suggested by the IMF and many economists. Critical voices and opinions are largely diffused. Resistance is particularly strong against the recommendation of further, rapid financial liberalization. As pointed out by Ha-Joon of Cambridge University, for many Koreans 'the ultimate solution lies in strengthening, not weakening the co-ordinating function of the gov-ernment – albeit in a more consensual and sophisticated way than before. . . . While it is unwise to suggest that a return to the traditional model is possible and desirable, the country's headlong dash towards the Anglo-American institutional model, half voluntary and half under IMF pressure, does not seem to be particularly desirable' (Ha-Joon, 1998, p. 230).

Notes

1. According to a survey by the Nihon Keizai Shinbun, winter bonuses paid by private companies in 1998 were down 2.9 per cent from last year. This is the largest decline since 1975.
2. As in a convoy of ships all the institutions have to proceed at the same speed that is the speed of the slowest one. The system provides protection for all the institutions but prevents competition.
3. At the end of December 1998, 18 major banks were reported to be planning to apply for less than 6 trillion yen. As for the procedures, a number of major banks that intend to obtain public funds have to amend their articles of incorporation before the issue of preferred shares: a process that can take months and require the shareholders' approval (*Nihon Keizai Shinbun*, 16 and 18 December 1998).
4. In the 1999 budget draft a key spending item is the 31.7 trillion yen earmarked for new Shinkansen (high speed train) lines in the Tohoku, Hokuriku and Kyushu regions (*Nikkei Weekly*, 28 December 1998).
5. The principal revisionists books and articles include Choate (1990), Fallows (1989), Johnson (1995), and Prestowitz (1988).
6. Sakakibara, after graduation from the Faculty of Economics of Tokyo University, joined the Ministry of Finance. From there, in the second half of the sixties, he went to the US to obtain a Ph.D at Michigan University in 1969.
7. According to Itami, 'employee sovereignty' implies that 'the firm belongs to the people who have committed themselves to it and worked in it for long periods. . . . They are the holder of *sovereign power*: the people who have the right to make decisions and the priority rights in the distribution of the economic products of the firms activities' (Itami 1994).
8. According to this research lead by Sakakibara, in Japan there are 40.5 civil servants (including local government employees and personnel of Japan Self Defence Forces) for every 1000 inhabitants, while in Western countries the number is respectively of 79.3 in the US, 78.3 in the United Kingdom, 78.3 in Germany and 95.4 in France (Sakakibara, 1995, pp. 32–3).
9. The author would like to thank Benedetta Trivellato for her help and support.
10. Chang Ha-Joon has argued, however, that the level of nonperforming loans in Korea at the eve of the crisis was not particularly high (Ha-Joon, 1998).
11. Labour has strongly resisted Hyundai's attempt to cut 8000 jobs in the car sector. In the end only a few hundred jobs were eliminated. At Samsung Motors workers resisted being absorbed by Daewoo by shutting down operations.

References

Bank of Japan, 'Monthly Report of Recent Economic and Financial Developments', (Tokyo, 30 November 1998a).

Bank of Japan, *Quarterly Bulletin*, (Tokyo, November 1998b).

Choate, P. *Agents of Influence*, (New York: Knopf, 1990).

Economic Planning Agency and Economic Council, *Social and Economic Plan for Structural Reforms*, (Tokyo, 29 November 1995).

Economist Intelligence Unit, *South Korea – Country Report*, 4th Quarter 1998.

Fallow, J. 'Containing Japan', *The Atlantic*, (May 1989).

Ha-Joon, C. 'South Korea: the Misunderstood Crisis', in K.S. Jomo, *Tigers in Trouble*, (London, Zed Books, 1998).

Horiuchi, A. 'Financial Fragility and Recent Development in the Japanese Safety Net', paper presented at the Conference on 'Regulation and Deregulation: Japan and Europe in the Global Economy', (Firenze, European University Institute, 1977).

Huntington, S.P. 'The Clash of Civilizations?', *Foreign Affairs* 72, No. 3 (Summer 1993).

International Monetary Fund, *World Economic Outlook*, September 1998.

Itami, H. *Jinponshugi Kigyou*, (Tokyo: Chikuma Shobou, 1987).

Itami, H. 'The "Human-Capitalism" of the Japanese Firm as an Integrated System', in K. Imai and R. Komiya (eds), *Business Enterprises in Japan: Views of Leading Japanese Economists*, (Cambridge, Massachusetts and London: The MIT Press, 1994).

Johnson, C. 'Trade, Revisionism, and the Future of Japanese American Relations' in C. Johnson, *Japan, Who Governs?*,(New York: W.W. Norton, 1995).

Keidanren, *An Attractive Japan, Keidanren's Vision for 2020*, (Tokyo: Keidanren, 1996).

Johnson, C. *MITI and the Japanese Miracle* (Stanford: Stanford University Press, 1997).

Kosai, Y. '"Minshu", "shijo-Keizai" o Tettei' (For a Thorough Democracy and Market Economy), *Nihon Keizai Shinbun*, (1 January 1997).

Krugman, P. 'Even worse than you think', *Financial Times*, (27 October 1998).

Miwa, Y. *Firm and Industrial Organisations in Japan*, (London: Macmillan, 1995).

Nakatani, I. 'Keizai-Taisei: Senshinkokugata ni' (The Economic System: Toward the Model of Advanced Countries), *Nihon Kezai Shinbun*, (9 January 1995).

Nakatani, I. *Nihonkeizai no Rekishitekitenkan* (The Historical Turning Point of the Japanese Economy), (Tokyo: Tokyo Keizai Shinposha, 1996).

Nihon Keizai Shinbun, *'Daikyosojidai e no Chosen'* (The Challenge of Mega Competition), (Tokyo: Nihon Keizai Shinbunsha, 1996).

Ozawa, I. *Nihonkaizookeikaku* (Plan for the Restructuring of Japan), (Tokyo: Kodansha, 1993).

Prestowitz, C.V. *Trading Places*, (New York: Basic Books, 1988).

Sakakibara, E. *Beyond Capitalism: the Japanese Model of Market Economics*, (Lanham, Maryland: Economic Strategic Institute, 1993).

Sakakibara, E. *Shinposhugi kara no Ketsubetsu* (Farewell to Progressivism), (Tokyo: Yomiuri Shinbunsha, 1996).

Sakakibara, E. 'Bunsekinaki Kanryoubashingu ga Nihon no Shakaishisustemu = Tsuyosa no Kiban wo Houkai saseru' (Bureaucrat bashing without analyses will destroy the basis of the strength of Japan's social system), in *Nihon no '97 Ronten* (Japan's issues for 1997), (Tokyo, Bungeishunju, 1996).

Sakakibara, E. 'Academic economists reveal vacuum of thinking on Japan's problems', *Financial Times*, (30 October 1998).

Sakakibara E. (ed.), *Nichi-Bei-Oo no Keizai-.Shakaishisutemu* (The Socio-economic Systems of Japan, the US and Europe), (Tokyo: Tokyo Keizai Shinposha, 1995).

Sakakibara, E. and Y. Noguchi, 'Okurasho·Nichigin-Ocho no Bunseki: Soryokusen-Keizaitaisei no Shuen' (Analysis of the Ministry of Finance-Bank of Japan Dynasty: the End of the All-out War Economic System), *Chuo-Koron,* August 1977.

Vogel, E.F. *Japan as Number One,* (Cambridge, Massachusetts: Harvard University Press, 1979).

Yomiuri Shinbun, 'Yomiuri Proposal for Restructuring the Cabinet and Administrative System', (Tokyo: Yomiuri Shinbunsha, 1996).

3
Southeast Asia Facing Economic, Political and Social Crisis

Benedetta Trivellato

The Southeast Asian countries at the centre of the crisis were for years admired as some of the most successful emerging market economies, owing to their rapid growth and striking gains in their populations' living standards. With generally prudent fiscal policies and high rates of private savings, they were seen as models for many other countries.[1] Even if there had been some forecasts of growth slowdown in the nineties,[2] few considered these countries likely to have become involved in a spiral of financial and economic crises. Even if widespread currency devaluations seem to have come to a halt, the aftershocks in the countries of the region are continuing.

This chapter highlights the outbreak, the evolution and predominant effects of the crisis in Southeast Asia (SEA). The main stages through which the crisis broke out in the region and developed in 1997–98 are summarized in the first section. Subsequently, economic and political effects of this evolution on SEA countries are analyzed, starting from countries which have been worst hit – Indonesia, Malaysia and Thailand – to the relatively less affected – Singapore and the Philippines – to those countries which are less integrated in the regional economy, and therefore suffered less from the direct impact of the turmoil – Vietnam, Laos, Cambodia and Myanmar.[3] The last section of the chapter evaluates the role played by the most important regional association, ASEAN, in dealing with the consequences of the economic and political crises, and by organizing an effective regional and co-operative response.

3.1 The outbreak of the crisis and its evolution until December 1998

After being targeted by some speculative attacks in 1996, the Thai baht came under renewed downward pressure at the beginning of 1997.[4]

This pressure was due to growing concerns regarding the sustainability of the US dollar peg in the face of a large current account deficit, high short-term foreign debt, the collapse of a property price bubble and an erosion of external competitiveness. Measures adopted by the government to ease the pressure were seen by markets as inadequate, due to their ineffectiveness in addressing the weaknesses in the financial sector, and equity prices continued to fall sharply. Other ASEAN countries were still relatively unaffected at that time, thanks to smaller current account deficits and a less serious export slowdown. But the deteriorating situation in Thailand brought rising concerns that the financial sectors in these countries might also be exposed in the property sector, causing a downturn in equity prices, particularly in Malaysia and the Philippines.

Pressures on the Thai baht re-emerged in May 1997, forcing the Central Bank to intervene in the markets and to introduce capital and exchange controls. As the intervention failed to restore confidence, pressures continued in Thailand while diminishing in other ASEAN countries through the authorities' intervention in exchange markets and higher interest rates. Due to continued speculative attacks, on 2 July 1997 Thailand abandoned its exchange rate peg against the dollar and allowed the baht to float. After having used most of the country's foreign exchange reserves in an effort to defend the currency, the Thai government was forced, on 28 July, to turn to the IMF to raise funds needed for financing trade and foreign debt servicing.

The fall in the baht raised doubts about the viability of exchange rate arrangements in neighbouring countries. Spillover effects spread quickly to the Philippines, Malaysia and Indonesia, where the authorities allowed the currencies to depreciate. The situation worsened in the following months, reflecting concerns about the effects of currency depreciation and higher interest rates on highly leveraged corporate and financial sector balance sheets, and about the commitment of the authorities to implement reform. The actual or only threatened imposition of capital controls further undermined investors' confidence. In October 1997 Indonesia was also forced to seek the IMF's support, in exchange for a commitment to close a certain number of ailing banks, cut government spending and balance the budget.

The beginning of 1998 was marked by a new round of devaluations, following Thailand's declared inability to satisfy IMF requirements. Confidence in regional markets was hit deeply by this announcement, prompting renewed speculative attacks on the currencies. By January

1998, the Indonesian rupiah had lost more than 60 per cent of its value in July 1997. The negative reaction of the IMF and the international markets to the 1998–99 budget presented by the government forced President Suharto to revise forecasts and to agree to give up new projects of industrial development as well as dismantle local monopolies, including those tied to his own family. This was not enough to restore investors' confidence and halt the currency's fall, and led to social tensions spreading across the country. The situation degenerated, causing violence particularly towards ethnic Chinese. Social conflict and economic crisis raised doubts about President Suharto's ability to stay in power, but this did not prevent the People's Consultative Assembly from re-electing him, during the March 1997 meeting, for the seventh consecutive term. However, continued worsening of social and economic conditions led to renewed and deeper conflicts, which brought about Suharto's downfall in May 1998 and saw the appointment of his deputy, B.J. Habibie, as the new President.

After a relatively calm period, the social and political effects of the crisis re-emerged in Malaysia and Indonesia from September 1998. Currency controls imposed by the Malaysian government brought some immediate benefits due to falling interest rates and capital repatriation, but also induced some observers to expect capital flights from the region for fear of other countries following Malaysia's example. The Malaysian government's intervention was not confined to the economy – in September 1998 Prime Minister Mahathir Mohamad sacked his Deputy, Anwar Ibrahim, on the basis of charges of sodomy and corruption, and had him arrested. This action, which Mahathir took because he perceived Anwar to be a growing threat to his position, provoked an immediate domestic and international outcry.

The continued deterioration of Indonesian economic conditions led, in September 1998, to renewed protests by students and intellectuals calling for Habibie's resignation. Demonstrations led to open conflict between the population and the army in November 1998, during a special meeting of the PCA. Called to settle the deadlines for the 1999 parliamentary and presidential elections, the meeting was seen by the students as a means of maintaining the status quo and confirming the army's role in politics. Further riots took place in December 1998 between Muslims and Catholics, reinforcing the perception that the political and social conditions in Indonesia were highly unstable, while its economic system is still far from showing signs of recovery.

3.2 Most severely hit: Indonesia, Thailand and Malaysia

Among SEA countries, Indonesia, Thailand and Malaysia have been the hardest hit by the crisis. The former two have been forced to turn to the IMF for financial support, while Malaysia introduced in January 1998 restrictive policy measures which have helped push the economy into recession. Nonetheless, the actual political and economic situation is very different in the three countries. If considered from an economic perspective, Indonesia and Thailand are suffering the most, while Malaysia is enjoying the breathing space conceded by the currency controls imposed in September 1998. From the point of view of political and social stability, Indonesia and Malaysia present the most worrying threats.

Indonesia's President Habibie faces the difficult task of restructuring both the nation's political and economic systems, in a situation where 100 million citizens are slipping below the poverty line, as GDP is estimated to have shrunk 20 per cent in 1998. Banking-sector reform is among the first priorities for economic recovery. Almost demolished by the Asian financial crisis, Indonesia's banking sector had grown to more than 240 private banks in mid-1997, it has now shrunk to as few as five major banks in 1999. Non-performing loans have reached roughly 60 per cent of total loans, according to government estimates, while high interest rates are suffocating even the healthiest institutions. Furthermore, the banks' woes have hurt other parts of the Indonesian economy. Trade finance is latent, because banks are unwilling to take loan risks, which hurts exports; Indonesia's retail and consumer markets have crashed following diminishing consumer confidence, falling incomes, and even the fact that shopping malls and shops were widely burned during the riots. The lack of an effective legal protection system, meanwhile, prevents creditors from seizing many of their debtors' assets. The restructuring of $80 billion in private corporate debt is another primary issue. As is the case with banking reforms, however, it has been undermined by social and political upheaval and the depressed value of the rupiah. Indonesian companies do not have the money to pay back their foreign parties, making debt rescheduling less useful in the short run. Ultimately, foreign lenders will have to agree to the writing down of parts of their loans to ease the debt impasse.

However, political uncertainty is seen as providing the largest threat to Indonesia's economic revitalization. In an effort to build support, Habibie has loosened media controls and released political prisoners. At the same time, however, he has been unable to halt perceptions that his government is an extension of the Suharto regime. Therefore, opposition to his rule continues, fuelling uncertainty over whether he can serve out his term, which ends in December 1999. For this reason, Habibie called in November 1998 a special meeting of the PCA, to ratify an election timetable that he hoped would allow him to stall for just a while longer. Issues discussed during the meeting included new rules to restrict a future President's tenure to two five-year terms; rules for holding elections and allocating seats in parliament; procedures for making collusion, corruption, and nepotism more difficult; and proposals for devolving more autonomy to some of the regions of the archipelago. The effort did not stop protesters, who considered the meeting a mere attempt to gain Habibie some temporary legitimacy and called for the President to step down. Demonstrations predictably caused the outbreak of violence between protestors and the army, further exacerbating resentment of the latter among the population.[5]

On the other hand, there is no real alternative to the current president. Some of the ruling Golkar's Party opponents, including Megawati Sukarnoputri, daughter of the country's first president, and Amien Rais, the head of a large Islamic group, are simply unable to reach an agreement on a candidate for presidential election, further weakening the organized opposition.

The role of the army is another major issue in the evolution of Indonesia's politics and security. Under the present system, Indonesia's police and military serve a dual role, called *dwifungsi*: besides serving the government, they are also a part of it. This was accepted in the 1960s, when communists were viewed as a constant threat and the armed forces were one of the most trusted institutions, but it is now rejected by many citizens. Tainted by revelations of human rights atrocities, the armed forces are the target of growing calls to remove themselves from politics, and their actual ability to maintain order under such attacks from the public remains in question.

With so little agreement on even the most basic questions, with the economy devastated and with racially motivated violence a constant threat, Indonesia is facing hard times. Few can guess what will happen if Habibie loses the election, or what the backlash on the streets will be if the election itself is delayed. But, if nothing else, democracy in Indonesia now has the opportunity to develop, which it has not had in recent decades.

For the time being, the economic effects of the regional crisis have been felt more deeply in Indonesia than in Malaysia, although this did not prevent the latter from sinking into its first recession in 13 years. After months of accusing currency speculators, Prime Minister Mahathir responded with drastic measures, including insulating Malaysia from international financial markets by putting controls on short-term capital movements and fixing the exchange rate. At the same time, he had to face the most widespread show of public dissatisfaction in his 17-year rule after having sacked Deputy Prime Minister Anwar Ibrahim. Nonetheless, it is unlikely that the disfavour will reach the point of threatening Mahathir's position in the near future: he blamed the recession on Anwar's austerity plan, which consisted of the same high interest rates and tight government spending measures that the IMF prescribed when it bailed out Thailand and Indonesia. Currency and capital controls imposed in September 1998 will not be effective unless Malaysia uses the time it has bought to restructure its ailing banking business. The economy would likely benefit from Mahathir's relinquishment of his nationalistic efforts and from the liberalization of the country's foreign-investment rules, particularly in the banking and finance sectors. International fund managers are currently particularly negative about Malaysia, which is not surprising given the locking-in of foreign investment funds under currency controls.

As far as the political landscape is concerned, Anwar has begun a legal battle to clear his name and show that he is the victim of a political conspiracy. The trial revealed the inner workings of Malaysian law enforcement and a political culture in which deference to authority could result in police abuse, which, in turn, could strengthen the call for reforms. The trial may produce more revelations that could further undermine Malaysian faith in Mahathir's governance, already shaken by the publicity over Anwar's sacking, arrest and alleged beating while in police custody. The constant use of the Internal Security Act alarmed many Malaysians, arousing suspicions that the law is being used to stifle political opposition. This could further reduce the people's loyalty to Mahathir and the ruling party United Malays National Organisation (UMNO). Much will depend on how fast the government can get the economy back on track.

Amid political and economic turmoil, an Islamic opposition party poses another challenge to the government. In the northeastern state of Terengganu, the popularity of the opposition Parti Islam (Pas) poses a serious challenge to the ruling coalition headed by Mahathir[6]. The resurgence of Pas is one indication of changes taking place in the political landscape. Observers doubt that Pas could win a majority in the federal parliament but do not exclude the possibility that it could secure control of several state governments of the Malaysian federation, and gain enough seats in the parliament for UMNO to lose its two-thirds majority. Some attribute Pas's recent gains mainly to UMNO's mistakes: the reason for the massive swing would be more of a protest vote than an actual shift in commitment to Pas's Islamist ideology. UMNO leaders recognize rising challenges to the party's position, but they are convinced that anger over Mahathir's handling of Anwar will fade in the coming months.

The threat posed by the crisis to Thailand's political stability is much weaker than to Indonesia's and Malaysia's, but the Thai economy is still far from showing signs of recovery. By October 1998, the baht had stabilized, foreign reserves had increased again, interest rates were down to pre-crisis levels, and inflation had been kept in check despite the currency devaluation. The situation may have stabilized, but Thailand's recovery is still distant, and many structural problems remain in place.

In many areas outside the banking sector, the pace of change has slowed. The IMF has been pushing for increased efficiency in the banks, but there is little similar pressure on other parts of the economy, such as limits on foreign investment. Unless restructuring of the financial sector is accompanied by substantial changes elsewhere in the economy, including reform of the legal system and of attitudes in corporate governance, the IMF efforts in the banking sector will loose efficacy. Even within the banking sector problems persist: interest rates may be down to a pre-crisis level, but risk-averse banks are not providing new loans. This means that many credit worthy companies cannot get new loans, and, with the relations between the banks and companies broken down and having lost the momentum of growth, it will be hard to get Thailand's economy moving again in the short run. Beyond internal reform, Thailand's economy is exposed to the effects of Japan's recession and the overall economic downturn in the region, as Asia accounts for about half of the country's exports and half of its inward foreign direct investment. Prime Minister Chuan Leekpai's government faces growing pressure due to the economic downturn. Opposition party members have repeatedly called for a debate on the government's ability to revive the economy, but the ruling coalition holds a parliamentary majority, and many analysts believe the real pressure on Chuan is more likely to come from voters, who are growing impatient for economic recovery. For now, though, the Chuan administration is still more popular among the middle class than any opposition alternative.

3.3 Relatively less affected: Singapore and the Philippines

Two very different SEA countries – Singapore and the Philippines – have been left relatively unscathed by the crisis, compared with the ones mentioned above. Singapore is a city-state, one of the richest of Asia's newly industrialised economies (NIE), ruled by an authoritarian and efficiency-oriented government which has transformed it into a regional hub for financial and business services. The Philippines is a less developed country among the ASEAN-4, the group of SEA countries considered to be the 'second-tier NIEs', at least before the crisis broke out in 1997. Nonetheless, it was its relatively limited integration in the global financial market and in the regional economy which limited the effects of the Asian crisis: the recession that the country is currently experiencing is mainly due to a sharp downturn in agricultural output because of the El Nino climatic phenomenon.

Singapore, like the rest of SEA, is experiencing bad times, but it is not suffering as much as Malaysia and Indonesia. In line with its high per-capita income – above that of many Western nations – there is still enough prosperity for conspicuous consumption. The economy's slowdown has showed how much Singapore depends on the well-being of its neighbours and the rest of the world: Indonesia's collapse has contributed directly to Singapore's fall in tourism, property prices and banking business, the slowdown in the world-wide computer business has led to thousands of Singaporeans working in the electronics sector being laid off, while exports to the rest of Asia are understandably decreasing.

The Singapore government, which has traditionally pushed companies and citizens to be productive, is appealing for more productivity gains coupled with lower costs. To help employers, the government will reduce the level of mandatory contributions they must make to employees' pension funds. Authorities are also hoping that Singapore will attract new investment because of the island's efficiency and sound management (there is no foreign debt). But others point out that one of Singapore's great strengths is as a regional service centre and now there is much less business to service. The difficulty for Singapore is that while it may have seen competition from Malaysia and Thailand effectively wiped out, those countries are the ones on which it relies for business, but the crisis has frightened away many clients and others are shifting their money further afield. The question is where Singapore will find new business opportunities in the next few years. Singapore might be well placed to service mergers-and-acquisitions activity, debt- and corporate-restructuring business and fund management, but it will be some time before Southeast Asia's firms can afford to pay for such services.

Therefore, traditionally conservative Singapore needs to embrace creativity and risk, but this raises a sense of ambivalence. On the one hand, the government recognizes that the greatest long-term opportunities lie in knowledge-based industries such as information-technology, biotechnology and medical sciences, as well as high-end services such as finance and logistics, and it is trying to make this city-state a more congenial place for the free-thinkers and entrepreneurs who drive these industries. But the government is unwilling to renounce its controls over political debate, which have effectively marginalized any opposition; nor does it plan to reduce its dominant role in the economy, exercized through land and pension policies and through controlling ownership of major companies. But a campaign to develop popular initiative cannot be entirely government-mandated: authorities cannot force the people to innovate and some say the key lies in changing social incentives Singapore previously has attracted foreign investors by offering high level infrastructure and wide tax breaks, but knowledge-based industries also need workforces with initiative. Singapore needs to change its image if it is to attract investors and innovators from the West's high-tech community, and it is therefore easing its lifestyle restrictions: by loosening up, planners hope they can create a comfort zone for software engineers and financial wizards, but, again, ambivalence emerges. Singapore's reputation for efficiency could be sacrificed, and in a country that depends so much on foreign investment, on trade with the region, efficiency is a key feature.

Economic growth is down also in the Philippines mainly because of the El-Nino effects, but the downturn is much more limited than that of its neighbours. President Joseph Estrada's task will be to encourage growth while coping with decreasing tax revenues that have put severe restraints on government spending. His pledges to spend heavily on rural infrastructure and agriculture will have to be scaled back to cut the budget deficit, but the government's focus on rural development is sorely needed: the drought has devastated the countryside, leading to starvation in some areas, and has in one season wiped out several years of income gains for the country's extremely poor rural population.

The fact that all the major Philippine banks still maintain healthy profits and single-digit bad-loan ratios is being underlined by the government as a sign that the economy is fundamentally sound and structurally different from those of Thailand, Malaysia and Indonesia. Still, the Philippines is struggling with the problems of an economy slow down. To keep banks healthy and protect the peso, the Central Bank has kept reserve provisions, capital requirements and interest rates high, draining liquidity from the market. While part of the economy had weakened following the crisis, the Philippines has benefited from two factors: first, Filipinos abroad repatriated US$ 6 billion in 1998, according to the Central Bank, 10 per cent more than in 1997. Second, exports keep growing fast while imports are not decreasing as much as in neighbouring countries, leading to a large improvement in the balance of trade. As Philippine exports are closely tied to US demand and vulnerable to fluctuations in the markets for computer parts and other electronic products, there are concerns that a slowdown in these markets could severely hurt Philippine exports. Still, direct investment in manufacturing for export continues to grow, so new production could to some extent compensate for a possible reduction in exports from existing businesses.

3.4 Indirect effects of the regional turmoil: Indochina

The indirect effects of the regional crisis have mostly been felt by a group of SEA countries, due to their relatively limited integration in the regional economy. These are the countries belonging to the Indochinese peninsula, that is Vietnam, Laos, Myanmar and Cambodia. The impact of the crisis on these countries is due to the fact that old problems, typical of their regimes (such as economic backwardness, isolation from the rest of the world, corruption, lack of freedom), have been exacerbated by the Asian crisis[7]. New problems relate to increased currency volatility, a slowdown in trade and foreign investment and a possible halt to the process of reform. The non-convertibility of the currencies and existing regulations on financial flows prevented direct pressure from speculators, but did not halt the effects of the regional slowdown. The main channels of transmission of the regional turmoil have been trade and investment flows, which have been steadily declining, as a sizeable percentage came from some of the hardest hit SEA countries. This is particularly damaging, given those countries' heavy dependence on international trade and foreign capital for economic development. A major problem stems from the widespread use of the Thai baht for border trade and for transactions in the so-called 'baht-zone', which groups neighbouring areas in Myanmar, Laos and Cambodia: the depreciation of the baht has badly affected trade flows between these countries. Authorities have signed bilateral agreements with neighbouring countries to offset the worst effects of declining trade, which are designed to reduce import duties, enhance barter trade and promote the use of regional currencies in other areas of trade.

Vietnam is feeling the impact of growing unemployment, falling exports and a downturn in foreign investment. Because trading in the Vietnamese currency, the dong, is controlled by the government, it has not weakened as much as other regional currencies. That means this country's main assets, cheap labour and exports, have become less competitive, while its biggest market is contracting: before the crisis occurred in 1997, more than 60 per cent of Vietnam's exports went to Asia. The country's main source of foreign investment is also shrinking, as Singapore, Taiwan, Hong Kong, Japan and South Korea account for more than 65 per cent of foreign investment. Gross domestic product is already eroding and without further reform it is likely to continue falling over the next few years. This is troubling, given that the present growth rate is hardly enough to keep up with the 1.4 million workers who enter the job market each year, according to the government. Nonetheless, Vietnam's growth figures (estimated to be 3–4 per cent for 1998) still look good compared with neighbouring countries' contracting economies.

Vietnam will have to make fundamental changes to avoid a deeper long-term crisis; it can still use the lag time to eliminate similarities with the nearby economies, such as lack of transparency, weak banks and overvaluation of assets. The leadership recognizes that further reform is unavoidable. Signs that the government is responding include increased concessions to foreign investors, a 16–17 per cent depreciation of the dong since the beginning of 1998 and moves to liberalize the export sector. But tougher reforms need to be implemented. Whether or not reform speeds up, a burden on the economy is represented by the fact that Vietnam's banks are riddled with debts, foreign exchange is scarce and the country has a current account deficit of 5 per cent of GDP.

The Asian crisis has caused considerable difficulties for Laos, which will likely be followed by a slowdown in some areas of the reform process. Some key reforms, such as restructuring state enterprises and banking sector reform, are not being implemented because of the related technical and political difficulties, but as the government recognizes that reform is crucial to obtain foreign donor and investors commitment, some progress will be made. The government has introduced some measures to encourage foreign investment, such as more generous tax breaks, but, as long as regional investors remain short of funds, these efforts are unlikely to have the desired effect. Furthermore, the regional crisis will lead to weak regional demand and low dollar prices for some of Laos's key exports. The Laotian banking system is unstable, while the government has lost control of monetary and fiscal policy. If the situation worsens, the risk of complication due to growing pressures to put more power in the centralized system and less in the market, might increase.

Myanmar is also facing a deepening economic crisis. Inflation has soared, growth is slowing and the lack of foreign exchange has forced the military junta almost to halt imports. Real incomes are falling, causing considerable frustration and discontent both in urban and rural areas, and resulting in mounting tensions: there is a risk that political protests will erupt once again. The government has shown no intention of tackling the deepening economic crisis by implementing the reforms proposed by the IMF and the World Bank. The junta had promised to speed up privatization, but the drastic shortage of foreign exchange and the collapse of the economy has overtaken them. Concerns about the new restrictions on trade and foreign exchange, combined with the regional economic crisis, will result in falling inflows of FDI in the coming years.

The Cambodian situation has been marked by political instability since the onset of the crisis: it was in July 1997 that Prime Minister Hun Sen ousted his co-Prime Minister, Prince Norodom Ranariddh, giving way to the elections which took place in July 1998 and were won by Hun Sen's Cambodian People's Party (CPP). The new government, led by the CPP and established only after a deal was reached in November 1998 between Hun Sen and Prince Ranariddh, is likely to continue to pursue the current economic policy, that is openness to foreign investment and trade liberalization. Recent membership of ASEAN will also lock Cambodia into the process of lowering tariff barriers. However, the possibility of an unstable coalition government implies that progress on structural reforms, such as privatization, banking sector reform and environmental protection, will slow down. This, in turn, risks bringing the government into conflict with international donors, including the IMF.

3.5 Regional response to the crisis: the role of ASEAN

There is a common feature in SEA countries' responses to the crisis: every country is going it's own way. With some exceptions, there has not been a concerted effort to exploit regional ties to overcome at least some of the effects of the crisis. The Association of South East Asian Nations (ASEAN)[8], one of the most important and long-lasting regional associations, has been unable to propose a solution to bail out this region. Its response to the crisis, including both immediate crisis management in unstable financial markets and the policy for longer-term adjustment and economy restructuring, seemed slow, inefficient and inadequate. This raises some questions about the role of regional co-operation frameworks, and of ASEAN in particular, as it has been in the recent past, and as it could be in the future.

However, in the last few months, member countries reached several agreements in response to the chaotic situation on the basis of consensus. In brief, the response included:

- Agreeing to establish an ASEAN monitoring and surveillance mechanism within the general framework of the IMF with the assistance of the ADB. Yet getting past the planning stage has been difficult, as some countries have expressed reluctance about passing on market-sensitive details to their counterparts.
- Supporting the use of regional currencies to promote intra-ASEAN trade; endorsing the use of Bilateral Payment Arrangement (BPA). The approach would initially be implemented on a voluntary basis, with a view to developing this facility into a multilateral arrangement.
- Accelerating the implementation of the ASEAN Free Trade Area scheme, with a plan to increase the number of products that will carry zero tariffs by 2002.
- Establishment of an ASEAN Investment Area, to remove barriers to investment from ASEAN countries by 2010 and by 2020 for non-ASEAN nations.

All of these responses certainly can help to lessen the chaos in SEA, but it is still unclear how effective these responses are and to what extent these proposals could be implemented.

The ASEAN summit held in Vietnam, in December 1998, once again ended up without significant proposals for action. Members were divided on many issues, including the admission of Cambodia: after the deal between Hun Sen and Ranariddh, Cambodia claimed to have a legitimate government, but some members wanted to see more evidence of political stability before admission. Therefore, ASEAN declared that Cambodia was destined for membership, but would join at an unspecified date in the future. The most worthwhile plan offered at the summit was the one proposed by Japan: a US$ 30 billion rescue fund for the region's battered economies. Even if Japanese officials admit that a major goal of the plan is to help the Japanese economy, it represents nonetheless a firm commitment compared with ASEAN's other endeavours.

The final Hanoi Declaration called for closer unity, dialogue and co-operation but avoided detailed calls for a new era of vigour and openness demanded by some of the bloc's oldest members – Thailand, the Philippines and Singapore. Instead, official statements stayed within ASEAN's tradition and played up the principles of consensus, consultation and non-interference in each others' affairs. Vietnam, Laos and Myanmar made it clear that they will stand up for their principles and interests, however unpalatable they may be to outsiders. Even if there has not been much progress, the situation does not appear completely bleak. The region's prospects for recovery depend largely on reforms which will be implemented by individual countries, as well as on the quality of their fiscal policies. Therefore, the main issues are long-term: ASEAN countries may not have achieved much at the December 1998 meeting, but at least their leaders did not turn back.[9]

Despite contingent reassurances that ASEAN leaders are at least showing a willingness to maintain their commitments, the lack of effective action has prompted criticism over ASEAN's structure and decision-making process. Two factors weigh heavily against the effectiveness of ASEAN's response to the financial crisis. One is that ASEAN is operated by consensus. This character has enabled ASEAN to survive in a rapidly changing environment, but after 30 years' operating on consultation and dialogue, ASEAN has fallen into a 'lowest-common-denominator' syndrome, which limits ASEAN's flexibility and initiative, because agreement has to be reached on the lowest consensus level. Limited by this syndrome, it is hard for ASEAN to find a rescue package on the basis of consensus in a time of urgency, such as the financial crisis. Another factor is 'non-interference' in one another's domestic affairs, one of ASEAN's founding principles. Although there are several reasons for the crisis, the weaknesses in some individual ASEAN countries' economic and political structures are believed to be fundamental to it. But under the prerequisite of 'non-interference' ASEAN cannot impose discipline on its members' weakness that is rooted in their internal political and economic systems.

Apart from being largely ineffective in providing a co-operative and common response to the Asian crisis, ASEAN might loose a relevant characteristic. Without regional cohesion, ASEAN's members might seek help individually from strategic powers in the neighbourhood. This would undermine one of the main features of ASEAN's regional role, that is a balancing power in a region that has historically been at the crossroads of superpower rivalry. Some regional powers are already trying to exploit the association's weakness to expand their influence. China, for instance, is widening its control on the disputed Spratly Islands and strengthening ties with Myanmar; Japan pledged a US$ 30 billion rescue plan for the region that seeks to remove the US dollar as the dominant currency. The problem is that ASEAN does not have the power, and now not even the unity, to formulate regional strategies to deal with the great powers.

The Asian crisis has produced changes: when the region was a hub of prosperity, ASEAN was treated with respect by major powers around the world. The crisis has forced member states to turn to their own individual problems, reducing ASEAN to the sum of its parts. There is no doubt that differences between members mean greater difficulties in achieving co-operation. In June 1998, Thai foreign ministry officials proposed that ASEAN should adopt a 'flexible' engagement policy in its relations with members, replacing the principle of 'non-interference'. The proposal, backed from the Philippines, was rejected because many members, including Indonesia and Myanmar, remained opposed to such a change in ASEAN's operating procedures, although the need for 'enhanced interaction' was approved. Individual member states developing ties with regional powers, like Thailand with Japan or Myanmar with China, offer a striking contrast to the region prior to the crisis. Before 1997, ASEAN enjoyed a more egalitarian relationship with the big powers; now, the association could become a means to obtain aid from developed countries more easily, and therefore, a centre for superpower rivalry.

The unstable political and security environment poses an important challenge to ASEAN. In the post-cold war period, ASEAN's threats come from both external and internal factors. The collapse of the bipolar system and the declining capability of US power provide more occasions for conflict between regional powers, such as China, Japan, and India; therefore, ASEAN has to learn how to accommodate the changing relations among great powers. Inside ASEAN, the unstable regional regimes also threaten ASEAN's future. The financial crisis has undermined the political stability of many ASEAN countries: in Thailand, the Chavalit government collapsed after it failed to cope with the crisis and was replaced by the Chuan government, whose fate is also dependent on economy recovery; in Indonesia, President Suharto resigned, raising questions about control of the country and how to restructure the deteriorating economy; in Malaysia, people have begun to question Mahathir's leadership; in the Philippines, former actor Estrada has become the new President, but how well he understands the economy is a crucial question; the Vietnamese economy is caught in an impasse; Myanmar is still under a military regime that is under attack by the West for human rights abuses; Cambodia finally has a new government, but the problem of political stability cannot be considered resolved.

Throughout its history, ASEAN has tried to maintain relative peace and stability among its member countries as well as in the entire Asia–Pacific region. This helped to create a favourable environment where rapid and sustained economic growth became possible. Economic development, in turn, brought about social progress and human development. Therefore, ASEAN's prosperity in the future will largely depend on whether it can go on consolidating the regional peace and stability. Furthermore, the economic environment is not favourable to ASEAN. Continued access to developed markets is becoming increasingly contingent on reciprocal access to ASEAN markets; trade and investment competition from China is arousing more and more concern. ASEAN is still too small to be effective in its external economic diplomacy: to increase its effectiveness, ASEAN needs to be part of a larger grouping within the pacific region such as APEC and act actively. But ASEAN is also too big to be effective for regional integration and co-operation: difficulties have already resulted from the processes of expansion and integration. ASEAN's expansion will no doubt enhance the international status of the organisation, but it may strain its cohesion. The proportion of trade with external partners, such as Greater China, Japan, South Korea and the US is much larger than that of intra-ASEAN trade. In this sense, ASEAN should integrate itself in the wider regional economic grouping such as APEC to exploit its potential fully.

Despite the growing prominence and influence which ASEAN has displayed in the regional economy and as an important means for member countries to effectively interact with other parts of the world, ASEAN is facing a series of challenges: how to preserve cohesion as membership expands, how to maintain ASEAN's purpose in the face of developing Asia–Pacific security and economic regionalism, and how to reconcile changing relations among the great powers. These challenges have to be met with the help of the world community through a rethink of the association and the economic role it plays.

3.6 Conclusions

The negative domino effect of the financial crisis proved how intertwined the ASEAN economy was, but ASEAN's influence in the economic field is fairly limited at present. Over the past three decades, so many cross-border links have developed through trade, direct investment, stock market investment, tourism and other means, that it is becoming increasingly difficult to isolate problems within the borders of a single country. This trend will lead to pressure to create an effective institutional structure within ASEAN for discussing problems that have cross-border implications like the financial crisis. This means that ASEAN's policy of non-intervention may have to be modified. At the same time, if the group insists on acting in a co-ordinated way only when complete consensus can be reached, the 'lowest-common denominator' will often be no agreement. However, there have been some positive signs of breakthrough in the domains of political and security co-operation.

The financial crisis has left ASEAN countries with two choices. One is to introduce more protection measures to secure a stable internal economic environment and reduce the risk coming from external sources. This may take the form of slowing down or pausing on the road to further economic integration. The other choice is to proceed on the road to integration and co-operation, ensuring that closer and faster integration is further developed as a source of strength in the open multilateral trading system. The second choice would be the better one: an open market can secure ASEAN outside support which is necessary to maintain sustainable growth; a closed market only makes recovery from the financial crisis more difficult. The only way to a regional recovery is a new burst of exports: this requires an outward-looking policy. Fortunately, ASEAN leaders had re-affirmed their commitment to a trade and investment regime that is increasingly integrated in ASEAN and open to the rest of the world, and resolved to speed up even further the process of internal and external liberalization. So, whether the financial crisis becomes an opportunity for ASEAN or a big challenge to its existence, will be a test for ASEAN.

Table 3.1 SEA countries: real GDP growth (%)

	1996	**1997**	**1998**	**1999 Forecast**
Indonesia	8.0	4.6	−15.3	−5.6
Thailand	5.5	−0.4	−8.5	−2.3
Malaysia	8.6	7.8	−6.0	−2.7
Singapore	6.9	7.8	0.8	−2.5
Philippines	5.8	5.2	−2.0	−2.9
Vietnam	9.3	8.8	4–5	n.a.
Laos	6.7	8.0	n.a.	n.a.
Cambodia	7.1	2.0	n.a.	n.a.
Myanmar	5.8	4.5	n.a.	n.a.

Source: IMF (1998).

Table 3.2 Indonesia: economic indicators

	1996	**1997**	**1998**	**1999 Forecast**
Consumer Price Index (%)	8.0	6.6	62.1	47.2
Current Account Balance (% of GDP)	−3.4	−2.4	13.1	10.7
Exchange Rate (Rp: US$)	2342	2909	8937	13447
Foreign Exch. Reserves (share of imports)	0.4	0.4	0.6	0.5
Export Growth Rate (%)	3.7	12.5	13.1	3.7
Unemployment Rate (%)	4.9	6.0	n.a.	n.a.
Investment Rate (% of GDP)	29.6	28.7	19.4	17.4

Source: IMF (1998).

Table 3.3 Thailand: economic indicators

	1996	**1997**	**1998**	**1999 Forecast**
Consumer Price Index (%)	5.8	5.6	9.2	7.8
Current Account Balance (% of GDP)	−7.9	−0.8	10.3	7.9
Exchange Rate (Bt: US$)	25.3	31.4	46.6	47.2
Foreign Exch. Reserves (share of imports)	0.5	0.5	0.6	0.6
Export Growth Rate (%)	−0.9	9.0	6.3	1.1
Unemployment Rate (%)	2.0	3.5	n.a.	n.a.
Investment Rate (% of GDP)	40.8	35.6	26.3	24.3

Source: IMF (1998).

Table 3.4   Malaysia: economic indicators

	1996	**1997**	**1998**	**1999 Forecast**
Consumer Price Index (%)	3.5	2.7	6.0	7.5
Current Account Balance (% of GDP)	−4.9	−4.8	1.4	3.3
Exchange Rate (Ringgit: US$)	2.5	2.8	3.8	4.2
Foreign Exch. Reserves (share of imports)	0.4	0.2	0.3	0.4
Export Growth Rate (%)	3.4	4.8	−7.2	−3.5
Unemployment Rate (%)	2.5	2.5	8.4	7.5
Investment Rate (% of GDP)	42.2	42.4	38.6	38.4

Source: IMF (1998).

Notes

1. See World Bank (1993).
2. Krugman (1994).
3. The country which is commonly named 'Burma' at the international level is here analyzed as 'Myanmar', the name given to the country by the military junta and used by ASEAN countries.
4. See IMF (1997).
5. 'Back on Indonesia's streets', *The Economist*, 14 November 1998.
6. 'Call of the Imams', *Far Eastern Economic Review*, 10 December 1998.
7. Capannelli (1998).
8. ASEAN was established in 1967 among five East-Asian countries (Indonesia, Malaysia, Thailand, Philippines and Singapore) with the aim of preserving national security and regional stability; unofficial but no less important also was the aim of defending the region from the threat of communism. ASEAN has now ten members (Brunei, Vietnam, Laos, Myanmar and Cambodia have been admitted), and after the end of the cold war has shifted its focus also towards co-operation aimed at liberalizing trade flows within the area (ASEAN Free Trade Area). An attempt to extend dialogue also at the security level has been made through the ASEAN Regional Forum, which allows participation also from non-ASEAN countries, like China, the US and the EU.
9. 'ASEAN looks to the new year', *The Economist,* 19 December 1998.

References

ADB, *Asia Responding to Crisis,* (Asia Development Bank Institute: 1998).

Akrasanee, N., 'Financial Crisis in Thailand: Causes, Consequences and Remedies', paper prepared for the Seminar on Asian Financial Crisis at the ADB 31st Annual Meeting in Geneva (28 April 1998).

'Asian Economic Survey', *Wall Street Journal,* 26 October 1998.

Capannelli, G., 'Old Problems and New Worries. How the Current Crisis Affects New ASEAN Members', mimeo, ISESAO, Bocconi University (1998).

Corsetti, G., P. Pesenti and N. Roubini, 'Paper tigers? A preliminary assessment of the Asian crisis', paper prepared for the NBER-Bank of Portugal International Seminar on Macroeconomics (ISOM), Lisbon, (14–15 June 1998).

Economist Intelligence Unit, *Country Reports: Vietnam, Laos, Myanmar, Cambodia,* 4th Quarter 1998.

Elek, A., 'Pacific Economic Cooperation: Policy Choices for the 1990s' in D.K. Das (ed.) *Emerging Growth Pole – The Asia Pacific Economy,* (Singapore: Prentice Hall, 1996).

Funston, J., 'ASEAN: Out of its Depth?', *Contemporary Southeast Asia,* Vol. 20, No. 1, (April 1998).

IMF, *World Economic Outlook – Interim Assessment* (December 1997).

IMF, *World Economic Outlook* (1998).

Krugman, P., 'The Myth of Asia's Miracle', *Foreign Affairs,* November/December 1994.

Montes, M., K. Quigley and D. Weatherbee, *Growing Pains: ASEAN's Economic and Political Challenges,* (New York: Asia Society 1997).

Petri, P., 'Historical Roots of the Asia-Pacific Interdependence' in D.K. Das (ed.) *Emerging Growth Pole – The Asia Pacific Economy,* (Singapore: Prentice Hall, 1996).

Suthiphand, C., 'Crisis and its Impact on ASEAN Economic Integration', paper prepared for the International Workshop on 'ASEAN-EU Relations: The Long-term Potential beyond the Recent Turmoil', Como, Italy, 22–23, April 1998.

United Nations 'The Asian Crisis: Toward Recovery and Reform', paper presented at the Expert Group Meeting: 'What have we learned one year into the financial crisis in emerging market economies?', New York, 21–23 July 1998.

World Bank, *The East Asian Miracle,* (New York: Oxford University Press, 1993).

World Bank, *East Asia. The Road to Recovery,* Washington D.C. (1998).

World Bank, *Social Consequences of the East Asian Financial Crisis,* Washington D.C. (1998).

4
Central Asia: The Illusion of a World Order

*Valeria Fiorani Piacentini and Gianluca Pastori**

The purpose of this chapter is to examine the interaction of the main players (that is the ex-Soviet CA republics of Kazakhstan, Kyrgyzstan – now officially Kyrgyz Republic – Tajikistan, Turkmenistan and Uzbekistan) and the peripheral actors (Russia, Iran, Afghanistan and Pakistan) in reshaping the regional strategic situation after the disintegration of the Soviet Union. In particular the extent to which the role of the internal and external influences can be characterized as proactive, reactive or passive is examined in terms of regional and collective security and present and future global implications. In this perspective, the following chapter has been organized into two distinct sections, the former aiming at focusing challenges and security issues which represent the geopolitical theatre where economic forces – exposed in the latter – act and interact.

4.1 The mercantile attraction

4.1.1 The main players

The sudden collapse of the USSR in 1991 created a regional power vacuum which suddenly left the officials of the five CA republics 'orphans'. The unexpected independence created an equal number of 'Founding Fathers of the Nation'. Thus, these new leaders suddenly found themselves facing challenges which they could neither avoid nor postpone, decisions which they could not refuse to take, all, however, being conscious of the vulnerability of their country and, above all, of its premature birth as a 'nation'. The situation also obliged the CA leaders to make some fundamental political choices, first of all that to dissolve national communist parties, or to put their own credibility in doubt. However, the change was merely formal, neither the men nor the structures could be substantially altered. Which fact can represent an element of internal and regional stability insofar as it can guarantee a painless transition from an old to a new regime. But what regime and on which features these Fathers of the Nation will mould the independence of their individual countries is still a puzzling question: the illusion of a new order within a new global village, or the disillusion of an old disorder?

It is true that the leaders of today reflect clearly the old soviet establishment – although these now officially go under the name of 'socialists'.[1] Yet, it is also true that the current leaderships – beyond all official labels – continue to be expression of traditional, local, political forces and of the interests (economic too) which these represent.[2] With independence, the five Republics have found themselves having to face Stalin's borders as a given fact and the Soviet socialist system as a given rule. Although the matter of 'borders' is a crucial question, however and notwithstanding the contrary opinion of some analysts, today there would appear to be no such question – insofar as none of the five ex-Soviet republics intend to open the thorny question of their respective territorial demarcation. Others appear to be the most urgent questions raised by the sudden independence of 1991.

A review of some key-issues helps to shape the main challenges which these countries have now to face:

1. to break out of their economic isolation. This target includes the restructuring of the economies of the individual countries based on single-crop agriculture and the exploitation of natural resources;
2. to attract foreign investment and aid;
3. to update the education and training of the autochthonous population in order to develop autochthonous administrative and technical officials, and reduce their dependence on minorities or ethnic-Slav groups;
4. to create financial and banking systems capable of supporting economic reconversion;
5. to introduce communication and transportation systems capable of providing regular and efficient links both within individual republics and with other states, in line with the new internal and regional economic programmes and new markets (roads, railways, airport, fuel, communications and telecommunications and so on);
6. to find a direct outlet to the sea;
7. to confront ecological problems which are getting dramatically

worse, thus exacerbating internal and regional stability and causing catastrophes in the agricultural-food sectors (Kazakhstan and
Uzbekistan);

8. to secure their frontiers so as to prevent the Afghan crisis from having
   a domino effect on the region with consequent risks for internal
   stability and the reconstruction process.

Within this broad framework one must not forget that there are at
least two other elements, strictly connected to these 'priorities', which
effectively constitute *condiciones sine qua non* for recognition by
the world community and that aid so essential to the *de facto*
independence:

1. the acquisition of a 'national identity' to justify independence and
   to structure this in terms of democratic choice;
2. the solution of problems created by the coexistence of different
   ethnic/cultural and religious groups within a given 'national'
   territory.

These last two points take us back to those specific realities that, with
independence, are re-emerging closely linked to social, political and economic groups, and interests. As many clues to the reading of individual regional situations, they intertwine with the challenges of the third
millennium and stress – or rather underline – the risks of fast violent
revolutionary political, social and economic changes *vis-à-vis* a gradual
auto-referential evolution. No analysis or effective valuation is therefore
possible without taking into consideration also certain local realities.
Today there is no doubt that the traditional local political forces represent ethnic-cultural structures that are deeply rooted in the image
and awareness that these populations have of themselves. Since 1993
the official labels have changed but, in substance, the mechanisms of
traditional power, its expression and means of interaction have not
altered.[3] Some elements in particular can be outlined:

1. the concept and structure of power, that – on both the central and
   the peripheral level – is still highly personalized;
2. the 'personality cult' – and related heroic myths – to the extent that
   these enable popular consensus to concentrate around the leadership; loyalty is never devoted to institutions but to the persons;
3. the recruiting of bureaucratic and technical officials is still carried out
   on the basis of traditional local forces according to traditional balances of power; it follows a widespread favouritism still based on
   clan–family and tribal links;

4. *vis-à-vis* the re-emerging clan-system, it is noteworthy that the absence of a 'national' Army – which would become the inevitable cause of revolts and military *coup d'état* – hand-in-hand with the consolidation of militias/police forces recruited from the clan/family group from which these leaders come;[4]

5. the 'Islam factor'. None of the five CA Republics have yet declared themselves officially to be 'Islamic'; the administrations and the judicial systems are secular. Islam is however an element of the local culture and is an Islam with vividly local overtones involving spiritually evocative features (sufism, mysticism, cult of local saints, and so on) and robust syncretisms with pre-existing traditions and cults. An understanding of these religious forces is, therefore, essential; it implies also an understanding with those political forces which Islam can express and becomes a *condicio sine qua non* for the stability of the region. 'Radical' Islam – or what is commonly called 'parallel Islam' – appears to be an 'imported' factor, ethero-directed, which plays on the ignorance and poverty of certain sections of the population and on those forms of cross-border and trans-national solidarity created by the confraternities.[5]

These points seem to evoke once again the traditional model of the Islamic District Paradigm, whose essential terms of reference are administration (Soviet/ex-Soviet current establishments), Islam (traditional Islam or radical Islam or a new secular Islamic model?) and Traditional Leadership. These appear to be the basic mechanisms by which means of power interact in states that define themselves as independent and modern. Within this picture, no forecast can be made without that force which in any status apparatus is the only experimentally discernible principle of authority, and is still represented by the Russian Army.

4.1.2 The Russian Federation

It follows that the other major protagonist – although only a peripheral subject – is Russia. Since the collapse of the USSR, Moscow's policy in the CA region has been in a state of flux and formation, remaining reactive rather than pro-active and, it would seem, lacking so far a coherent agreed-upon vision. However, the ex-Soviet Republics yet still remain at the core of Moscow's national interest and security. So as to create a stable base for facing the inevitable period of transition from a state of 'imposed' to a state of 'true' independence. Since the very beginning (3 November 1993) Moscow's 'new military doctrine' underlined a kind of right–duty to intervene in the internal affairs both to protect the ethnic-Russian minorities and for reasons of Russian national security, given that these republics constitute a sort of buffer-zone for the defence of Russia.[6]

Since that period, despite the fact that Russia still lacks a univocal policy towards the five republics often adopting *ad hoc* measures for dealing with them, facts (including the recalled military initiatives) have shown a steady shift in favour of an active approach by Moscow to this area,[7] viewed as:

1. yet still falling within her legitimate sphere of influence and 'vital interests';
2. a major element in Russian relations with the countries of Southwest Asia, especially those geographically close to the CIS southern borders, and those which seek a new and more active role and involvement in the region, such as Turkey, Iran, Pakistan, Saudi Arabia and, at present, Afghanistan.

Among the political factors which still forge a close link between Moscow and Central Asia, we may include:

1. the present establishments in power are expression of the old *nomenklatura*, which still is the backbone of the individual administrations, which in their turn represent current regional economic forces and traditional power groups (see also above);
2. the destiny of numerous ethnic-Slav peoples living in CA (important also for the individual economies, which they continue to provide with technological expertise and various kinds of technical personnel);
3. the obvious difficulties of continuing to receive refugees;
4. questions of regional security which require also effective military interventions (such as the Tajik civil war, the Afghan crisis) and concern for the effect that such events could have on Russia herself;
5. the 'radical-Islam factor'; given the globalisation of the media and the porosity of the frontiers, serious worries exist about the uncontrollable resurgence of radical Islam in neighbouring regions and the effect that this could have on the Russian Muslim population as well as on the security of the Federation's border (as the Chechen crisis has well shown and as indicated by Pakistan's equally aggressive policy, terrorism, narco-trafficking, and so on).

This political picture seems in turn to guarantee close interests and ties of an economic and financial nature which continue to link Moscow to the ex-Soviet Republics and *vice versa* (see below).

Let us now analyze briefly the most recent events in Russia and their impact on her CA policy. On 18 August 1998 Moscow announced that the rouble was in free-fall. A crisis thus began which was financial and political at the same time, destined to have far stronger repercussions on the CA theatre than did the Asian crisis. The crisis of August to early September 1998 may, in fact, be interpreted – beyond its economic and financial connotations – as a wilfully political one. In other words, it is more than likely that it represented the final stage in a long drawn-out struggle between the President and the Duma, aimed at bearing on the former to obtain greater powers for Parliament and the political forces holding the majority in the latter.[8] Finally, on the 10 September 1998, the nomination of Primakov, formerly Foreign Minister and exponent of the old Soviet administration.[9]

In our opinion, it seems that the scenario drawn by some analysts of a return to the pre-1991 stance is to be discounted even if there is some 'touching up' of Russian economic policy which will without doubt carry some global impact. The SU is history. It is unthinkable that the process of economic renewal now under way in Russia may suffer a dramatic reversal. It seems also that any sudden drastic change would be technically inconceivable from either the economic–financial stance or that of international politics (the World Bank, the IMF, the EU, which has invested greatly in the renewal and continues to do so in one way or another in order to avoid further chaos in view of the serious crisis looming in the agricultural–food sector on the eve of winter 1998–99) But – beyond all this – the Asian ex-Soviet republics now play a major and decisive role in making a return to pre-1991 state of affairs most unlikely.

Let us re-consider the previous paragraph. The difficult and delicate process of reconstruction under way in CA could not, today, be suddenly brought to halt. The five 'Fathers of the Nation' appear determined to follow the road to political independence, which means also economic and financial independence within the CIS and an opening up to the West. As already outlined, such process is under way, although its lines are so far those of a moderate and gradual re-conversion and transition (see below). Therefore, in CA, Primakov may represent, more than a novelty, the consolidation of a foreign policy which he carried forward as Foreign Minister with continuity, coherence and a firm hand,

and which had a decisive impact on the Asian theatre, too. In that sense, Moscow has achieved certain goals which in no way indicate a break with the Soviet past (one need only think of the Russian position in Syria; Moscow's policy in relation to the 'Turkish push' in Asia; her position in relation to allied 'intervention' on the occasion of the second Iraqi crisis (February 1998); and the Balkans, the UN reforms, NATO, and – last but not least – her equally determined stance regarding the Afghan crisis and Pakistan's regional policy). This, however, does not represent adequate reason to fear a 'renaissance' of the old, Soviet colonial empire.

Thus, analysing the CA theatre pragmatically, we cannot help but recognize once again that Moscow still has notable interests in this region, not only of an economic nature, and that it has still a role to play. However, beyond the myths aroused by Russian nationalists, it does not seem likely that even an old exponent of the Soviet class like Primakov can realistically believe in an 'involution' towards a past by now firmly behind him. *Vice versa*, Primakov seems to be considered by the CA élites not only as a valid card to be played, but also as one meriting respect for his ability and experience. In this light, a possible political CA scenario today is represented by a Moscow's more assertive policy in support of Russian interests in CA: first and foremost, the definition and stabilization of yet still fluid frontiers; consolidation of stability of the current regimes; limitation (as far as possible) of all interference by external subjects (be these regional – as in the case of China, Turkey, Iran or Pakistan – or 'out of area' as in the case of Saudi Arabia or the US); preferential regimes with Europe; the solution of current conflicts by means of negotiations – where possible – or by resorting to the Army where necessary or indispensable (as in Tajikistan).

To conclude, it is well possible that – under Primakov – some ties will be forged anew, especially if certain specific factors are taken into consideration: first and foremost, the fact that too few years have passed since the independence of the five ex-Soviet Republics to have already formed and trained new administrative/bureaucratic structures and experts in the most various fields. Consequently, the still relevant role that ethnic-Slav populations continue to play at the level of CA élites and economies, and, by extension, in the Russian economy with which these still interact. Along with these two points, one must not forget other structural factors, such as the financial and banking system; food-supplies and some areas of agriculture (especially cotton); communications (railway, roads, airlines); certain industrial and technological sectors; internal and external order and security – both essential for orderly economic and financial action and interaction.

4.1.3 Other peripheral actors: the Islamic Republic of Iran, Afghanistan and Pakistan

Russian security strategy in CA obviously is not synonymous with the security of all the five new independent states, neither with the security strategy of other peripheral subjects. Present involvements may reflect different ranges and degrees of individual emotions and interests (that is, political, economic, social). Therefore, to complete this picture in all its essential terms some partners in the regional political games will be given consideration.

The Islamic Republic of Iran has always been sensitive and reactive to CA, although in a cautious manner. In an overall evaluation of Tehran's policy, certain key factors must be considered:

1. First and foremost, certain geographical and cultural advantages (such as its lengthy borders with Turkmenistan and in particular that Iran – potentially – may guarantee an easier outlet to the sea for Turkmenistan and Uzbekistan; historical and cultural ties with certain persophone areas of CA such as Tajikistan, Bokhara and Samarkand in Uzbekistan).
2. These positive factors are, however, counterbalanced by negative considerations, such as: the lack of communication routes linking the country with the CA basin (roads, railways capable of supporting significant commercial traffic, and so on); the lack of financial and technological resources with which to boost the economic efficiency of the region; the presence on Iranian soil of groups of ethnic Turks, 'related to' ethnic turcophone groups of CA; the fact that the Persian-speaking peoples of CA are mainly Sunni, which would make extended propaganda by Tehran difficult and any cultural penetration supported by the religious element extremely unlikely; the historical incompatibility between the Shi'a state model and the 'secular' political model of CA; lack of financial and technological resources necessary for an effective economic development of the region.
3. The long war with Iraq, the impact of which is still strongly felt in demographic and economic terms.
4. The Afghan crisis, which continues to keep Tehran involved in both border-guard operations along the country's eastern frontiers and internally (refugees, aid of various kind to the Coalition of the North, prevention and repression of drug-trafficking, and so on).

5. The crisis in the oil sector, due to low world prices combined with high costs extraction and transportation for Iran.

6. The political importance which the Gulf area continues to represent compared with the CA theatre (complex problems connected with oil, with oil-producing states, Tehran's repeated demands for greater negotiating power within OPEC, reconciliation with Saudi Arabia, the mediating role performed when Iran held the Presidency of the Islamic Conference, and so on).

Khatemi's rise to power (summer 1997) as the result of a popular vote reflects precise economic and power groups within the country who want a return to normal political and economic relations with the West. The tenacious policy approach had been planned and programmed for years (that is, before Khatemi Government came to power) and carried forward by the Tehran administration through various parallel mechanisms and different official/officious channels. The shift of power produced new open priorities. One of the new Khatemi Government's first objectives was economic revival; thus, normalization of relations with the West (especially Europe) became an essential starting point, which Tehran is now pursuing actively through a low profile policy (notwithstanding some internal political tension, due, it would appear, more to the 'metabolization' of some fringes of Islamic militias). Significant pointers in this direction are the brake put on aggressive and/or provocative actions (such as support for international terrorism or religious intransigence), the reduction and/or elimination of possible causes of friction with neighbours and the multifarious openings for dialogue (even of an inter-cultural/religious nature).

Considered and analyzed in this global context, the CA policy of Tehran leads us to surmise that Tehran's unwillingness to be more directly involved in CA affairs will continue for some time to come. Iranian activity in CA continues to be predominantly motivated by matters of economics and security: improving relations with certain countries of the same region and elsewhere (Turkmenistan, Uzbekistan, Russia, India, China); bilateral and multilateral initiatives in the political framework of collaboration in regional organizations (ECO, Conference of Islamic Countries, the Islamic Bank and so on); a solution to the Afghan crisis;[10] an alternative route to CA oil and gas. CA is, however, still a 'sensitive area'. Not to be excluded from CA is certainly a political goal; understandable especially if one considers the 'complex of encirclement' that afflicts Tehran in relation to the Turkish peoples, and the 'complex of isolation' as far as the international community is concerned. However, a sudden about-face by the Islamic Republic of Iran in relation to this region (as some experts have denounced with increasing alarm) is equally improbable. Tehran's policy continues to be characterized mainly by pragmatism and by priorities that Iran gives to multilateral initiatives. Equally, although the 'Afghan Question' is openly denounced by Tehran, little credibility can be given to the hypothesis of any direct confrontation, and Tehran's statements reflect a policy which remains unaltered: any solution is to be looked for above all in the context of multilateral negotiations which involve the players of the region and those out of area principally interested in maintaining regional stability.

As regards Afghanistan and Pakistan, the active efforts of some Pakistani forces (in particular the ISI) have forced some hands, leading to the fall of Mazar-e Sharif in the northern area controlled by the Uzbek warlords and reducing the area controlled by the Coalition of the North forces – supported by the Iran and the Russian Federation – to little more or less than 10 per cent of the Afghan territory (as at end July 1998). The reunification of the remaining 90 per cent of the territory under Pashtu political control (that is the Taliban regime) represents an enormous crisis factor for the region.

New lines have emerged that, although do not imply new forms of opposition or firm alliances, nevertheless reflect clear bewilderment and division as to which policies should be adopted. On the one hand we have:

1. the Russian Federation, the Islamic Republic of Iran and India greatly worried about:
   - the strengthening of Pakistan and the economic groups currently in power there (whose basis would appear to consist of the production, refining and exportation of drugs – heroin to the West and opium to the East, and, in lesser quantities, cannabis, marijuana and so on);
   - the porosity of the frontiers;
   - the presence and exportation of a radical Islam state model (that of the Taliban), which constitutes a highly destabilizing factor both within the five ex-Soviet republics and for other regional players, including the People's Republic of China (PRC).
2. Uzbekistan, concerned principally about:
   - the exposure and instability of its borders with Afghanistan on the one hand, and with Tajikistan on the other, this latter still torn by civil war which has reduced control of the regular forces (that

is Russia's 201st Motor Rifle Division reinforced by other special
rapid intervention forces including Kazakh, Kyrgyz and Uzbek
units) to little more than the capital Doshanbeh. It should be
noted that Tashkent never officially supported the Uzbek warlords,
and does not appear to have lent them either military or other
aid, or shelter;

- drug-trafficking (today largely under control and mainly diverted
  via the Osh region to Kyrgyzstan and to Turkmenistan);
- the presence of illegal capital and a hidden economy which is
  difficult to control;
- the radical Islam factor of the Taliban regime, seen as a threat to
  the Uzbek socio-political model.

3. Kyrgyzstan, which would appear to have a new role to play in the
   lucrative drug traffic (Osh region);
4. the Coalition of the North (Rabbani-Mas'ud's Government), today
   reduced to a handkerchief of rocks and mountain ravines, and,
   therefore, less and less credible as a *de jure* authority representing
   Afghanistan;
5. the PRC, which looks on in consternation at the spread of the
   Kashmir crisis, the success of radical Islam, the exporting of revolutionary forces, the Indo-Pakistani nuclear proliferation – all factors
   representing serious threats to the security of her frontiers and the
   stability of her peripheral regions.

On the other hand we have the Federal Republic of Pakistan, with
financial backing from Saudi Arabia and other, uncertain sources. The
Pakistan government was the first to officially recognize the Taliban government in 1997, soon followed by Saudi Arabia and the UAE.

The recognition was not followed up either from the final reunification of Afghanistan nor from the expected increase in Pakistan's
internal stability and economic growth. This chapter almost wholly
omits Pakistan's situation and position within the framework of the
subcontinent equilibria and economics. However it would be a mistake
not to mention Islamabad's role in CA and the impact of its CA policy
on the stability of the country itself.

On the contrary, the situation got progressively worse. Over the last
year it has been possible to witness:

1. a worsening of tension in Kashmir, with a subsequent worsening of
   tension between India and Pakistan;
2. a disturbing structural frailty in Pakistan as a united nation in terms
   of ethnic-cultural unity;

3. an endemic state of internal guerrilla warfare, both inter-ethnic and inter-tribal (Sind and Baluchistan);
4. an ever more important role played by the army – the positive balancing factor in internal politics and guarantor of the unity and survival of the country;
5. the resurgence of Islam as a political force, including the most radical (Pakistan is voting on various articles of its constitutions which foresees a strict return to *shari'a* – the Islamic law).[11]

Tensions and rivalries with India – aimed also at achieving a more relevant role in the sphere of the United Nations – came to a climax in the late spring of 1998 with the nuclear experiments. Embargo followed which, for Pakistan, meant a sharp deterioration of the country's economic situation and a spiral of internal disorder and power struggles within limited ranks of large economic groups. Almost unprecedented limits were reached in both political favouritism and corruption, while the Clinton administration went on hammering, with ever growing insistence, on Pakistan's collusion in international terrorism. This culminated in the US reprisals against terrorist bases in Afghanistan linked to Osama bin Laden and Saudi financing in August 1998. The disorder and poverty of the region – aggravated by natural disasters – today present a danger which is beginning to arouse serious disturbances. There have also been signs that advanced and nuclear technologies may escape Government control and be placed on the open market.

Such a situation has increased the political and diplomatic isolation of Islamabad and the Taliban regime. With regard to the latter, however, while anything but popular, it does represent a reality which cannot be ignored. It is difficult to foresee the scenario if this regime – unpopular but strong at the moment – can succeed in bringing about the longed-for reunification and pacification of the region; the aim of economic and financial projects with entirely different objectives. Since the summer of 1998 alliances and strategies have once more been placed in doubt. And it is a fact that the CA region – rather than looking towards the Afghan territory for its 'outlet to the sea' – has turned its attention once again towards the west–east links through China,[12] while multilateral negotiations have recently regained strength.

4.1.4 Conclusion

We may well assert that, within this schematic scenario, the 1998 Asian crisis does not seem to have had specific impacts on the regional asset. The approach to this region differs significantly from the approach to other Asian regions. Central Asia is still under the subsequent reeling from the collapse of the Soviet Union and power vacuum. But no approach to CA can yet ignore the Russian reality. Elements of rivalry are emerging, but, in this course, the different partners have to take into account the West – primarily the US – as well as other partners in the regional games. Political factors are intertwining with increasing urgency with economic ones, hand in hand with new terms/concepts of globalization, liberalization, the free market and so on. But these are not the major issues at stake in the region. Globalization does not represent the key either to order and stability nor to freedom and democracy. Too strong are the emotions, too deep are the crises (economic, social, ethnic-cultural, political, religious and psychological, too) which the region is experiencing. Notwithstanding this background, rational forces and an international balance of interest seem to be prevailing so to allow one to speak, at the opening of the third millennium, in terms of gradual evolution toward new social and political structures and, in their turn expression of rational balances of powers and economic interests towards a new order (whether global or regional) and a new future.

4.2 Coping with transition – Central Asia between Russia, China and the West

4.2.1 A troublesome problem

Generally speaking, the Asian crisis seems to have only marginally impinged on CA, bearing little direct impact on most of its leaderships' choices. The problems that the ex-Soviet republics of Kazakhstan, Kyrgyzstan, Tajikistan, Turkmenistan and Uzbekistan are facing now are thus quite different from the ones which are facing, for example, Japan, Korea or the other south-eastern economies, relating mainly to their need to put once and for all the Soviet experience aside and lay the foundations of true market systems.

The origin of these problems can be traced back to the sudden collapse of the USSR, in 1991, that forced the fifteen 'successor states':

1. to shift from planned to market economies, transferring to the private sector all the means of production formerly owned by the state, liberalizing prices and fares, and opening up their systems to free competition;
2. to build up new financial structures through the introduction of national currencies, the institution of central banks and boards of

Table 4.1 Central Asia Republics' GDP – selected years (at purchasing power parity in $ billion)

	1989	**1991**	**1995**	**1996**	**1997**
Kazakhstan	71.8	72.3	40.0	41.2	42.8
Kyrgyzstan	11.1	11.2	6.0	6.5	7.0
Tajikistan	9.9	9.7	4.0	3.9	4.1
Turkmenistan	10.0	10.5	6.8	6.4	4.8
Uzbekistan	44.5	48.8	43.9	45.4	47.4

Source: Official data.

control, and the setting up of intermediation networks previously almost nonexistent;
3. to widen, strengthen and modernize their productive and distributive apparatus, injecting foreign capital, skills and technologies, turning where possible their natural resources to account, and updating their obsolete infrastructures;
4. to overhaul the Soviet system of national specialization, and build up new commercial networks, both inside and outside the CIS;

thereby starting a wide-ranging transformation of their socio-economic structures. In CA this was, from its very beginning, a particularly painful process. During the Soviet period these states were, in fact, tightly entwined within the system of a planned economy: they were net beneficiaries of budgetary allocations and subsides for cotton, minerals and energy transfers; Russia offered them preferential access to its markets and institutions; and among them almost no direct links existed but some low level trans-border trade. In this context, the end of the Soviet rule meant a sharp decline both in GDPs (see Table 4.1) and in living standards, a peaking of inflation to three digits figures and a sudden collapse of commercial exchanges.

In 1996 the situation began to recover. Kazakhstan and Kyrgyzstan introduced new macroeconomic stabilization programmes while Turkmenistan and Uzbekistan made efforts to increase diversification in production and extend their commercial relations (Chenoy 1997; Haghayeghi 1997; Kaser 1997). Almost everywhere legislation relating to foreign investments and joint ventures was re-defined, fiscal benefits for investors extended and currency controls loosened. Although privatization affected only marginal sectors, the role of state diminished. In Uzbekistan, in 1997, 63 per cent of GDP was produced by non-state businesses, compared to 54.7 per cent in the previous year. In

Kazakhstan, by March 1996, roughly 11 500 firms were privatized, five of which were defined of 'strategic relevance'. In Kyrgyzstan, in spring 1997, large shares of Kyrgyztelecom and Kyrgyzaltan were ceded to private ownership, though quarrels slowed down the dismissal of Kyrgzenergholding (EIU 1996, 1997, 1998). But the market building process is still in its early stage. Only in few cases has a legal framework been developed guaranteeing businesses against undue interference by the authorities. The uncontrolled creation of new banks has fuelled mistrust, while lack of qualified personnel, cumbersome procedures and difficulties due to tight state controls continue to limit their functioning greatly (recently, in Kyrgyzstan an attempt at rationalization began, but it does not yet appear to have borne any fruit). Lastly, still unconvertible national currencies continue to limit exports, influence business choices and favour the growth of a lively black market (in Uzbekistan, for example, in October 1998, the official bank rate was of 120 *sum* to the dollar while the 'market' one wavered between 250/300:1) (Sachdeva 1997).

Currently, therefore, the CA leaderships find themselves suspended between two contrasting needs. Insofar as their success and credibility are founded on their ability to guarantee living standards comparable to that enjoyed in the Soviet era (ensuring them, for example, free access to health and education, welfare provisions and a series of good such as water, gas, electricity, and so on), their entry into the world market seems essential. On the other hand, the widespread uncertainty characterizing the region makes this a fairly risky option (Brill Olcott 1995; Webber 1996; Bakshi 1998). Finding an answer to this dilemma, has thus become their first priority. This is the reason why, while none of them seems to hope for a re-integration of the old Soviet area, all (though with differing enthusiasm) are pleased to extend their network of relations to both Russia and other partners (Webber 1997; Gumpel 1998). But what is the real strength of the different options? Is Russia still a useful partner for CA? What role can the West play? And – in a wider prospect – what role China can play, which has been, for long time, trying to extend its influence to Kazakhstan and Kyrgyzstan?

4.2.2 Russia – the emperor's new clothes?

The role that Russia can play in CA is mostly linked to its Soviet heritage. As is widely known, until 1991, Russia was the core of a strong 'imperial' system, within which CA fulfilled the task of providing everything its economy needed to work smoothly. Within this framework, cotton was thus introduced as a main crop in Uzbekistan, oil and gas

Table 4.2   Russia's share of Central Asian trade – selected years (%)

	1991 (a)	**1995**	**1996**	**1997**
Exports				
Kazakhstan	89.5	42.3	44.5	33.9
Kyrgyzstan	87.8 (b)	25.6	30.4	16.4
Tajikistan	44.8 (b)	12.7	16.3	16.2
Turkmenistan	85.8	7.7	62.4 (c)	43.6
Uzbekistan	81.8 (b)	18.8	22.9 (a)	32.0
Imports				
Kazakhstan	92.8	49.0	55.0	46.0
Kyrgyzstan	95.5 (b)	21.9	19.9	26.9
Tajikistan	77.2 (b)	17.0	11.4	9.2
Turkmenistan	83.8	9.4	10.1	10.0
Uzbekistan	84.6 (b)	24.9	32.1 (a)	19.9

(a) Share of CIS on CA exports/imports.
(b) 1992.
(c) In 1996 gas exports to the CIS countries are included in the total for Russia, probably as the gas was sold on the Russian border.
Source: Official data.

pumped from Kazakhstan and Turkmenistan and ore mined almost everywhere in the region to feed its *kombinats* and let them grow according to *Gosplan* – often unrealistic – prescriptions (Pomfret 1995). This managed economy left marked traces in the region, although different from republic to republic (Apostolou 1994). Russia, for example, is still an important trading partner (see Table 4.2), buying from CA a high proportion of its raw materials and semi-manifactured goods, and in turn selling most of the consumer goods it produce. It plays a key role also in other fields.

1. First of all, the Soviet system of economic planning favoured a convergence of all resources (both material and financial) towards the centre which then redistributed them according to pre-established objectives. The infrastructure network of CA is therefore still oriented towards Russia. Western investments have barely affected this state of affairs, mostly because they have been aimed, first and foremost, at the oil and gas sector (Devereux and Roberts 1997). Moreover, even when large, they have often been entangled in the political fetters (both national and international) limiting the region. In this context, the situation in the Caspian basin is typical, where every initiative has run aground when faced with the conflict over access and

exploitation rights to the platform (Forsythe 1996; Miyamoto 1997; Ruseckas 1998).

2. Second, the professional expertise of Russian and Ukrainian technicians has, since the very beginning, been essential in CA industries. Although independence has not been followed by the feared exodus of such technicians (Moscow – well aware of its inability to cope with a massive immigration – threw all its weight into competing with the local leaderships to avoid discrimination against their Slav minorities) and notwithstanding the fact that – in Gorbachev's years – there was an increase in the number of native technicians, such a dependence does not seem to have significantly decreased. (It is worth noting that there is a similar situation in the military field where, even after the formation of the 'national' armies – mainly enrolled among the followers of the various leaders in power – many ethnic Slavs continue to hold high rank.) (see above in this chapter).

3. Last, despite the more or less voluntary introduction of national currencies, the CA republics continue to be strongly affected by fluctuations in the rouble value, sharing with Moscow a general interest in its stabilization. Despite the hopes of many leaders, the introduction of national currencies has not, in fact, entirely isolated their territories and, as has been repeatedly shown, inflationary tendencies are still transmitted from one republic to the others.

Thus, although formal relations between core and periphery have gradually been replaced by more informal links, overall, the situation does not seem to have changed greatly since the times of the USSR. Economically, Russia continues to play a pivotal role and strongly affect CA's performance. Again, more than one decision taken in the region has strengthened Moscow's grip. The process of privatization, for example, has represented, on the one hand, the means by which patronage has been extended and reinforced, the handing over of privatized industries to state managers enabling them to ensure not only their political but also their economic future. But, at the same time, the homogeneity existing between these managers and some elements of the *nomenklatura* now on the rise in Moscow, is playing an increasing role in further connecting the two areas. In this perspective, Russian *atouts* in the region have increased. Although it is yet still too early to affirm that such an increase will shape CA's future, nevertheless it seems meaningful to point out how it seems to be pushing Russia and its former tributaries towards a growing – albeit conflictual – integration (Johnson 1998).

4.2.3 The West – gold at the end of the rainbow?

The West is the second main reference point for CA republics. Between 1991 and 1994, direct investments from the West represented an important share of the Republics' income (see Table 4.3), while the subsequent technological transfer enabled them to re-industrialize, update their technologies and – in some cases – open up production in previously ignored sectors. In this period FDIs interested a wide range of sectors:

1. low cost/low tech consumer goods, either to be sold *in loco* or exported; many clothing industries, for example, invested in Uzbekistan where they could count on an easy access both to cheap labour force and raw materials;
2. infrastructures, although with the limitations mentioned above;
3. semi-manufactured goods (textiles, metal works, basic chemical works, and so on);
4. mineral (the extraction and initial treatment of ferrous and non-ferrous minerals, such as iron, copper, gold and uranium) and energy fields (mainly oil and natural gas); the latter, in particular, being the most visible, leading to a greatly distorted perception of CA's economic role (Jaffe and Manning 1998–99).

The somewhat ambiguous nature of privatization of land and state industries, together with the lack of clear regulations of private property, have instead slowed down entrance into the mechanical and agricultural/food sectors (the tobacco sector is an exception, where important investments have been made in Kazakstan, Uzbekistan and Kyrgyzstan) (EIU 1995, 1996, 1997). But, since 1996, Western commitment seems to have changed, and notable differences have appeared both between the republics and the sectors. Central Asia continues,

Table 4.3 Central Asia Republics' net FDIs as a percentage of GDP – selected years (%)

	1993	1994	1995	1996	1997
Kazakhstan	3.8	5.8	5.2	4.5	n.a.
Kyrgyzstan	n.a.	n.a.	n.a.	n.a.	n.a.
Tajikistan	n.a.	n.a.	n.a.	n.a.	n.a.
Turkmenistan	3.0	3.8	4.4	5.8	3.9
Uzbekistan	0.4	0.9	1.5	1.0	0.4

Source: Official data.

therefore, to have decrepit telephone lines. The provision of energy remains uncertain, given both the poor conditions of many stations and the endemic commercial wars. Transport suffers from the appalling state of both roads and railways. Despite the development of national companies (or possibly because of this), the cost of air travel and transport (often the only efficient means of communication for those wishing to travel from one republic to another), is still high and the standard of service unreliable, a problem further exacerbated by the poor quality of the airports. Moreover, with the independence, corruption appears to have increased, due both to the high degree of patronage involved in the choice of officials and to the increasingly evident emergence of links between institutional heads and the leaders of the ever greater 'informal' sector.

Almost the same arguments apply to the international financial institutions. Carried along by the crisis in the USSR, these institutions (to a large extent a reflection of the role played by the West at the level of international finance) extended extensive credit to new states on the basis of some general promises of renewal and reorganization of their respective economic systems. The first rouble crisis and the decision of the republics to swiftly leave the Russian currency area made this commitment even greater. Between 1993 and 1994, therefore, the IMF offered wide financial concessions to Kazakhstan (more than $160 million in STF in two years and $170 million in stand-by facilities); Kyrgyzstan ($62 million as an extraordinary payment to support the new national currency and access to ESAF) and Uzbekistan ($140 million as a first instalment of STF, later integrated with further payments, to finance the creation of a national currency and support the process of market transition) (EIU 1995).

In close harmony with the evolution of the US *weltpolitik*, however, also the IMF has had to review its position. In 1996, it thus asked Ashkhabad for repayment of credits accorded as a result of what it considered the clear decline in the process of economic reconstruction (EIU, 1997). Even if such a radical stance does not appear to have been taken elsewhere in the region, it does however seem significant that, since that date, the position of the Fund has become more and more cautious and stricter criteria have been applied in conceding financial assistance. Although it appears extremely improbable that international financial bodies could abandon the ex-Soviet republics of CA to their fate – given also the dramatic political consequences which such a decision could have – it is clear that the republics will have to face far more stringent conditions in the years to come.

4.2.4 China – in the shadow of the dragon?

Both politically and economically, the dissolution of the USSR posed Beijing a dilemma very similar to the one posed CA leaders. Can China open its doors to CA? In other words: are CA republics reliable partners for China, both in the economic and political fields? Beijing's policy towards the region seems still to be cautious. Of course, CA can make an important contribution in fuelling Chinese economic development, importing Chinese goods and selling to it most of the resources that China needs. Moreover, there is a strong tradition of trans-border trade between China (mainly the Xinjiang Uighur autonomous region) and Kazakhstan and Kyrgyzstan eastern *oblasts*. But, on the other hand, Beijing is aware of the danger represented by people of common ethnic origin living on the two sides of a border and by the spread of the Islamic message from CA, both elements serving to strengthen its Uighur minority's separatist claims (Munro 1995).

For their part, CA republics have repeatedly shown their eagerness to deal with China (Melet 1998). China is one of Kazakhstan's main trading partners (see Table 4.4), and also Kyrgyzstan and Uzbekistan have strong economic ties with Beijing, despite official figures which often underestimate the extent of this phenomenon. For example, during a conversation with the author held in Tashkent in October 1998, Uzbek authorities asserted that the black market annually creates 'wealth' to the value of 50 per cent of the country's GDP, and that most of such items come from China. Although this estimate is not confirmed by any official figure, it gives a fairly clear idea of the true nature of the international integration of this republic. This does not, however, give

Table 4.4 China's share of trade with Kazakhstan and Kyrgyzstan – selected years (%)

	1992 (a)	**1993**	**1995**	**1996**	**1997**
Exports					
Kazakhstan	16.3	11.6	5.9	7.4	6.9
Kyrgyzstan	36.6	16.4 (b)	16.8	13.8	5.2
Imports					
Kazakhstan	43.6	16.9	0.9	0.8	1.1 (c)
Kyrgyzstan	23.1	0.0	0.0	0.0	0.0

(a) Share of trade outside the FSU.
(b) 1994.
(c) Jan./Nov. only.
Source: Official data.

any indication of the interest shown by Chinese authorities in the republic, nor does it help to understand which factors really influence decisions taken by Beijing. Above all, this does not help to understand what is the real feeling among CA leaders, who (it has been noted above) seem neither to consider the possibility of linking their destinies to that of a regional partner, nor to view the creation of a regional system of alliance or economic co-operation as a credible prospect or alternative.

From this point of view, while there is certainty about Chinese intention and ability to play a major role in CA, there seems to be much less than this about the attitude that Russia, the West, and CA itself will assume in the area. Railways, pipelines and roads linking – through China – Middle Asia to the Pacific could dramatically shift the regional balance of power, projecting Chinese wealth and influence far westward, not only to the Caspian but to the Gulf and the Middle East. But, such a scenario seems, at least, unrealistic, despite the signing – in 1997 – of a \$4.4 billion memorandum of understanding with Kazakhstan to build pipelines to Iran and China in exchange for oil and gas concessions and a 51 per cent stake in Kazakhstan's state controlled oil production company. A far more credible scenario seems a step-by-step policy of economic co-operation, aimed at strengthening the existing web of trans-border relations, thus reinforcing Chinese influence over the region and protecting its internal security (Kasenov 1997a–1997b).

4.2.5 Conclusion

To draw any conclusions is at the same time difficult and dangerous. Yet – from the remarks of this chapter – one element seems to emerge. The country that, today, has more interests at stake in CA is Russia. CA seems to act as a buffer isolating Moscow from the turbulence of radical Islam, which Russia shows to fear so greatly, and as the front line for a Russia in which the war against narcotics is attracting ever increasing attention. Central Asia represents a precious supplier and an important market for the products of Russian industry. Russia can, moreover, provide the CA republics with the means they need to emerge from the isolation in which they find themselves today. The main problems of this phase of transition are that of communications and access to the sea. Here, only Iran has, to date, taken concrete steps to offer itself as a viable alternative to Russia. Iran has invested extensively in the CA republics, especially in Turkmenistan. The effort made to open the Mashad/Sarakhs railway in the spring of 1996 is worthy of note, especially if one bears in mind the difficult conditions of the Iranian economy. Although overrated, the linking of the Turkmen and Iranian railways so far represents the only attempt made by the republics to emerge from their isolation. On the other hand, the regional players, who are those with the greatest interest in promoting the development of the CA republics, are also those with the greatest problems in getting the funds required to finance it. Pakistan, Turkey and Afghanistan, *uti singuli*, are not capable, today, of helping the development of CA economies or of promoting a wider process of regional aggregation. Their political activity also continues to be, to a great degree, ineffective and their role seems not to be able to go far beyond that of merely carrying out orders originating in other contexts, as occurred in Pakistan in the case of the Taliban operation. Russia alone has the industrial apparatus required to satisfy the many demands of the republics (and *vice versa*), and only Russia can guarantee them the possibility of buying goods at prices far below those of the international markets. Hence, for CA today, renouncing Moscow means, facing, in an entirely unprepared state, a far worse crisis than that – already serious – which they have been going through, as well as losing the chance of benefiting from the few weak signs of recovery which are beginning to be seen.

Therefore, independently of what it's leadership is, or may be in the foreseeable future, only Moscow would appear to be both capable and willing to take on a region in which, today, the burdens far outweigh the benefits. Moscow, seriously bound up with internal problems, is still searching for her role in the post-bipolar world. The CIS is an instrument which needs a long period of time to become entirely efficient and is far from representing what the then Foreign Minister, Primakov, defined 'a part of a process of multi-level, multi-rate integration'. In this light, the only chance for Moscow to regain the prominence it holds necessary is to move autonomously by means of bilateral and multilateral agreements like that with Kazakhstan, Kyrgyzstan, Belarus and the Ukraine, signed in March 1996, to bring into being the so-called 'Community of Integrated States'. If and when this proves to be a successful policy, it can in no way be established *a priori*. The difficulties faced in offering her counterparts the same level of technology as the West, the unwillingness to pay in hard currencies for goods acquired from its neighbours (an unwillingness stemming above all from difficulties in obtaining such currencies), the constant fear of an involution of its shaky regime, are factors which place Russia at a disadvantage compared to her competitors. On the other hand, for it's leadership it is essential to escape this impasse. Positions taken since

1996 clearly show how Russia is aware of this and how, notwithstanding the difficulties involved, it is trying to develop a coherent policy in the region. The road to be taken is, however, a long one, as the recent tendency to entrust foreign affairs – both in political and economic field – to people close to the presidential entourage, clearly shows.

Notes

* Valeria Fiorani Piacentini wrote section 4.1 while Gianluca Pastori wrote section 4.2 of this chapter.

1. In some republics the process of creation of an autochthonous political class is more advanced than in others. Tajikistan still finds itself in the total chaos of civil war, involving a marked Russian military presence which, in turn, is a factor that influences political and economic choices. Turkmenistan, given its limited population – is a case apart.

2. It was Stalin who drew the geopolitical map of Central Asia. The radical change began in 1924. Stalin's strategy of 'frontiers' and 'great migrations/deportations' had the precise aim of controlling and governing a vast empire whose ethnic-cultural diversity was the cause of continuous revolts and bloodsheds by means of alterations in ethnic-demographic ratios both within individual republics and among them. This policy made it possible to reduce the possibility of regional unity in both economic and ethnic-cultural terms which would constitute the inevitable prelude to claims for independence. Thus, five Republics were created, nominal seats of five nationalities to be identified with the majority ethnic group of the area. The masterpiece of this *divide et impera* policy, however, lay in the delineation of the borders!

3. For instance, the political-economic balance of power in Kazakhstan is still a reflection of the traditional balance of power between the three 'Hordes' – Great, Medium and Small. Likewise, the ratio/balance of power in Uzbekistan still follows the traditional balance between the Turko-Uzbek and the Tajik elements. Similarly in Turkmenistan the Tekke and Yamut tribes still control the core of the country.

4. Although in some republics (Uzbekistan, Kyrgyzistan, Kazakhstan) there are military units highly specialised, the Army proper – that is an institutional military structure – in at least four of the five Republics is constituted by units of the Federal Republic of Russia, who are stationed in one form (current agreements of the CIS) or another in one or other of the Republics.

5. For the present, Islam in its radical expressions is officially outlawed. In some regions it represents a source of serious tension and conflict, such as in Tajikistan, in Uzbekistan – where the Naqshbandiyyah – whose main centre is near Bokhara – has still a strong impact on the local population, and in Kyrghizistan.

6. Notwithstanding the agreements signed by the CIS on security and peacekeeping, the military doctrine of Russia – formally defined 3 November 1993 – and other later formulations referring to peacekeeping/peace-making/

peace-enforcing and so on, interventions, including those with NATO – relations between the institutional organisms of CIS and the Russian Ministry of Defence are still rather ambiguous. As already stated, Russian armed forces have gradually increased their role (also political) in Central Asia; the new 'interventionist' role of Moscow, pinpointed Moscow's right–duty of interference in the internal affairs of the ex-Soviet republics, both for the protection of the ethnic-Slav minorities and for reasons of Russian national security. These principles saw their immediate application in Tajikistan.

7. Although more than one specialist and analyst draws the pessimistic scenario of a 'Russia to pieces' (see Limes, No. 4/1998).

8. The fact that the Army did not interfere when the crisis was at its climax may be significant. The official statement by the Commander-in-Chief himself and the speaker of the Ministry of Defence was that 'it was involved outside the capital in its traditional seasonal activities of collaborating with the rural population during harvest time'.

9. The absolute majority obtained by the appointed premier in parliament, his programme and the list of ministers (some of whom came as a total surprise) seem to stress the *pro tempore* Duma's victory – as well as the 'political' nature of the crisis. Moreover, repercussions at the level of world public opinion and certain international financial and political fields (such as the World Bank, Central European Bank, BERS, the EU, Clinton Administration, some CA leaders, Asian financial organizations and so on) are a further indication of the close relationships between Russian internal affairs and bordering or more distant regions.

10. The deepening of the Afghan crisis and the Taliban victories at the end of July 1998 (together with Pakistan's active policies in this sector) have placed the entire eastern frontier of Iran in question, dramatically exacerbating existing problems (drug-trafficking, refugees, communications and so on). It seems inevitable for Tehran to review its CA policy, as may be seen by the manoeuvres which took place between August and September 1998, accompanied as they have been by an unprecedented mobilization in Khorasan and Sistan. However, true armed intervention does not seem likely. The Afghan region is too remote, too inhospitable, others have already failed, and, moreover, such initiative would provoke immediate reactions from other nations (the US and EU and, possibly, Turkey). Therefore, it does not seem likely that there will be any radical change in Tehran's policy in relation to a direct military intervention in the Afghan region, more probable is some tactic aimed to exercise a psychological pressure or impact.

11. This point – object of careful analysis – is commonly viewed as a move by the weak Sharif government as a means of polarizing public opinion in a period of serious internal crisis and international isolation. It can also be indicative of the government's wish to please and placate the Pashtu population.

12. An article announced (*International Herald Tribune*, 7 December 1998) that Unocal Corporation has withdrawn from the consortium that planned an US\$ 8 billion pipeline system traversing war-torn Afghanistan (the project was started around 1994, Unocal joined it in 1995). There was to have been a 1600 km oil pipeline and a companion gas pipeline, in addition to a tanker-loading terminal in Pakistan's Arabian Sea port of Gwadar. Other pointers

seem to signal that the Afghan route can become more and more improbable in the short term: a report from the Centre for Strategic Studies of Kyrgyzistan, for example, points out in 1997 the east–west route via China as the more convenient both on the political and economic levels; reports from the Presidential Institute for Strategic and Regional Studies of Uzbekistan follow the same line, stressing that it is almost impossible to solve the region's greatest problem and transport gas and oil from Turkmenistan across Afghanistan to Pakistan. Many industry officials and analysts are now questioning the wisdom of having planned such a huge infrastructure project across a war-ravaged country like Afghanistan.

References

Apostolou, M.A., 'The Problems of Creating Economies in Central Asia', in Anoushiravan Ehteshami (ed.), *From the Gulf to Central Asia: Players in the New Great Game* (Exeter: University of Exeter Press, 1994), 58–73.

Bakshi, J., 'No Single Power or Power Centre Can Have Exclusive Sway Over Central Asia', *Strategic Analysis*, XXII (1998), 119–41.

Becker, A.S., 'Russia and Economic Integration in the CIS', *Survival*, XXXVIII, No. 4 (1996–97), 117–36.

Brill Olcott, M., 'Sovreignty and the "Near Abroad"', *Orbis*, XXXIX (1995), 353–67.

Chenoy, A.M., 'Political and Economic Process in the CA Republics', *International Studies*, XXXIV, No. 3 (1997), 301–12.

Devereux, J. and B. Roberts, 'Direct Foreign Investment and Welfare in the Transforming Economies. The Case of Central Asia', *Journal of Comparative Economics*, XXIV (1997), 297–312.

Dyker, D., *International Economic Integration for Central Asia* (London: RIIA, 1997).

EIU (The Economist Intelligence Unit), *Country Profile – Central Asian Countries* (London: The Economist Intelligence Unit, 1995, 1996, 1997, 1998).

Forsythe, R., *The Politics of Oil in the Caucasus and Central Asia* (London: IISS and Oxford University Press, 1996).

Garnett, S.W., 'The Integrationist Temptation', *The Washington Quarterly*, XVIII, No. 2 (1995), 35–44.

Gumpel, W., 'Economic Development and Integration in Central Asian Republics', *Eurasian Studies*, V, No. 13 (1998), 18–32.

Haghayeghi, M., 'Politics of Privatization in Kazakhstan', *Central Asian Survey*, XVI (1997), 321–38.

IPIS (Institute for Political and International Studies), *Central Asia and the Caucasus Review* (Tehran: IPIS – Institute for Political and International Studies, 1998 – in Persian).

Jaffe, A.M. and R.A. Manning, 'The Myth of the Caspian "Great Game": The Real Geopolitics of Energy', *Survival*, XL, No. 4 (1998–99), 112–29.

Johnson, L., *Russia in Central Asia: A New Web of Relations* (London: RIIA, 1998).

Kaser, M., *The Economics of the Republic of Kazakhstan and Uzbekistan* (London: RIIA, 1997).

Kasenov, O., *Central Asia on the Eve of the 21st Century: The Second 'Great Game'?*

(Center for Strategic and International Studies, Kainar University, 1997a, *mimeo*).

Kasenov, O., *Potential Export Routes for Kazakhstan's Oil* (Center for Strategic and International Studies, Kainar University, 1997b, *mimeo*). *Limes*, No. 4, 1998.

Melet, Y., 'China's Political and Economic Relations with Kazakhstan and Kyrgyzstan', *Central Asian Survey*, XVII, No. 2 (1998), 229–52.

Miyamoto, A., *Natural Gas in Central Asia* (London: RIIA, 1997).

Munro, R.H., 'China, India, and Central Asia', in Jed C. Snyder (ed.), *After Empire. The Emerging Geopolitics of Central Asia* (Washington D.C.: NDU Press, 1995), 121–35.

Pomfret, R., *The Economies of Central Asia* (Princeton: Princeton University Press, 1995).

Ruseckas, L., 'State of the Field Report. Energy and Politics in Central Asia and the Caucasus', *AccessAsia Review*, I, No. 2 (1998), 41–84.

Sachdeva, G., 'Economic Transformation in Central Asia', *International Studies*, XXXIV, No. 3 (1997), 313–27.

Webber, M., *The International Politics of Russia and the Successor States* (Manchester and New York: Manchester University Press, 1996).

Webber, M., *CIS Integration Trends* (London: RIIA, 1997).

5
At the Foot of the Himalayas: India from the 'Hindu Equilibrium' to an Asian Regional Power?

Paolo Panico and Gianni Vaggi[1]

5.1 The subcontinent: some features of the South Asian economies

In East Asia, 1997 will be remembered as the year of the financial crisis. After 30 years of very high growth rates, three ASEAN countries and South Korea plunged into deep economic crisis. This crisis overshadowed other events: the fiftieth anniversary of the independence of South Asia, or the partition of British India into two separate States: the republics of India and Pakistan, whose eastern part became Bangladesh in 1971. International attention remained focused on SA in 1998 due to the nuclear tests of India and Pakistan and the ensuing sanctions. These tensions notwithstanding, SA was the fastest growing region of the developing world after China. Its growth rate was 4.6 per cent in 1998 and it is expected to reach 5.5 per cent in 1999–2000 (*World Bank News*, 13 October 1998).

This chapter explores some of the social and economic features of the large countries of South Asia. As shown in Table 5.1, India is by far the biggest economy of South Asia, and the only one that might lead a process of regional integration, as will be discussed later in this chapter. Not only is South Asia already home to more than 1.2 billion people but, given the expected population growth, it will reach almost 1.8 billion in the year 2015 (UNDP 1998, statistical appendix, table 47). This fact puts considerable strain on the use of land and natural resources. Population density is very high and it reaches the highest levels in the world in cities like Calcutta, with more than 88 000 inhabitants per square km. At the same time, the share of urban population is lower than in sub-Saharan Africa and the process of urbanization is still taking place.

Table 5.1 The three big countries of South Asia

	Bangladesh	**India**	**Pakistan**
Population (million, 1997)	124	961	137
Population growth rate (1990–97)	1.6	1.8	3.1
Population density (people per km^2)	920	313	169
Rural population (%, 1997)	81	73	65
Life expectancy (years)	59	63	65
Per capita GNP (US$, 1997)	270	390	400
Average annual growth rate (% 1990–96)	2.7	3.8	1.1
Per capita GNP at PPP (US$, 1997)	1050	1650	1590
Population with less than 1 US$ a day (%)	28.5	52.5	11.6
Agricultural value added as a % of GDP (1997)	30	27	26
Exports as a % of GDP	16	12	16
Gross domestic investment as a % of GDP	17	25	19
Military expenditures as a % of combined health and education expenditures	41	65	125
External debt (million US$, 1996)	16083	89827	29901
External debt (present value, as a % of GDP)	30	22	39
Current account balance (as a % of GDP)	–5.1	–1.1	–6.5

Sources: The World Bank 1998/99 and 1998c, UNDP 1998.

South Asia has a very high percentage of irrigated land, at 27 per cent much higher than East Asia's 10 per cent. Irrigation was a crucial component of the 'green revolution', but it is also an indication that some opportunities to increase domestic food output have already been exploited. With the exception of Sri Lanka and the Maldives, all the states of SA have a very low Human Development Index (see UNDP, 1998 statistical appendix, table 1). Gender-related inequalities are remarkable, even by third world standard, but SA is also the only part of the world in which women have been prime ministers for a considerable period of time, and where they still play a significant political role (Sri Lanka, Bangladesh, India and Pakistan). Contrary to many developing countries, elections have been held regularly in the four mentioned states, and the military have never seized power in India.

South Asia is the area with the highest number of 'poor' – more than half billion people – and the fight against poverty will be the main challenge for years to come. Economic growth is slower than in the rest of Asia. Even though the investment levels are not particularly low for developing countries, the SA economies are still relatively closed to foreign trade and find it difficult to increase their share in the world trade. This fact is mirrored in the poor conditions of the current and trade accounts of the three countries, which are particularly worrying in Pakistan and Bangladesh. These two countries had large foreign debt levels in the eighties and they were hit by the debt crisis of that decade. India reached a very high stock of debt later in the eighties and in the early nineties. The structure and terms of foreign debt in the three countries are not as bad as those of Latin America: a high proportion of the debt is concessional and less than 20 per cent is at variable rates, thus less sensitive to changes in international interest rates. A decline in concessional lending and an increase in debt instruments at variable rates were recently recorded in India and Pakistan (World Bank 1997a, p. 43).[2] Defence expenditures are a very high percentage of GDP in the region: they reach 6.1 per cent in Pakistan, the highest rate in Asia excluding the Middle East and North Korea, and are much higher than the expenditure on health and education.

The economies of SA are marked by two further features. First, the occupational structure of the labour force has been stable over a long period of time (see World Bank 1997a, pp. 11, 65). In particular, the people employed in agriculture are still two thirds of the labour force in India and they only slowly decreased from 73 per cent to 63 per cent between 1965 to 1989, at a time when there was a considerable growth in the service sector. Second, SA has suffered from the collapse of the Soviet Union and the crisis in Eastern Europe since 1989. In the case of India, exports to Russia and Eastern Europe went down from more than 20 per cent of total exports in the eighties to 4.2 per cent in 1992–93; the share of imports decreased from more than 10 per cent to 2.5 per cent (see *Economic Survey 1993–94*, Statistical tables p. 94). Pakistan was hit by the retreat of Russia from Afghanistan and the cuts in American support to anti-communist guerrillas. The US and the EU are now the main economic partners of SA, but India and Pakistan have been trying to redirect their foreign trade between 1989 and 1996, with a view to enhancing their economic relations with the booming economies of EA, a region with significant FDI in SA. It remains to be seen whether this process has began and will continue after the 1997–98 crisis of that region.

5.2 India: the slow elephant of Asia?

A popular image of India is that of an elephant, not only because of its size but also because of its slow motion, particularly with respect to the EA 'tigers' and more recently to China. It is common to make comparisons with the spectacular economic growth of South Korea, where real per capita GDP (at prices of 1990) increased by ten times between 1960 and 1995, whereas in India it merely doubled. The annual growth rate of real GDP in 1980–93 averaged 9.6 per cent in China against 5.2 per cent in India. The size of the country is thus seen as no excuse for a slow economic pace. Economic growth was particularly low in the 30 years after independence, with a meagre annual average rate of 3.5 per cent up to 1980 (Parikh 1997). It improved to 5.7 per cent in the eighties and it has fluctuated between 5 and 7.5 per cent since 1991–92 (see *ibid.* and World Bank 1998a, p. 1).

However some remarkable social and economic achievements of the post-independence period must be remembered. Famine has been eradicated through state intervention and public works securing purchasing power to the rural poor; the 'green revolution' made India a net exporter of cereals. In fact, the Indian economy grew faster between 1947 and 1991 than it ever did during the colonial period, and with much lower fluctuations than in other parts of the developing world, notably Latin America. Moreover, inflation was always under control and definitely low by developing country standards. Starting from 1947, the India economy became the most important example of a non-communist planned economy system, following the import–substitution approach of Mahalanobis and Nehru's vision of socialist self-reliance. The second and third five-year plans of 1956–66 led to massive investment in basic and heavy industries, a strategy which led to an increase in the incremental capital–output ratio from 2.8 in the fifties to 6.2 in eighties (see UNIDO, 1990), with damaging effects on productivity. This policy was not opposed by India's industrial houses, that enjoyed the artificial protection of tariff walls.[3] Many economic areas, such as heavy manufacturing, banking, civil aviation, power generation and telecommunications, were closed to the private sector and foreign investors. India's licensing regime, the so-called *permit raj*, compelled companies to seek permission to invest or launch new products. Many key prices were state-controlled (steel, fertilizers, petroleum products), subsidized credit was extended to favoured users and many industrial enterprises were state-owned.

India has a diversified industrial production and export base but, as a consequence of her inefficient industrial system, India's share of world manufacturing exports declined from 2 per cent in 1950 to 0.45 per cent in 1990 (Ahluwalia 1998, p. 248). The infrastructure sector performed poorly in the same years, which contributed to the poor performance of the organized manufacturing sector, where total factor productivity declined at an annual rate of 0.5 per cent between 1960 and 1980. It increased by 2.8 per cent per annum after 1980.

The responsibilities of the planning system in braking the Indian economy are clear but there are some further components. Jalan (1991) indicates three common features of 19 developing economies which grew more than an average 6 per cent from 1965 to 1989: increasing domestic savings rates; high literacy levels; and the absence of balance of payments crises. In India gross domestic savings increased from 10.4 per cent of GDP in 1950–51 to 23.6 in 1990–91, but there were frequent balance of payments crises in 1957, 1966, 1981, 1991. Furthermore, nearly half of the adult population is still illiterate (two-thirds of adult women), whereas some EA countries had good schools and high literacy records at the very beginning of their economic development process. In 1960 South Korea and Thailand enjoyed literacy rates (68 per cent and 71 per cent, respectively) significantly greater than the present Indian one (51 per cent). The relative neglect of basic education in India did not favour the labour-intensive, export-oriented manufactures which have boomed in EA.

A political economy outlook, allowing for India's diverse social structure in terms of religion, caste and community, is crucial to understand the peculiarities of the Indian economy in the Asian context. Deepak Lal (1988) identified the causes of India's low growth rate – which he called the 'Hindu equilibrium' – as being the unique social structure based on Indian castes that has shaped economic activity in the subcontinent since 1500 B.C. The Sanskrit words corresponding to what is ordinarily termed 'caste' are *varna* and *jati*. *Varna*, which literally means 'colour', is the well-known distinction among Brahmins, Kshatriyas, Vayshas and Shudras. Along with this, Indian society is organized into several thousands of *jatis*, that can be directly translated as 'occupations'. Indeed, most *jatis* have traditionally been identified with some specific profession or craft for centuries, and some of them have in turn become to powerful business communities. Accordingly, the social interaction of an Indian individual is mediated through the network of kin and associates belonging to the same *jati*, the so-called *biradari*.

In his economic analysis of the Indian castes, Panini (1996) argues that this social system managed to thrive even during the years of socialist planning, while a radically different model of society was advocated and pursued by the country's political leadership. The extensive regulations enacted by the Indian government in the first 40 years after independence encouraged a strong network of connections to either successfully exploit or circumvent those same regulations. Accordingly, managers and employees were recruited from the same *biradari*. Furthermore, the bias against large-scale businesses and anti-competitive practices led to the proliferation of small-sized businesses, often created around *biradari* clusters. Indian industry is best characterized in terms of family businesses, rather than independent firms. A recent analysis by Dutta (1997) shows that 99.9 per cent of all Indian companies and, most noticeably, 75 per cent of India's largest corporations, are owned and controlled by individual families. This means that the main decision-making positions are occupied by family members and the preferred relations within the family's *biradari*. Accordingly, the Indian market can be described as neither competitive nor oligopolistic. The meaningful dimensions of industrial organization in India are those of co-operation within the same community, or cluster of families, and competition among rival *biradari*s. This applies even to the few world-known Indian industrial brands such as Birla, Tata, Goenka, Agarwal and the like, who often own but a tiny proportion of their group undertakings. Nevertheless, the interplay of cross shareholding and loyalty within each *biradari* can effectively prevent an outsider from taking over an Indian business or entering a 'guarded' market.

Due to the pre-1991 *'permit raj'*, those Indian business houses diversified their activities in as wide a gamut of industries as they could obtain licences for. The outcome is not unlike the poorly focused, oversized conglomerates of Indonesia, Korea and Japan, one of the factors that ushered in the financial crisis of 1997 and 1998.

Furthermore, land reform was never completed in India, even though it was a priority at the time of independence. Land reform is now mainly a state-level issue, but in some states of the Gangeatic valley agriculture is still carried out in feudal conditions, giving rise to interlocked markets of land and credit (Bhaduri, 1983), where chronically indebted peasants are forced eventually to sell their lands. Thus many states witnessed land concentration and an increase in the number of landless households, so that per capita land availability in India is one of the lowest in the world. The 'green revolution' was limited to some parts of India, mainly the Northwest, largely because social group of independent and relatively wealthy cultivators already existed. Land reform has been found to be an important element into establishing positive inter-sectoral linkages

between agriculture and industry and so to increase agricultural productivity in South Korea, Taiwan, Japan and post-1978 China.

Finally, it must be remembered that since 1947 India has been a
democracy with regular elections. The relationship between economic
growth and democracy in Asia is a tricky matter (Wade 1990). India's
central government had often to appease different classes and contain
social unrest, thus acting as a conflict manager (Bardhan, 1984) rather
than taking a more direct developmental role (Chakravarty, 1987). For
many years the Congress Party had been the main political forum. The
rise of the Hindu nationalist Bharatiya Janata Party (BJP), and the formation of coalition governments in the nineties, turned the composi-
tion of different political claims to negotiations between many political
parties, but the role of the central government as conflict manager does
not seem to have changed.

5.3 Regional diversity and cohesion: the Indian states

The economic performance and development perspectives of India rely
on the individual economic management and policies of its states. In
fact, many of the 26 states that (together with six Union Territories,
including the capital Delhi) make up the Indian Union, have a size
exceeding that of the largest countries in Europe, either in terms of
population or area. Independent India inherited the administrative
organization of the British raj, based on 16 large and multi-ethnic states,
resulting from the gradual take-over and amalgamation of previously
independent principalities and kingdoms. A thorough reorganization
along ethnic and linguistic bases was undertaken in the fifties, starting
at the break-up of the former state of Madras into Tamil Nadu and
Andhra Pradesh (1953). The process continued in the sixties, as the
former state of Bombay was split into Maharashtra and Gujarat (1960),
while a predominantly Hindu state, Haryana, was separated from
Punjab, where the majority of the population belong to the Sikh religion, in 1966. The state of Himachal Pradesh was separated from Punjab
in 1971, while in the north eastern regions of the country two small
states, Nagaland and Meghalaya, were created from the former large
state of Assam (1963 and 1972, respectively). Furthermore, some Union
Territories have been promoted into states since the early seventies.

Accordingly, ethnic and linguistic specificity is the key determinant
of the current territorial administration of post-independence India.
Significant differences can be recognized in terms of social and economic outlook as well. Table 5.2 provides an outline of economic and
social indicators for the 14 largest Indian states. Female literacy rates

Table 5.2 The largest Indian states: the main social and economic indicators

State	Population (million)	Per capita income (US$)	Life expectancy (years)	Female literacy rate (%)
Uttar Pradesh	150.7	200	57.9	25.3
Bihar	95.4	146	57.6	22.9
Maharashtra	86.4	490	63.1	52.3
Madhya Pradesh	75.2	229	55.5	28.9
West Bengal	73.6	251	59.8	46.6
Andhra Pradesh	72.0	289	60.6	32.7
Tamil Nadu	58.4	335	60.8	51.3
Rajasthan	48.4	238	58.2	20.4
Karnataka	48.2	301	62.7	44.3
Gujarat	44.8	411	59.9	48.6
Orissa	34.4	191	56.2	34.7
Kerala	31.0	279	71.3	86.2
Punjab	22.1	521	65.5	50.4
Haryana	18.2	459	62.7	40.5

Note: Population projections were developed by the World Bank for the financial year 1995–96 based on the latest available Indian census (1991). Per capita income calculations are based on state per capita GDP expressed in Indian rupees, then converted into US dollars at the average exchange rate in the same financial year – life expectancy at birth and female literacy ratios are the 1991 census figures.
Source: The World Bank (1997b) and *India at 50* (1997).

are consistently lower than the corresponding figures for males, hence they provide a sensitive benchmark for state education records. The abysmal educational conditions of many Indian states would be best portrayed by the rural female literacy ratio. With the sole exception of Kerala, these figures are ten percentage points lower than the corresponding rates exhibited in Table 5.2. Accordingly, rural female literacy rates are below 50 per cent in all Indian states but Kerala, a worrisome record since the percentage of rural population in India is about 75 per cent.

A clear correlation can be identified between health and education standards such as those exhibited in Table 5.2 and the economic welfare of Indian states. The richest states in terms of per capita income, such as Punjab and Haryana, Maharashtra, Gujarat and Tamil Nadu, rank equally high in terms of their social indicators. Conversely, the poorest states are the worst performers with regards to literacy rates and health conditions. A significant indicator is the state of Kerala, where a successful educational policy leading to almost universal literacy brought about a remarkable improvement in living standards, including a successful reduction in population growth. Nevertheless, due to the concurrent structural and political imbalances in the state, these achievements failed to translate into a prominent economic performance. A strong need for improved health and education standards is anyway confirmed by the figures above. India cannot reasonably aim at a leading regional role in Asia if its literacy rate barely exceeds 50 per cent. This requires increased, focused investment at the state as well as the central government levels, within the existing, tight budget constraints.

Further differences can be recognized with regards to economic structure and performance. The most industrialized states of Punjab and Haryana, Maharashtra and Gujarat, Tamil Nadu and Karnataka, have an established tradition in select industries, such as machinery, textile, cement, automotive, leather and software, respectively. These are among India's most competitive industries and their development in select states and regions can be traced to the development of the corresponding skills by specific castes and communities. Local skills and specialization, as well as infrastructural endowments, are the key determinants of the Indian states' ability to attract FDI, an essential source of capital inflow after the main criteria for state financing were modified in 1991.

The ability of Indian states to levy taxes is restricted by the Constitution to a few indirect taxes, mainly in the form of excise duties, import (or countervailing) duties and sales taxes. Accordingly, state financing has traditionally relied on revenue sharing with the central government, based on each state's income level and its planned development goals. The proportions of revenue sharing and the scope for direct transfers are recommended by the Financial Commission, an independent body periodically appointed by the President of India for a five-year term. Until 1991, a 'gap-filling' approach prevailed with this respect, that is, states were granted the necessary resources to match their actual budget deficits. At the same time, market borrowing was highly restricted, to the extent that the phrase was specifically used to indicate captive loans extended by state-owned financial institutions as part of their statutory liquidity requirements for development programmes approved by the central government. Recommendations in thus regard were given by the Planning Commission.

This system was complemented by borrowings from central government and it had the merit of establishing a predictable, transparent set-up which avoided major financial default at state level. Accordingly, this system was instrumental in insulating the Indian states from the impact of the Asian financial crisis of 1997 and 1998. At the same time, this framework allowed the redistributive mechanisms which should have led to a balanced development across the Indian Union. Nevertheless, the pre-1991 state financing system had a major shortcoming, insofar as it discouraged financial discipline. The 'gap-filling' approach, based on actual instead of normative deficits, as well as the provision that new programmes would be fully funded for the first five years, led to a proliferation of low-return investment projects. A number of programmes were thus initiated by the Indian states without an appropriate coverage of their operating and maintenance costs, either in terms of tariff schemes or the underlying tax base.[4]

There are several examples of the detrimental effects of such a lack of financial discipline at state level. For instance, Rajasthan, one of India's poorest states both in terms of natural resources and per capita income, exhibited an impressive growth rate of 6 per cent during the eighties. This was mainly as a result of government provision of goods below cost, which inevitably led to the eventual state's inability to operate, maintain, let alone renovate, its infrastructure. A major effort in reforming power generation, water, and fiscal policy at large was then initiated by the government of Rajasthan in the early nineties. In the case of Haryana, state subsidies to deliver underpriced electric power in the early nineties amounted to the cost of setting up a 500-MW power plant. This led to a thorough review of the state power generation policy in 1996.

Indeed, infrastructure, a well-educated and disciplined labour force, and an attractive mix of fiscal incentives are the main factors leading to an investor-friendly environment, on which Indian states are currently competing. FDI is a key source of upgraded technology and the capital inflows necessary to cover the existing state budget deficits. It is perhaps too early to identify some 'winners' in this process, though the highest-income states (Maharashtra, Gujarat, Punjab and Haryana) and the four southern states of Tamil Nadu, Karnataka, Kerala and Andhra Pradesh are undoubtedly the preferred targets for foreign investors.

5.4 From the planning experience to liberalization

Despite the many economic and social differences among the Indian states, the present outlook for the Indian economy is greatly influenced by a major and comprehensive new economic policy package adopted by central government in 1991. The then prime minister Rajiv Gandhi made a modest attempt to reform the planning system in 1985 and he tried to boost demand through a surge in public investment and a more expansionary fiscal policy. The result was a rapid demand-driven growth followed by inflation and a balance of payments crisis. In June 1991, India faced a tremendous foreign exchange crisis: reserves were down to the value of two weeks' imports, while inflation was at 13 per cent, one of the highest levels since 1947. The Gandhi liberalization favoured an increase in the import of consumer durables rather than investment goods, without an adequate rise of exports. This, in turn, boosted external borrowing.

The incoming Prime Minister Narasimha Rao, also under the pressure from the IMF, implemented a more decisive reform of the old planning system, making the year 1991 a turning point for the Indian economy. The new programme was made up of two complementary parts: macroeconomic stabilization and structural adjustment, namely liberalization of the production structure of the economy. Stabilization was aimed at improving the fiscal deficit and the balance of payments. The gross fiscal deficit of the central government decreased quickly from 8.3 per cent of GDP in 1990–91 to 5.9 per cent in the following fiscal year and it remained roughly stable up to the estimated 5.6 per cent of 1998–99 (World Bank 1997a; 1998a, p. 92). Budgetary conditions have improved since 1991, also because of the remarkable cuts in capital and development expenditures, while the consolidated gross fiscal deficit of the states have almost trebled since 1990–91.[5] The consolidated public sector fiscal deficit, including the centre, the states and public enterprises, has remained unchanged since 1991–92 and it has always been above 9 per cent of GDP. Subsidies on diesel and kerosene still have a significant weight in the budget of public oil companies. To sum up, many expenditures were delayed and others were transferred to the states, which do not have enough tax capacity yet.

The other side of the macroeconomic stabilization programme was a cut in the current account deficit, which was achieved mainly through a devaluation of the rupee *vis à vis* the US dollar and a severe import squeeze. The deficit fell from 3.4 per cent of GDP in 1990–91 to 0.7 per cent the following year, while during the same period foreign exchange reserves increased to 3.3 months' worth of imports. The rupee has been kept on a downward 'crawling peg' system with the US dollar since 1991, with a slight devaluation year on year, which has taken the exchange rate from 26–27 rupees per dollar in 1992 to 42 in December 1998. No major sharp devaluation has taken place since 1991, however: during the 1997–98 EA crisis the rupee lost a mere 10 per cent of its value in 1997 and another 10 per cent in 1998 (IMF 1998, Figure 2.8).

As regards the structural reforms, it can be seen that the economic liberalization process is certainly slow but still continuing, nothing resembling the 'shock-therapy' experienced by Russia and Eastern Europe since 1989. The major aspects of this process are de-licensing of investment and production as well as opening-up to private investors in many industries, including power, steel, oil refining, air transport, telecommunications and mining. In addition to that, a reform of the tax system is under way, aiming at a simplified structure and lower rates. Many import controls have been removed and there has been a sharp reduction of tariffs, even though India's average tariff is still twice as high as the average in most of EA. FDI has been encouraged, through the establishment of joint ventures with an Indian producer, which is still regarded as the best way of investing in the country. Liberalization of capital markets is slower, and the various governments have been trying to attract funds from non-resident Indians, up to now without much success.[6]

As far as the social sphere is concerned, the liberalization process initiated in 1991 is perhaps the most powerful policy set-up leading to an eventual 'annihilation of caste'. Paradoxically enough, the modernization effort unsuccessfully pursued with socialist techniques might best be achieved via the opposite policy prescriptions. Increased competition is likely to enhance the value of innovation and efficiency, as opposed to networking and connections. The creation of new job opportunities is likely to reduce the scope for caste-based recruiting.

A free flow of commercial information, as a result of liberalization, opening-up and the abolition of licensing, is likely to reduce the value of private information of the kind available within a closed *biradari*. All these processes are bound to gradually replace impersonal, 'neo-classical contracting' for the existing, caste-determined 'relational contracting' prevailing in India.[7] Of course, these mechanisms are embedded in the peculiar Indian social structure, given the initial distribution of resources and capabilities, which requires additional caution in order to prevent harmful and potentially disruptive social and political outcomes.

To the many limitations of India's process of economic liberalization we can add the slow pace of privatization, also due to the difficulties in finding a solution to the problem of the employees of public-sector enterprises, the so called 'exit policy'.[8] Some advancement in this direction may take place however, since the BJP cabinet relaxed its previous *swadeshi* (self-reliance) rhetoric and declared its intention to press ahead with an ambitious programme of public assets divestment. If privatization is to bring more revenues to the central government, though, most of it can be expected out of the sale of some reputable quasimonopolies such as the telecom provider VSNL, the Container Corporation (Concor) and the Oil and Natural Gas Company (ONGC).

5.5 Sectoral imbalances and development perspectives: the present tasks and the road ahead

Overcapacity is perhaps the main reason for the slowdown of Indian industry, both private and public, in 1998. Excess capacity was built into most industries after 1991, exploiting the possibility of access to state-of-the-art technology and capital goods. Due to ineffective planning and licensing, excess capacity was a common feature of several Indian industries even during the '*permitraj*'[9] and in some cases it was retained thanks to a bailout by India's largest institutional investor in industry, the Unit Trust of India. As a result, overcapacity is present in many heavy industries such as steel, cement, aluminium, as well as oil refining, cars, hotels and a number of industrial good. Private domestic investment in such industries is therefore not to be expected in the near future. The only 'winner' in Indian industry appears to be software, matched by a few select industries where India has some recognized brand names, at least at a national or regional level, such as edible oils and detergents. Even though some blue chips of the Indian software industry, such as Infosys, Satyam and Pentafour experienced a drop in their stock value, most companies are still recording sales increases of 40 per cent above 1998 levels. Accordingly, the market capitalization of the most prominent Indian software houses is still impressively high.

Another factor hindering the growth of Indian industry is the number of bottlenecks created by the lack of appropriate infrastructure in transport, telecommunications and power generation. The ongoing opening-up of the sectors above to foreign entrants, and in some cases to private players, may speed up the upgrading of Indian infrastructure to a level conducive to a resumption of direct investment growth. As pointed out previously in this chapter, significant investment is required in the areas of health and education as well. Even though the need for a carefully directed investment activity by India's government is quite clear, the resources available to India's public sector are severely constrained. The existing budget deficit of 6 per cent of GDP is well above the planned 4 per cent figure. Additional pressure created by the states has led to an overall public sector borrowing requirement of 10 per cent in the financial year 1998–99. Furthermore there is no clearly decreasing trend in the domestic debt–GDP ratio, which is stuck around 60 per cent. Interest payments are already a very large and sensitive component of the overall fiscal deficit. Savings and investments have slightly increased to more than 25 per cent of GDP during the nineties, but the very low level of public saving is worrying (Ahluwalia 1998).

A thorough reform of the tax system, aimed at expanding the actual tax bases might be the way to strengthen the centre's investment capacity as well as to ease the states' fiscal crisis. A large fiscal deficit is likely to trigger a mounting inflation trend. The consumer price index increased from less than 6 per cent in early 1997 to more than 16 per cent in December 1998. This surge in inflation is quite worrisome, especially because it is taking place at a time of low and decreasing prices of raw materials and oil, on imports on which India is still strongly dependent.

Recurring macroeconomic imbalances show up also in the balance of payments, with a large negative trade balance which is transformed into a less negative current account balance thanks to the invisible items. Even though the current account deficit ratio to GDP reaches the apparently modest rate of 2 per cent – much smaller than Thailand's 8 per cent in 1996 – still it could create problems (World Bank 1996b). To sum up, in spite of the importance of India's domestic market, the country shows some of the features of a small open economy with a foreign exchange constraint, that is, it is highly sensitive to variations in the prices of imports and interest rates. Foreign financing has not been a major problem yet, but a high proportion of portfolio investments to FDI, at least with respect to China, were recorded in 1995–96 (World Bank 1995, pp. 42, 48).

On the other hand, the relative inward orientation of the Indian economy – with exports totalling as little as 6.5 per cent of GDP – proved beneficial in limiting the country's vulnerability to the Asian crisis, and to the US sanctions imposed after the nuclear tests of May 1998 in Pokhran (Rajasthan).[10] At the same time, though, a drop in demand by the region's recessionary economies, as well as a fiercer competition from the same SEA countries, whose currencies devalued far more than the rupee, jeopardized the Indian chances for sustained export-led growth. Competition relates not only to consumer goods, for which a 4 per cent increase in import duties was imposed by the last budget, but also to heavy industrial items such as cement (Indonesia) and steel (South Korea), with a further erosion in the price-making capacity and profit margins of India's major public sector players in the same industries. The direct impact on trade of the sanctions imposed on India by the US was small, but the indirect effect may be significant. The World Bank postponed several loans and direct aid, while credit and guarantees were not extended by the US Export–Import Bank, Eximbank, which may have a negative impact on some big infrastructure projects, from power to telecommunications. As a result, external commercial borrowings are currently inaccessible to several Indian businesses, given the existing spread of 700 to 800 basis points over LIBOR (London interbank offered rate), while the domestic prime rate is in the region of 13 per cent upwards. The increase in interest rates is further aggravated due to a downgrading of India's sovereign rating to the level of 'speculative grade' by Moody's rating agency in June 1998.[11] This, in turn, brought about an increase in the cost of external borrowing, further restricting Indian firms' access to capital sources.

More expensive money, coupled with the downturn of Indian equities and real estate (Bombay's Sensex index collapsed after April 1998, while the price of commercial properties dropped by 50 per cent in Bombay, 25 per cent in Delhi and Bangalore over the last three years) are responsible for a depressed domestic demand. The hardest hit of India's consumer base is the urban middle-class, whose savings were mostly held in the form of stock investments and real estate. The only segment of the Indian population that may nurture a demand-led recovery are the rural rich, thanks to a satisfactory harvest following a more benign monsoon season than 1998. But the propensity to consume of India's rural middle and upper classes is impaired by a number of resisting habits and traditions.

The number of potential Indian consumers is as debatable as that of her poor. The well-off middle and upper-middle class may be at most 20 per cent of the population, thus around 200 million people, but this is a very optimistic estimate. The top 5 per cent of households roughly 50 million consumers, make up the really rich market. Probably those potential spenders with Western tastes and consumption standards are in the range of 100 million people. Whatever the potentiality of the domestic market, India still has some major economic and development problems to tackle and their solution cannot be delayed. A country still hosting some 25 per cent of the world poor can no longer afford to be trapped in the so-called 'Hindu rate of growth'. In fact, India needs a growth rate of about 7 per cent if it is to rescue increasing shares of its population from their 'below-poverty-line' conditions.

A GDP growth between 5.5 and 6 per cent for 1998 and 1999, would be a satisfactory record in comparison to India's neighbours in SEA. An acceleration would be beneficial however, though it faces a number of structural constraints. Growth can be expected to continue at good, though not impressive levels: the objective of an average growth rate of 7 per cent over the long run may be difficult to achieve, which may lead to serious problems in the fight against poverty. In fact, India's major problems are linked to human development: rapid growth is necessary but it may not be enough to alleviate the conditions of more than 300 million people living below the poverty line. Structural and macroeconomic adjustment must continue but the size and quality of the 'safety nets' needed to shield the poor from the possible hardships are awesome. Infrastructural bottlenecks in telecommunications, power generation, distribution, housing, health and education all serve to hinder human development.

5.6 Lessons from the experiences of liberalization and adjustment in India and in East Asia: the revenge of the elephant?

It may be interesting to compare some aspects of the liberalization-cum-adjustment process undertaken by India in the nineties with the financial crisis of EA in 1997–98. India had to partially restructure its foreign trade in 1991–92, due to a debt and liquidity crisis which – even though it was not as dramatic as that of Indonesia in 1997 – was by no means an easy task. The adjustment took place with much smaller losses in growth than those experienced by EA in 1998. Cutting expenditure is always costly: GDP growth fell from 5.4 percent in 1990–91 to less than 1 per cent in 1991–92, but it bounced back to 7 per cent in 1994–96, an amazing performance for the Indian economy. Industrial output did even better, with average growth rates around 10 per cent. The current account deficit is still slowly decreasing, external debt declined from 34 per cent of GDP in 1991–92 to 27 percent in 1996–97. The improvements in the debt–service ratio were even more remarkable: from 32.4 per cent of gross current receipts in 1990–91 to 23.2 per cent in 1996–97 (World Bank 1998a, p. 77). Reserves are more than US$ 26 billion and can cover more than seven months of imports. India's external position is strong and it is most unlikely that the country will suffer the sort of financial crisis experienced by its EA neighbours, as well as Russia and Brazil in 1997 and 1998.

Exchange rate management, with the rupee floating downwards since August 1995, led to a controlled depreciation and avoided any large real exchange rate appreciation which was one of the causes of the EA crisis (Milesi-Ferretti and Razin 1996).[12] It is true that the Reserve Bank of

India (RBI) had to intervene in defence of the currency in November 1997 and January 1998, when the rupee was under attack; both interest rates and cash-reserve ratio were increased and the currency fell a few percentages points (World Bank 1998a, p. 13). The existing controls on capital movements prevented easy borrowing from abroad and the inflows of short-term, 'hot' money that took place in Russia, South Korea and Indonesia, hence India scores well in terms of this vulnerability indicator (World Bank 1998b, p. 8). It is now widely recognized that full liberalization of the capital account has to be preceded by a consolidation of the domestic financial system and the credit sector in particular (Fisher 1997).

To sum up, moderate growth rates by Asian standards, and capital and exchange rate controls, sheltered India from the Asian contagion. The 'slow elephant' of Asia was not caught by the fever of 'short-termism' which took many emerging markets. Development takes time, even economic growth takes time in SA and sometimes this can be an advantage. There have already been bubble crises in the Bombay (Mumbai) stock market, but their real impact has been almost negligible: the effects of good and bad monsoons on GDP is still much greater than that of stock exchange volatility. Nature and population still set the time in the Indian subcontinent, but India cannot stay still and watch the crises of the EA miracle countries; things are changing and fast even for India.

5.7 India and the world: any chance for sub-regional leadership?

A closer look at the form and structures of India's foreign relations, especially in the economic sphere, allows a better understanding of the context and the constraints within which India may play a role as a regional leader in SA after the 1997–98 turmoil. The main sub-regional institution for mutual co-operation in SA, where India has a natural leading role – if only because of the sheer size of its economy and population – is the South Asian Association for Regional Co-operation (SAARC), formally established in 1985 between India, Pakistan, Bangladesh, Sri Lanka, Bhutan, Nepal and the Maldives. The association seeks to promote the improvement of human well-being in the seven SA countries and it actually succeeded in mobilizing public opinion towards sensitive issues such as drug trafficking, the environment and terrorism. This reflects the overall goal of the association to promote SA peoples' self-reliance.

In respect of trade and security – the two main dimensions of the world's major international associations of this kind, such as APEC, NAFTA, the EU – SAARC cannot be seen as a significant regional player, Indeed, as far as security is concerned, some border controversies exist with all the major partners of SAARC, namely. Pakistan, Bangladesh and Sri Lanka. The unanimity rule, originally designed to limit the otherwise inevitable pre-eminence of India over the association, ultimately grants each member country an effective veto and actually prevents the effective functioning of SAARC.

The hostilities between India and Pakistan date back to 1947, the year of partition and have their source in the deep-rooted rivalry between Hindus and Muslims. Even since the ground for open conflict has been control over Kashmir, with open war both in 1947 and in 1965. As far as Bangladesh is concerned, the conflicts with India refer to the Farakka dam, built in 1975 and deemed to be one of the main reasons for the yearly floods that occur in Bangladesh during the monsoon season. A related issue is access to India's far east, that is the states located northeast of Bangladesh, which cannot easily expediently be reached from the rest of the country without crossing the territory of Bangladesh that, in turn, views it as a threat to its national sovereignty. The Hindu secessionist movement in Sri Lanka (the 'Tamil Tigers') allegedly enjoy the support of India's southern state of Tamil Nadu against the country's Buddhist Sinhalese government. This has led to some embarrassment over time, especially when India tried to play the role of referee in an attempt to settle the dispute. Rajiv Gandhi's murderer was a supporter of Tamil extremism.

Given these political pre-conditions, it is almost natural that a reasonable free trade area cannot be created easily in SA. The SAARC trade arm, SAPTA (SA Preferential Trading Agreement), was signed in 1995 and it provides for the application of preferential trade tariffs on selected items to the other SA countries. Nevertheless, intra-regional trade in the SAARC area amounts to as little as 3.5 per cent of the seven countries' aggregated trade volume. The main reason is, again, the negligible share of trade between the two largest partners. India's trade with Pakistan accounts for less than 0.2 per cent of the total. Accordingly, a regional leadership role cannot be taken up by India in SA until the decade-long dispute with Pakistan is settled. Therefore, the political importance of SA remains limited, as the region is naturally meant to gravitate around India, at least in economic terms. India's role in Asia as well as in the international world order has to be re-devised in the post-cold war era, when 'non-alignment' is no longer a meaningful option in international

politics. India is not one of the 'economies' making up the APEC conference, though it is a full dialogue member of ASEAN. Some territorial
disputes between ASEAN member countries such as the Philippines,
Indonesia, Vietnam and Malaysia on the one hand, and China on the
other (such as the Spratly Islands) indicate the desirability of bringing
'the world's largest democracy' closer to ASEAN interests. For the same
reason the investment flows from Singapore intensified after the mid
nineties, especially in the southern states of Tamil Nadu and Karnataka
(Bangalore). At the same time, India's main trading partners and
investors are US and the EU. It is therefore essential that the BJP
abandon its *swadeshi* rhetoric in favour of a pro-growth, truly open-door
economy. The main challenge facing the current Indian administration,
though, is the trade-off between its fragmented, multi-community
domestic constituency and the outside world expectations for the
country.

Notes

1. Gianni Vaggi wishes to acknowledge the financial support of the Italian Min-
    istry of University and Technical Research (MURST) and the hospitality of
    St John's College, Cambridge.
2. Workers' remittances play an important role in the balance of payments of
    all the countries in SA.
3. The average import–weighted tariff was 128 per cent in 1990 and 20 per cent
    seven years later (World Bank 1997a).
4. In order to allow for each state's revenue potential, the Tenth Financial Com-
    mission set the level of central government transfers to the states as a pro-
    portion of normative, instead of actual deficits.
5. Aggregate state deficit was 34 per cent of the central government fiscal deficit
    in 1990–91, whereas it reached almost 52 per cent in 1997–98 (World Bank
    1998a, p. 94–5).
6. Investments, both portfolio and FDI, by expatriate Indians peaked to almost
    700 million dollars in 1996, but they decreased to little more than
    200 million in 1998 (*The Economist*, 25 July 1998).
7. These phrases are used to mean transaction cost economics, as specified by
    Williamson (1985). This view is shared by most analysts of contemporary
    India. For a contrasting view, possibly flawed by a limited reference to the
    Indian social structure, see Ghosh (1998), which provides a thorough survey
    of the economic debates on liberalization in independent India.
8. Privatization was not considered particularly important in attracting FDI in
    EA (World Bank, 1996).
9. A survey by the Industrial Licensing Policy Inquiry Committee (ILIPIC)
    found out that several companies were producing in excess of their licensed
    capacity as early as 1969. See Chaudhuri (1998).
10. It may be noticed that the recession of 1993–94 was overcome thanks to an

export-led recovery, based on export growth rates in the region of 20 per cent. Although, Indian exports have declined by 17 per cent as of May 1998, compared to the corresponding figure for the previous year. At the same time, Indian imports are show on the increase, which increases the prospect of a widening trade deficit for the country, adding to the existing structural pressures on the exchange and interest rates.

11. Long-term bonds and notes were rated Ba2, while bank deposits Ba3 and short-term bonds and notes were rated NP, 'not prime'. For comparison sake, the corresponding ratings for China were A3, Baa2, and P2, respectively.

12. The real exchange rate appreciated by a modest 3 per cent between 1992 and March 1998.

References

Ahluwalia, I.I., 'L'economia dell'India e le sue prospettive' in *L'India contemporanea* (Turin: Edizioni della Fondazione Giovanni Agnelli, 1998).

Bardhan, P., *The Political Economy of Development* (Oxford: Basil Blackwell, 1984).

Bhaduri, A., *The Economic Structure of Backward Agriculture* (London: Academic Press, 1983).

Byres, T.J. (ed.), *The Indian Economy. Major Debates Since Independence* (Delhi: Oxford University Press, 1998).

Chakravarty, S., *Development Planning: the Indian Experience* (Oxford: Oxford University Press, 1987).

Charlton, S.E.M., *Comparing Asian Politics. India, China, and Japan* (Boulder, Colorado: Westview Press, 1997).

Chary, S.N., *Mera Bharat Mahaan (My India is Great)*, (Delhi: Wheeler Publishing, 1997).

Chaudhuri, S., 'Debates on Industrialization' in Byres (ed.), *The Indian Economy. Major Debates Since Independence* (1998).

Dobbin, C., *Asian Entrepreneurial Minorities* (Richmond, Surrey: Curzon, 1996).

Drèze, J. and A. Sen, *India. Economic Development and Social Opportunity* (Delhi: Oxford University Press, 1995).

Dutta, S., *Family Business in India* (Delhi: Response Books, 1997).

Economic Survey 1993–94 (Delhi: Government of India, Ministry of Finance, 1994).

Fischer, S., *Capital Account Liberalisation and the Role of IMF* (Washington D.C.: The International Monetary Fund, September 1997).

Ghosh, J., 'Liberalisation Debates' in Byres (ed.), *The Indian Economy. Major Debates Since Independence* (1998).

India at 50. Facts, Figures and Analysis 1947–1997 (Madurai: Express Publications, 1997).

Institute of International Finance, *Capital Flows to Emerging Market Economies* (January 1998).

IMF (International Monetary Fund), *World Economic Outlook* (Washington D.C., September 1998).

Jalan, B., *India's Economic Crisis: the Way Ahead* (Oxford: Oxford University Press, 1991).

Lal, D., *The Hindu Equilibrium* (Oxford: Clarendon Press, 1998).

LaRue, C.S., L.I. Rudolph, S.H. Rudolph and P. Oldenburg (eds), *The India Hand-book. Prospects onto the 21st Century* (Chicago: Fitzroy Deaborn Publishers, 1997).

Lewis, J.P., 'Some Consequences of Giantism: The Case of India', *World Politics*, 43, 3 (1991) 367–89.

Lewis, J.P., *India's Political Economy* (Delhi: Oxford University Press, 1997).

Lin, L. and O. Acosta-Ruiz, 'Regional Growth Opportunities in Southern India', in Tan, *et al.* (eds), *Business Opportunities in India* (1996).

Milesi-Ferretti, G.M. and A. Razin, 'Current Account Sustainability: Selected Asian and Latin American Experiences', *IMF Working Paper* No. 110, Washington D.C. (1996).

Panico, P., 'Entrepreneurial Culture and Economic Development: some Cross-Asian Comparisons' Paper presented at the Third Conference on East Asia – EU Business (Como, 23–25, April 1998a).

Panico, P., 'India. Gli Squilibri di un Subcontinente', *Politica Internazionale*, 1 (1998b).

Panini, M.N., 'The Political Economy of Caste' in Srinivasan (ed.), *Caste. Its Twentieth Century Avatar* (1996).

Parikh, K.I. (ed.), *India Development Report 1997* (Delhi: Indira Gandhi Institute of Development Research, Oxford University Press, 1997).

Rutten, M., and C. Upadhya (eds), *Small Business Entrepreneurs in Asia and Europe* (Delhi: Sage Publications, 1997).

Srinivasan, M.N. (ed.), *Caste. Its Twentieth Century Avatar* (Delhi: Viking Penguin Books, 1996).

Tan, T.M., A.M. Low, J.J. Williams and R. Zutshi (eds), *Business Opportunities in India* (Singapore: Prentice Hall, 1996).

UNCTAD, *Trade and Development Report, 1996* (New York and Geneva: United Nations Publications, 1997).

UNDP, *Human Development Report* (New York, 1998).

UNIDO, *India New Dimensions of Industrial Growth* (Oxford: Basil Blackwell, 1998).

Wade, R., *Governing the Market* (Princeton: Princeton University Press, 1990).

Williamson, O., *The Economic Institutions of Capitalism* (New York: The Free Press, 1985).

The World Bank, *India: Economic Reform and Growth* (Washington D.C., December 1995).

The World Bank, *Managing Capital Flows in East Asia* (Washington D.C., 1996a).

The World Bank, *India-Five Years of Stabilization and reforms: The Challenges Ahead* (Washington 28 August, 1996b).

The World Bank, *South Asia's Integration into the World Economy* (Washington D.C., 1997a).

The World Bank, *India. Sustaining Rapid Economic Growth* (Washington D.C., 1997b).

The World Bank, *India – 1998 Macroeconomic Update* (Washington D.C., 1998a).

The World Bank, *East Asia – The Road to Recovery* (Washington D.C., 1998b).

The World Bank, *World Atlas* (Washington D.C., 1998c).

The World Bank, *World Development Report* (Washington D.C., 1998/99).

Part II
International Issues

6
Facing the Environmental Problems in Changing Asia

Maria Julia Trombetta

6.1 The role of the environmental crisis in geo-political and geo-economic equilibria

The emerging ecological crisis and above all, the growing awareness of the seriousness of the situation, both at a local and global level, could alter the geo-political and geo-economic equilibria. The problem is becoming more evident throughout Asia, both for the seriousness of the environmental problems – differing region by region – but which are equally relevant and growing in importance, and for the increasing role of the area in the world economy and in strategic balance.

The recent financial crisis and the weakness of the newly independent states in CA show the fluidity and the vulnerability of a continent searching for it's role. Ecological issues, often set aside in the name of development and economic growth or marginalized when faced by other priority issues, could increase even more the vulnerability of the system and suddenly present unexpected costs. Environmental problems strike and impoverish the state not only economically: absolutely since they de-legitimate the state and relatively because they change balances. Effects on the environment are not uniform and if it is difficult to assert that these changes could be an absolute gain for a state, losses could be relatively more or less serious, depending on the vulnerability of each system.

The environmental problem, on the one hand, is a constraining factor, because it imposes costs on the state, on the other it is a tool in the international arena. The ecological interdependence underlines issue linkages and then it subordinates compliance to other benefits or, on the contrary, it builds trust on co-operation. Sometimes actors are looking for the additional benefit of a good reputation in compliance, sometimes they hope to attract foreign investment or they try to use environmental standards as a benchmark.

Two aspects are remarkable and will be analyzed: the implications for security and the relationship between the spread of international environmental politics, and the globalization of the economy.

6.1.1 The Environment as a security problem

Environmental degradation rarely is an exclusive cause for violent conflict but it contributes notably to determine competition for resources, flows of refugees, decrease in economic growth and political instability, and hence it plays a significant – albeit complex – role in shaping relations among states and regional security.

Homer-Dixon (1991) individualizes three different kinds of environment-related conflicts, linking them with different theoretical models. i) The conflicts caused by the shortage or by the deterioration of resources. It is not a new phenomenon, the access to resources has always played a relevant role when determining the security of states. New aspects are the nature of the resources, the reason for the degradation and the entity of the phenomenon. The problem of shortage concerns even more resources which are considered renewable, such as water, fish-stock or forests. ii) The conflicts caused by population displacement, due to environmental degradation that makes some regions unable to support their autochthonous population, which flows within and beyond the borders. Different ethnic and cultural groups are obliged to cohabit in narrow areas, suffering stress or deprivation and hence conflict could spring up. iii) The conflicts due to relative losses of welfare. The environmental problems could determine, both in the industrialized countries and in the developing ones, a decrease in the ability to produce wealth, and hence in the standard of living. This diminution, and above all its rate, could determine tension and political instability.

The environmental problems generally threaten the developing countries more seriously because they are more vulnerable, but the consequences of such problems are reflected in the security of the developed countries. The mechanisms could be manifold and phenomena of political instability or local conflicts could have strategic repercussions, especially following the end of the cold war.

6.1.2 The spread of international environmental politics and the globalization of the economy: a future harmonization of standards or environmental dumping?

Economic globalization is changing the nature of environmental management. While it increases the influence of market forces on the making of environmental policy, it subjects national environmental policy to the role of international economic institutions. This creates new imperatives for states: not only to co-operate internationally so as to manage global resources but also to co-ordinate domestic environmental policy, not to be priced out or to lose attractiveness for FDI (Zarsky, 1997).

On the one hand environmental policy, altering costs of production, changes competitiveness. Unless policy measures are taken, environmental costs are not reflected in the market price but are borne socially, today or in the future. A country, which takes measures to internalize its own environmental costs or to protect its environment, could be priced out of export markets or lose attractiveness as a production site for foreign investors.

On the other hand growing green consumerism and product standards, to promote consumers' safety, imposed by state regulation push to converge in environmental policy. The mechanism is still weak: US and EU standards differ radically. Environmental standards for production and resource management, which have a greater effect on the environment than product standards, are ineffective since states are prohibited by the WTO from unilaterally imposing process and production methods (PPM), and eco-labelling, introducing the possibility of discrimination among products on the basis of production process, is disputed (Zarsky, 1997).

Moreover, the process of globalization is far from being really global and economic integration is largely regional. This implies that convergence in environmental policy is more likely at regional level.

6.1.3 The extent of international environmental politics

Even if social, political, economic processes and changing behaviour related to environmental change extend far beyond the realm of international environmental politics, the spread of international environmental politics and its effects are based on how the perception of ecological crisis and interdependence could change international regimes or the set of 'norms, principles, roles, decision-making procedure around which actors' expectations converge' (Krasner 1982).

However, environmental issues are largely institutionalized: UNEP has strengthened its mandate; many conventions have entered into force; several countries have created institutions and environmental legislation. A decentralized action, not only at national but also at local level, has been developed as the success of local 'Agenda 21' demonstrates. But this is not a homogeneous process and industrialized countries have reached more meaningful achievements than developing countries. According to Levy, Keohane and Haas, (1993:339) international institutions play a relevant role and fulfil three catalytic functions in development and spread of international environmental politics. Institutions boost concern at different levels of society, creating, collecting and disseminating shared scientific knowledge, legitimizing and de-legitimizing states' practises. Institutions enhance the contractual environment, providing bargaining forums and monitoring compliance with agreements and treaties. Institutions contribute to national policy response, improving domestic capability, for instance, transferring resources and technologies or providing technical assistance.

However, the spread of international environmental politics and it's effects on Asian economic and security scenarios face a set of problems. First, the difficulty to check compliance and the lack of enforcement. This has a twofold consequence: the effects of 'official' international environmental policy cannot be overestimated but, since everybody pays lip service to environmental problems, they could contribute to trust dialogue and confidence building. Second, while an international, albeit weak, framework for environmental multilateralism already exists, it is not integrated either with security organizations or with international economic governance. Concerning the former, the USSR's proposal at the UN to create a sort of 'Environmental Security Council', largely instrumental, has no consequences.[1] Concerning the latter, since 1991 GATT/WTO has included environmental issues on its agenda, first with a working group and since 1994 with the standing Committee on Trade and Environment (CTE). In spite of the aim of CTE to create a transparent, non-discriminatory, environmentally sound trade policy, it has focused only on whether and when unilateral or multilateral trade restrictions on environmental ground are permissible, debating on trade restrictions within multilateral environmental agreements and eco-labelling. Another means by which environmental protection is balanced with economic activities is the mechanism of the Environmental Impact Assessment (EIA). EIAs, intended to study the potential environmental consequences of a project, theoretically provide a forum for mediation of different interests and assure a proper assessment of costs and risks, bringing environmental concerns to economic decisions on FDI, but there is no international requirement that countries have EIAs at national level.[2] In the private sector, innovative institutional approaches are emerging; the most significant is the Environmental Management Standard (EMS), generated by the International Organization for Standardization (ISO). This voluntary standard provides guidelines for industry to monitor and to improve environmental management. However, the key to the success of ISO standards is broader regulations and the institutional context in which companies operate.

A third set of problems relates to the real extent of international environmental policy and its multilateral versus bilateral dimension. The late nineties are characterized by the growing importance of bilateral and regional relationships, which involve environmental politics too. The end of the cold war removed the strategic incentives for environmental co-operation. The main motivations for development assistance have failed and the industrialized countries are reconsidering, for instance, the role of ODA[3] and, generally, the fact of being engaged globally; they prefer to focus on regional initiatives, such as the recent Japanese engagements on environmental issues with China. Unlike the accident at Chernobyl, recent serious fires in Indonesia or severe floods in China underline more the local dimension and the differing vulnerabilities of the stricken systems than the global dimension of the environmental problems. Unavoidable, local and regional threats, dictated by geographical proximity, gain greater importance. This is the new dimension of environmental security and international environmental politics, strictly connected with the growing regional economic integration. This does not mean that the global dimension is vanishing but these new dimensions are to be considered.

6.2 Environmental issues in Asia

To analyze environmental issues in Asia and to identify those factors which are already effecting security, a regional perspective is preferred, considering that the main dimension of environmental issues is still regional, strictly connected with the existence of eco-regions and the growing regional economic integration. NEA, SEA, the Indian subcontinent and CA are analyzed. Special attention is devoted to China and Japan, for both their peculiarity and relevance.

6.2.1 North East Asia

The main environmental problems in the region are atmospheric and water pollution, degradation of marine resources, deforestation, desertification and soil erosion, and the storage of radioactive waste. The primary regional problem is acid rain, due to high levels of sulphur emissions from coal-burning power plants and factories, mainly in China and North Korea. Depending on the season and atmospheric conditions some countries may be both originators and recipients of acid rain, especially North Korea. Acid conditions occur also in Japan and southern China, producing tensions between the two countries.

Marine pollution takes place in an area of overlapping and contended maritime jurisdiction, rich in fish resources. The Yellow Sea receives large amount of pollutants, including hydrocarbons, heavy metals, industrial and agricultural chemicals and sewerage, both from coastal cities and the Yellow and Yantze rivers. The Sea of Japan suffers a high rate of pollution due to oil spills and radioactive waste dumping.[4] The risk of significant political and military competition for diminishing marine resources is emerging as a security issue: illegal fishing, territorial/economic exclusive zone encroachments and maritime incidents in NEA have been increasing regularly (Dupont, 1998). There were about 700 incidents of illegal fishing by Chinese ships in South Korea's territorial waters in 1995. North Korean patrol boats have crossed into South Korean waters to protect their fishing fleet, and Russia despatched a Kara-class cruiser to the East China Sea to halt attacks on its vessels (Dupont 1998). Maritime incidents involving fish resources are linked to intractable disputes; fishing rights in Diaoyo/Senkakus are relevant,[5] while the Kurils lie in the middle of one of the world's richest fishing grounds.

A scenario of geographical, ecological, economic interdependence progressively emerges with the integration of northeastern Russia, an area rich in natural resources, with technology and capital intensive economies, such as Korea and Japan. The globalization of the economy, the strong competition for capital, the lack of political will and of institutional tools, instead of leading to convergence in environmental standards change into ecologically destructive actions and lead to over exploitation of natural resources. Ecological dumping is a probable scenario. This phenomenon is potentially destructive: it involves economy and security. According to Hayes and Zursky (1993) a 'pollution haven' strategy, if pursued by all the developing countries of NEA, could imply a vicious circle of standards lowering competition, with long-term social costs and rapid resources depletion. Second, companies and industries attracted by the 'pollution haven' are generally non-dynamic, unable to innovate. They do not bring technology transfer or knowledge spillovers, which are necessary to sustainable, self-generating economic growth. Third, products manufactured or extracted from pollution havens may face environmental barriers in the increasing conscious market of OECD (Hayes-Zarsky, 1993). Timber resources may be especially vulnerable: Greenpeace has already targeted unsustainable logging practises by South Korean and other foreign companies in the Siberian forests.[6] Threats to security could occur when local actors emerge against the ecological marginalization.

Over recent years a great number of treaties and conventions have been signed by the states of the region, but compliance is low and difficult to check. Emerging regional environmental management include: the UNEP's Northwest Pacific Action Plan, instituted in 1989, the Northeast Asian Environmental Program and the Sub-regional Technical Co-operation and Development Program. The Tumen River Area Development Programme, launched in 1991 to foster co-operation and economic development has led to a 'tragedy of the commons' scenario and it 'may serve as a greater source of conflicts than co-operation' (Woodrow Wilson Center, 1998, 60).

6.2.1.1 China, the dirty giant

The way in which China manages its resources and pollution amid economic growth is of vital importance to the global environment and regional stability.

First, both the dimensions and the rate of growth of environmental problems are impressive both for population size and energy policy. This makes China able not only to condition the size of environmental problems at regional and global level but also to compromise the effectiveness of any environmental policy. China is already the second largest contributor to greenhouse-gas emission and its emissions are growing. Moreover, the seriousness of the problem could cause strains and political instability. The Chinese are still effected by a plethora of domestic environmental problems ranging from scarcities of water and arable land to air and water pollution, from flooding to desertification, all of which could contribute to population movements or health problems[7] and de-legitimize the state. Two environmental issues in China outweigh the others and are attracting the attention of national and international communities: preservation of water supply and energy policy. Both will fully manifest their effects in the future and both require infrastructure and investment.

Second, China, since the late 1980s, has used environmental problems as a tool to establish itself as the pre-eminent voice for the developing countries and play a regional role, while Western countries, and
above all the US, made little effort to understand either the seriousness
of the Chinese ecological problems or how best to conduct environmental diplomacy with China.

The first wave of environmental action dates from 1972 when China
attended the United Nations Conference on Human Environment.
However, environmental issues were not considered a serious problem,
following the strategy: 'Grow first and clean-up later'. During the late
1980s and early 1990s there was a significant growth in Chinese interaction with the international community on environmental issues
(Economy, 1997). On the one hand, it provided China with access to
new technologies and funds. China has received the largest amount of
Montreal Protocol funding, totalling over US$ 100 million, and also
over US$ 120 million of Global Environment Facility funding (Woodrow
Wilson Center, 1998: 69). On the other hand, the influence of the international community remained constrained. Scientific and environmental officers pursued assistance from the international community
while diplomatic officials worked to restrict any official obligation on
the part of China (Economy, 1997).

In international negotiations China reiterated a set of principles
including: environmental protection should not be achieved at the
expense of economic growth; the developed countries are responsible
for global environment change and sovereignty must be respected. In
1991 China convened the 'Conference of Developing Countries on
Environment and Development' in Beijing to develop a united bargaining position for UNCED. Chinese leadership pursued a strategy which,
ignoring the potential detrimental effects on the country in the long
run, 'maximized China's potential to continue its rate of rapid economic
growth while assuming a high moral ground' (Economy 1997, p. 39).

The Chinese environmental protection apparatus is relatively weak
and lacks in co-ordination. Environmental legislation has been developed but is inefficient, both because of administrative fragmentation
and for the lack of separation between polluter and controller.[8] Even if,
since 1979, a greater effort has been made to create an environmental
framework and that in 1997 environmental crimes entered Criminal
Code, enforcement is low. In this context new elements have recently
emerged: a growing consciousness of ecological issues is highlighted by
the ninth five-year plan (1996–2000) which includes environmental
investment of 450 billion yuan (accounting for about 1.3 per cent of

GNP in the same period)[9] and by administrative reform in March 1998 which elevated the State Environmental Protection Administration (SEPA) to the rank of ministry. Serious floods in summer 1998[10] exacerbated the urgency. On the other hand there are the contrasting effects of economic reforms and financial crisis, and the new role of environmental politics in the China/US relationship.

China's economic reforms have focused on increasing the role of price signals and reducing trade protection. From an analytical perspective the impact of trade liberalization on the environment could be either positive or negative. Positive effects include more rapid penetration of cleaner technology and enhanced production efficiency; on the other hand China's comparative advantage could be in pollution intensive industries. World Bank (1997b) highlights that China has been and remains a net importer of pollution intensive goods (with the only exception of ozone depletion substances). However, China is going to import resources from other 'resources-extraction havens' such as Russia or Myanmar. While the one year moratorium on conversion of forest land imposed after the recent floods reduces by 10 million cubic metres national production, Chinese companies are currently providing to Myanmar technical and financial assistance in the construction of roads along Myanmar northeastern frontier in exchange for wood (Talbott and Brown, 1998:57).

While shutting down state owned enterprises (SOEs) is an important step in enhancing China's energy and resources efficiency, its environmental impact is ambiguous; because the entrepreneurs, being under less control could exploit the environment for economic profit. However, the real problems are township and village enterprises: largely unregulated TVEs' emissions generally contain a higher level of pollutants than emissions from SOEs. A conservative estimate holds that TVEs discharge approximately half of the total industrial wastewater that is monitored, or more than 10 billion tons (Woodrow Wilson Center, 1998: 30). However, the greatest problems are massive infrastructure projects such as power and water plants deemed necessary to improve the economic environment. Foreign investment fell as a consequence of the financial crisis; the ADB estimates that China has US$ 800 billion worth of infrastructure needs, but many of these loans today are being redirected to China's neighbours (CES, 1998:65).

The Chinese position on environmental problems, especially climate change, in the early nineties was allowed through the lack of leadership by US and Japan, which did not exercize pressure to persuade China to take pro-active measures (Economy 1997). Recently both the US and

Japan have realized that environmental co-operation could promote their security and economic interest in the region. While Japanese engagement with China on environmental issue dates from 1989, the American one is more recent. Clinton, during his visit in China, under-lined the importance of environmental issues and co-operation, thus entering a new phase in the US–China environmental relationship. It is too early to evaluate the results of this change but certainly it gives a higher priority to environmental issues on the Chinese policy agenda: a growing environmental market open to US investment, and probably an increasing Chinese engagement with regional problems.

6.2.1.2 Japan and the politics of a 'ecological-predator'

Japanese rapid economic growth policies in the fifties and sixties so ignored the environment that by the 1970s Japan was considered to be one of the most polluted countries in the world. Environmental crisis such as asthmatic diseases (Yokkoichi Athsma) caused by air pollution and organic mercury poisoning (Minamata disease) emerged in many parts of the country. As a result of policy change Japan rapidly estab-lished one of the world's most successful air pollution control programmes.

However, Japan's environmental policy has focused on pollution control and energy efficiency and it is in these areas that Japan has been successful; most achievements have been local, made possible by the use of end of pipe control technologies. Until recently Japan did not pay much attention to resources recovery and material recycling. It is one of the largest users of natural resources imported from other countries, and, since the eighties, Japanese industries have been shifting their manufacturing process from Japan to other Asian coun-tries. In the nineties Japan entered a new phase of environmental aware-ness and emerged as a prominent international player, addressing pro-actively global problems such as global climate change and bio-diversity loss.

The reason for this change is twofold. First, the Japanese environ-mental policy model produces environmental technology which needs markets; environmental technology research and development accounts for more than 60 per cent of national R&D spending, Japanese industries are world leaders in the market for flue-gas desulphurization/denitrification equipment (ESCAP, 1995). Second, there is a growing need for an international cleaner image and of regional stability. Japanese global environmental initiatives are mainly the result of bilateral agreements in the Asian Pacific region, finalized to secure supply of raw materials, new markets for Japanese technology and to minimize regional threats to environment and security, both from trans-boundary pollution and competition for resources.

This change and its extent are clearly highlighted by the ODA policy. Since 1989 Japanese ODA has focused on environmental issues. By 1991 Japan has provided more than 407.5 billion yen in aid in the environmental field (Yamamoto 1994). Specific areas subject to Japanese Environmental ODA generally include, water supply and sewage systems, disposal facilities, air and water pollution monitor systems, energy and forestry conservation, as well as fostering of human resources. Three environmental centres were established through the grant aid programme in China, Thailand and Indonesia as well as The Japan–China Friendship Environmental Protection Center (technical co-operation) and the Biodiversity Conservation Project in Indonesia (Grant Aid).

6.2.2 South East Asia: confidence building?

The rapid economic growth, the great differences among countries and economies still based on the exploitation of the natural resources under-line the need to make compatible environment and development. The problem is made worse by the financial crisis that, on the one hand, increases the competition and that makes it more difficult to reconcile a sustainable exploitation of natural resources with the ability to attract foreign investments, on the other it decreases enforcement of environ-mental law and increases social instability, implying a growing pressure on environmental resources.

The major environmental problems in SEA vary from country to country but include: land degradation (desertification, salinization, water logging); deforestation (loss of 1.3–1.9 million of ha per year); water pollution (water quality problems in tropical climates, untreated domestic sewerage, and eutrophication), and bio-diversity loss (marine and coastal habitat). Atmospheric pollution, including acid rains which are less remarkable than in the north, already seriously strike Thailand, Cambodia, Vietnam and will be more and more important in coming years.

The awareness of environmental issues became of concern to SEA governments in two waves: the first, dating back to the UNCHE in 1972, implied an institutional implementation, the second, dating from the eighties, was introduced by Western donors, attaching conditions to their aid. Interest in environmental problems varies from country-to-country. Malaysia is the most advanced country of the region in environmental management; while environmental movements in Thailand are very active. Also in Laos and in Vietnam the environmental problem has recently gained a place in the political agenda, at least for Asian standards. However, there are two trends which limit environmental policies: first, Asian leaders consider environmental concern as a sort of Western imperialism and they believe that prescribed environmental measures meet Western needs and do not correspond with Asian priorities. Where the environmental movement is significant, such as in Indonesia, where the Indonesian Environmental Forum Whali[11] is probably the most powerful environmental NGO in SEA, environmental activists face the stigma of being branded as 'anti-development'. Second, environmental problems are frequently considered local concerns with little broad significance. Nevertheless the economic integration and the increasing environmental sensibility push toward the homogeneity of the environmental standards.

There is a growing diffusion of the EIAs, even if they differ considerably, from the recent and rudimentary system in Vietnam, to the developed and detailed one in the Philippines. EIA faces two problems. First, public involvement in the decision process is low: in these countries the traditional view is that the government is the trustee of the land and resources, and even if protests against major projects, such as the Bakun Dam or the Irin Jaya's Freeport, testify the existence of a growing environmental consciousness, they also show the failure of EIAs to prevent conflict or to legitimize governments' decisions. Second, it is likely that standards converge at a low level. There is also a growing diffusion of ISO 9001 and ISO 14001 certifications. In spite of the financial crisis, in Thailand in December 1997 certifications were 39, with a 400 per cent increment in six months, and 15 certifications in Indonesia. ISO certification is considered a benchmark to compete in international markets. However, the crisis will have a retarding effect on certifications, which are generally the result of former investments.

In 1998 the situation is already worsening. The crisis has deeply affected the investments in environmental infrastructures, however, international programmes have not been compromised, indeed they have gained a relatively greater role. As a result of the crisis the output of the industrial plants has declined, reducing industrial emission; however, pollution might increase because factories adjust their abatement effort in response to the lower regulatory inspection and enforcement, and higher pollution control cost. The World Bank estimated that in Indonesia the output of the operational plants has declined by around 18 per cent and since the start of the crisis pollution intensity for organic waste in industrial effluents has increased by 15 per cent (WB, 1998).

However, the greatest environmental implication of the financial crisis is connected with its social consequences. Financial crises are *per se* able to induce conflict and social strife. Environmental degradation could add a new dimension to the problem. First, recession implies a greater pressure on the environment and its resources, which are destroyed in a short time perspective. Second, social strife and conflict could imply a vicious circle of environmental degradation–productivity loss. On the one hand, social crisis sets aside environmental issues, on the other, environmental degradation could galvanize latent conflict both at national and regional level. Environmental problems could jeopardize the capability and the legitimacy of the state, especially when they are rooted in rapid economic growth that exploits the environmental resources heavily such as in Indonesia. At the present, there are no environmental components in the Indonesian riots, but corruption and nepotism, which are behind both deforestation and the recent forest fires, remain unrestrained.

The severe forest fires in 1997 and early 1998 had significant political and economic repercussions for Brunei, Malaysia, the Philippines and Thailand, and they strained relations between Indonesia and its ASEAN neighbours. The economic costs of the fires for Indonesia, Malaysia and Singapore were estimated at US\$ 1.4 billion in short-term health care, loss of tourists revenue, and reduced industrial and agricultural production (Dupont, 1998). Even so, the regional response to the Indonesian fires suggests that environmental problems would be most likely to prompt closer co-operation rather than confrontation (Dupont, 1998:16). ASEAN Environmental Ministers in April 1998, set up a fund to assist Indonesia in fire-fighting and to 'control and channel additional and complementary resources from region and internationally'[12] determining the first serious regional attempts to face environmental problems.

At the regional level, since 1978, ASEAN has established an Expert Group on the Environment, the ASEAN Senior Officials on the Environment (ASOEN) and started the first ASEAN Environment Programme (ASEP 78–92), replaced in 1992 by the ASEAN Strategic Plan of Action on the Environment. Since 1993 APEC has likewise introduced environmental considerations into its programme (Conference of Vancouver 1994, FEEP Framework for action on Environment, Economic

Development, Population, 1998). The attempt of APEC to integrate environment and economy underlines the perspective to frame environmental problems in the region. The results nevertheless appear rather scarce. The Asian countries play an insignificant role in the formation of the environmental agenda and the suggested solutions often involve the export of environmental services by the Western countries. States are worried that the ecological considerations could slow down the economic growth and, furthermore, formal co-ordination mechanisms and institutions are lacking.

The environmental interest of the EU in Eastern Asia is limited to the possibility of supplying environmental services and technology by European firms. The geographical distance removes the perception of ecological interdependence and threat to European environmental security is perceived to be low.

6.2.3 The Indian subcontinent

The environmental problems for the Indian subcontinent are connected mainly with population growth and the pressure on natural resources. The arable soil becomes scarcer and scarcer; there are problems of erosion, desertification and deforestation. The lack of resources in the rural areas pushes the population toward the urban centres. The rates of growth of the Indian cities are double those of other national averages, and this determines high levels of localized pollution, shortage of water and energy and lack of sewerage systems. Many areas of the region are threatened by global warming: the rise of the level of the sea could submerge densely populated areas such as exist in Bangladesh, with resultant flows of refugees. Catastrophic events, mainly floods, are particularly serious given the extreme vulnerability of the territory and the lack of instruments for social security.

The situation is explosive; the competition for scarce resources is added to ethnic and class conflicts. In the urban centres the citizens oppose the arrival of new inhabitants; in the rural area autochthonous groups oppose the exploitation of their own resources by central government, such as Sikhs in Punjab or against the settlement of immigrants in Assam. Environmental conflicts also threaten the stability of the region and new disputes could be added to the existing ones, for instance for the waters of the Ganges. At the regional level there is the South Asia Co-operative Environment Programme (SACEP) that involves Afghanistan, Bangladesh, Bhutan, India, Iran, Maldives, Nepal, Pakistan and Sri Lanka. However, the activities sponsored by ADB, GEF, UNDP and UNEP are more remarkable.

6.2.4 Central Asia: an ecological black hole

The desiccation of the Aral Sea – one of the major man-made ecological catastrophes – is the legacy of the former Soviet planned economy that imported the cotton monoculture, an inefficient irrigation system based on canals vanishing into the desert and an excessive use of fertilisers. Since the sixties the sea has changed in area, volume and salinity: it's level has dropped by 16.5 m, it has lost three quarters of its volume shrinking by 56 per cent, while salinity has multiplied to 30 g/l. The environmental problems in the Aral Sea basin include severe climate change, primary and secondary salinization due to over-irrigation, loss of deltaic ecosystems and salt storms. Contaminated drinking water contribute to serious diseases and high infant mortality rates, while the degradation of soils and the exhaustion of water resources have severely reduced agricultural production.

The situation is complex: CA is characterized by a high share in agricultural production, low industrialization and high population growth. Hydrological conditions allow the externalization of the cost of over-exploitation to downstream countries, however a reduced inflow not only affects the riparian of the water body but also regions hundreds of kilometres away, which suffer poisoned dust from the Aral Sea and climate change. The collapse of the USSR and the constitution of five republics with new political borders have divided the region and the previously shared water resources. While there is now no central authoritative power that can manage water dispute, the number of political decisionmakers has increased and different economic priorities have emerged, connected with different territorial distribution of resources. Uzbekistan does not control one single source of the main rivers, essential for its large irrigation system; Kazahstan is rich in fossil fuel and raw materials and has vast agricultural potential but lacks water; Turkmenistan has a small population, lots of oil and gas but largely depends on water flowing throughout Uzbekistan; upstream countries like Kyrgyzstan and Tajikistan are water-rich but resource-poor and depend largely on a safe supply of fossil resources.

Access to water resources has already led to interstate dispute, such as the Toktogul case in 1993,[13] or the contentions about the distribution of water in border zones. However, following the disintegration of the USSR, CA theoretically gained the possibility of managing the new international river basin, within the framework of eco-regional co-operation. During the Soviet era the whole region had been a 'national sacrifice area'[14] to produce cotton, prejudicing the traditional local economy based on fishing and agriculture. Although, in 1992, the five republics established the Interstate Coordinative Commission for Water Resources ICWC,[15] the institutional framework after independence remains based on the administrative structure of the Soviet period. Nevertheless the first agreement on water distribution, signed after independence in 1992, recognizes common tasks such as rational use of limited water resources to ensure socioeconomic development in the Aral region and formally recognizes the Aral Sea as the sixth demander (without fixing a quota). In 1993 the Interstate Council for Aral Sea (ICAS)[16] and the International Fund for the Aral Sea (IFAS) were established, financially supported by the members, which have to allocate 1 per cent of their state budget annually. However, until 1995 the countries of the basin paid only 15 per cent of their commitment, and Turkmenistan and Tajikistan did not contribute at all (Klotzli, 1997: 427). In the Declaration of Nukus the heads of states urged the international community to assist them in implementing strategies to save the Aral Sea. But there is a great difference between political concerns demonstrated at international level and country-specific policy.

Independence has brought fragmentation and the possibility of conflicts, while it has set aside environmental problems. Many factors traditionally associated with environmental conflicts are present: productivity loss, an increasing gap between the rich and the poor, higher competition for resources, while ecological consciousness and the perception of the threat are very low. The seriousness of the problem is only perceived at local level and it often conflicts with national priorities. The principle of 'sacrifice area' is repeated at republic level for example in the Karachalpakian Autonomous Republic where water need is sacrificed by Uzbekistan to supply water to Turkmenistan in exchange for oil.

The second ecological tragedy in CA is the Caspian Sea. Endowed with an oil rich basin (about 200 million barrels of oil, 16 per cent of the earth's potential oil resources) and one of the planet's most productive water bodies, the Caspian Region is characterized by many settlements along the coastal line, seriously threatened by three main categories of environmental problems: water pollution, fisheries depletion, and a significant rise in sea level (about 2.5 m since 1978). Flooding has damaged or ruined buildings and other infrastructure, and threatens the oil fields and radioactive waste storages. The presence of oil attracts many interests but it does not enhance the ability of the states to deal with the environmental problem. On the contrary, the presence of strong financial lobbies and the concentration of high income worsen the environmental situation and weaken the new states.

The debated question 'is the Caspian really a sea or just a lake?' involves economic interests and instrumental ecological considerations. If it is a lake the nations that border it would control the undersea wealth out to 45 miles from their shores, the remainder would be treated as an international seabed. If it is considered a sea the whole seabed is sliced into pieces. Adzerbaijan, Kazakhstan and Turkmenistan, which have the biggest energy fields off their own shores, want the whole of the Caspian to be divided into sectors. Russia and Iran, having less oil and gas off their Caspian shores, insist on concerns for the environment and highlight that the problem will be best addressed under joint sovereignty. An opportunistic position since Russia was and is by far the largest polluter.[17] In this context prospects for environmental co-operation are limited. The growing interest of Western companies might increase the environmental standards of oil installations, at least compared with those of the Soviet period, but environmental issues could become the catalyst for violent conflicts.

In CA, as well as other former Soviet regions, independence was followed by a precipitous decline in official and popular support for environmental co-operation, both at national and international level. The independence was characterized by persistent administrative and economic crisis and by a drop in the already weak environmental consciousness and demand for environmental protection. First, given the widespread unemployment, low wages and high inflation, people have little attention left over for the environment even in those areas where the situation is most critical. Second, a sort of fatalism, coupled with leadership corruption, increases inertia. This combination of indifference and instability made it difficult for external actors to find willing and able partners in the new states. The role of the NGOs like Green Salvation could be conclusive: they can work at different levels and they serve as a vehicle through which local consciousness could be addressed internationally. However, environmental movements are utterly dependent upon external financial and organizational assistance. Moreover, the end of the cold war removed many incentives for environmental co-operation both in former USSR and Western countries and the priorities for CA on environmental problems ended to accord with the Western ones, and in the future, the environmental crisis is likely to worsen dramatically. In this case environmental problems might become a catalyst for other latent tensions and conflicts among the ethnic and clan discontinuities, running across existing borders, repeating at regional level the ecological debates which accomplished and accelerated the dissolution of the USSR. The interests of the EU in the region are high but European environmental initiatives are limited even if a remarkable environmental component characterizes the TACIS Plan.[18]

6.3 Conclusions

Environmental problems differ widely region by region, as well as their security and trade implications. In NEA environmental dumping and 'pollution havens' are a probable scenario, not only between industrialized and developing countries but also within the latter, especially in Russia and along Chinese borders. In SEA co-operation on environmental issue can contribute to confidence building, however, there is the risk of convergence at low standards, and environmental 'black holes' like Cambodia or Myanmar, could weaken regional efforts. In SA latent conflicts could be exacerbated by environmental change, competition for fresh water or flows of refugees, while in CA, in spite of the seriousness of the problem, both for the persisting economic interdependence and the presence of higher priorities, environmental issues are largely set aside and environmental initiatives are frozen.

Environmental issues have a growing role in determining the future scenarios, especially at regional level and in developing countries. However, as Levy (1995) suggests, viewing the world through a narrow environmental lens may be inadequate to prevent or manage violent conflicts, likewise to view the world through the lens of conflict could be inadequate to manage and understand environmental problems in their social, political and economic complexity.

Notes

1. There are only a few unilateral initiatives like that of the US Defense Department or the Canadian Foreign Office and a few NATO pilot studies.
2. The Eposo Treaty requires EIAs only if there are trans-boundary effects.
3. The ODA target is 0.7 per cent of GNP of the industrialized countries.
4. In 1993 Russia admitted that the USSR had dumped civilian and military radioactive waste in the Sea of Japan.
5. About 40 000 tons of fish with an estimated marked value of US$ 65 million a year (Taiwan's national fishing association).
6. A. Rosencratz and Scott, 'Siberia's Threatened Forests', *Nature*, Vol. 355, No. 6358 (1992) quoted in Hayes and Zarsky.
7. According to the World Bank about 178 000 people in major cities suffer premature death each year from pollution; mortality rates from chronic

pulmonary disease are five times those in the US. Estimates also are that pollution damage equalled roughly 8 per cent of Chinese GDP in 1997 (World Bank, 1997).

8. The Chinese Government structure itself hampers environmental enforcement. First, the structure is multi-level with a functionally-defined hierarchy; each unit in the environmental hierarchy is subordinate to the territorial government at its own level, rather than environmental bureaucracy at the next territorial level. Many territorial governments have officials that have become entrepreneurs. As a consequence the entrepreneurs control the regulators. Secondly, the vagueness of the standards coupled with a lack of comprehensive enforcement regime have created a system where many environmental regulations are the result of deals between local protection agencies, SEPA, local governance and the polluting enterprises themselves.

9. NEPA, 1997 quoted in CES, 1998, 76.

10. Even if flow rates were below historic highs, water levels were setting records because of silting. Dikes are built only to counter floods that might come once in 10 or 20 years (US Embassy Beijing 1998).

11. Over 330 environmental groups are affiliated to Whali.

12. 'ASEAN Pool fire-fighting Efforts', *The Australian*, 6 April 1998, quoted in Dupont, 1998 p. 16.

13. In summer 1993 Kyrgyzstan retained half the water allocation granted to Uzbekistan in its reservoir of Toktogul releasing it in winter to produce electricity; the surplus had not even reached the Aral Sea, but was dammed up by the frozen lower course of the Syr-Darya and vanished into the Aidarkul depression (Klotzi, 1997).

14. Term coined by Boge, quoted in Klotzi, 1997, p. 426.

15. ICWC incorporates the two basin associations BWOs founded in 1986.

16. ICAS consists of 25 senior officials from the five republics and convenes twice a year (WB UNDP UNEP, 1994), CIS has an observer status in the Council (Kotzli, 1997:427).

17. Iran, which has declared that any undersea pipeline would be a disaster for sturgeons and migrant birds, depend on fisheries resources and pushes for a shorter, cheaper pipeline across Iran, vehemently opposed by US.

18. WARMAP programme (Water Resources Management and Agricultural Production).

References

Dupont, A., 'The Environment and security in Pacific Asia' *Adelphi Paper* No.319 (1998).

Economy, E., 'Chinese policy-making and global climate change: two-front diplomacy and the international community' in M.A. Schreurs and E. Economy (eds) *The Internationalisation of Environmental Protection* Cambridge University Press (1997).

ESCAP, *State of the Environment in Asia Pacific* Bangkok (1995).

Haas, P.M., R.O. Keohane and M.A. Levy, *Institution for the Earth: Sources of effective International Environment Protection*, MIT Press (1993).

Hayes, P. and L. Zarsky, 'Regional Cooperation and Environmental Issue in Northeast Asia', Nautilus Report to IGCC, UC San Diego (1993).

Homer-Dixoy T.F., 'On the threshold Environmental Changes as Causes of Acute Conflict' in *International Security* Fall 16(2) pp. 76–116.

Klotzli, S., ' "The Aral Syndrome" and Regional Co-operation in CA: Opportunity or Obstacle?' in N.P. Gleditsch (ed.) *Conflict and the Environment*, Kluwer Academy Press (1997).

Krasner, S., 'Structural Causes and Regime Consequences: Regimes as Intervening Variables' in *International Organization*, 36 (2) (1982).

Levy, M., 'Time for a Third Wave of Environmental and Security Relationship?' in *Environmental Change and Security Project*, Report No. 1 Woodrow Wilson Center (1995).

ODA Summary 1997 Minister of Foreign Affairs of Japan, http://www.mofa.go.jp/policy/oda/summary/1997.html.

'Yangtze Floods and the Environment' US Embassy Beijing August Report (1998) http://www.ncdc.noaa.gov/ol/reports/chinaflodding/cinaflodding.html October 1998.

Yamamoto, W., 'Japanese Official Development Assistance and Industrial Environmental Management in Asia' paper presented at Workshop on Trade and Environment in Asia–Pacific September 1994.

China Environment Series The Woodrow Wilson Center CES 1 (1997), CES 2 (1998).

World Bank, *Clear Water, Blue Skies: China's Environment in the New Century* The World Bank Press (1997a).

World Bank, *Surviving Success: Policy Reform and the Future of Industrial Pollution in China* (March 1997b).

World Bank, *Impact of Financial Crisis on Industrial Growth and the Environmental Performance in Indonesia'* (July 1998). http://www.worldbank.org/nipr/work_paper/shakeb/index.htm 19/10/98.

Zarsky, L. 'Stuck in the Mud? Nation-State, Globalization and the Environment' (1997). http://www.hautilus.org/papers/enviro/zarsky_mud.html

7
Security Implications of the Asian Crises

Marta Dassù and Stefano Silvestri

The Asian financial crisis and its economic implications at both the regional and the global levels have been thoroughly analyzed. Nevertheless, the scenarios are still uncertain. In particular, it is far from certain whether, and if so for how long, China's leadership will be able to stand by its choice of not devaluing the renminbi, on which it has built a good part of the country's new credibility as the key regional stability player. It is equally unclear how and when Japan will be in a condition to overhaul its banking and financial system, and emerge from the critical condition which has kept Tokyo from playing a constructive and positive role in the crucial phase of the Asian crisis. However the situation may develop, the economic repercussions of the Asian crisis will continue to be a topic of analysis and international debate.

The Asian financial crisis, however, calls not only for a fresh analysis of the clichés regarding Asian economies, but also for a new look at the relationship between the economy and security in the region. Up until the summer of 1997, for instance, the Asian tigers' economic health was considered to be one of the main guarantees of stability in the region – a region which, unlike Europe, lacks solid institutions for security. The financial crisis has changed this equation. While the economic convulsions in EA have not taken on the proportions of a security crisis, it would be premature to dismiss this possibility outright (Dibb *et al.*, 1998). Reasons for concern abound.

In evaluating how the economic crisis could alter the security equation, an important element should be taken into account: the relationship between the economy and security has never been linear. For example, one of the consequences of economic growth has been the military build-up of recent years, while one of the early effects of the crisis has been the opposite, namely a reduction in resources to modernize the military apparatus. As this chapter will show, while economic growth had generated a 'confident' nationalism in the area, the crisis that started in 1997 has, in some cases, resulted in an 'unconfident' nationalism, born out of weakness rather than strength.

The scenario has to be differentiated, though, according to the way in which the individual countries have reacted to the crisis. Most importantly, the China 'exception' has to be written into the equation. On the one hand, the PRC has drawn distinct diplomatic advantages from the Asian shock, while on the other hand China's own economy reveals many of the same structural difficulties that have confronted the Asian countries which were hit by the crisis (a weak banking system, for example, and a huge bad debts problem). So, while it is undoubtedly true that China has been successful – up until the end of 1998 – in escaping from the domino effect (for a number of reasons, ranging from the non-convertibility of the Chinese currency, to financial market controls), a contagion cannot be totally ruled out.

For the time being, the economic difficulties that have beset South Korea and Japan have tended to shift the co-ordinates of regional stability in favour of the PRC. While China has been seen mostly as a part of the solution to the crisis, Japan has largely been perceived as being a part of the problem. All of this is unfolding against a backdrop in which old and unresolved territorial disputes add to the variety of reasons for uncertainty or tension: the prospect of a collapse of the North Korean regime, the issue of nuclear proliferation, the emergence of ethnic and national pressures and the persistence of local conflicts. Moving from the assumption that the political tensions and the strategic changes generated by the financial crisis will not remain confined within EA and SEA, but will inevitably tend to weigh heavily upon the international equilibrium in the next century, this chapter will review the changes in the security scenario, by assessing first the political dimension of the crisis and then its effects on the Asian balance of power.

7.1 The political dimension of the Asian crisis: legitimacy at risk

The ramifications of the economic crisis extend far beyond the relative positioning of the major powers. In countries large and small, the events of 1997–98 have also transformed domestic policies. These changes have security implications, both for internal cohesion and for relations with neighbouring countries. The extraordinary economic growth in the region had bolstered the nation-building process, and strengthened the legitimacy of regimes and leaders. The economic shocks have prompted Asian publics' frustration and loss of faith in national development strategies, raising the question of whether their governments retain the legitimacy and support they need to restore business confidence and economic recovery.

The political effects of the economic crises vary quite substantially across countries in the area, with the consequences being most severe in Indonesia, less severe in Thailand and Korea, and much less severe in the Philippines and Singapore. Any tendency to generalize, therefore, should definitively be avoided. The differences in severity of the consequences can be explained in part by the greater or lesser legitimacy of the respective political systems and incumbent governments in Asia. In an established political system, the right to rule may only be claimed on the basis of conformity with established rules and procedures. Where this is not the case, as in several SEA states, then rulers may rest their claims on their performance in terms of economic development, political and social stability, national unity, as well as on charismatic authority, projected goals for the society or politically-defining moments.

While such bases may legitimate specific governments for a limited duration, on their own they cannot provide the framework for a more durable system of authority. Authority claimed on one or more of these bases will necessarily be narrow, conditional and open to contention with changes in circumstances. A fundamental challenge confronting Asian countries, in particular SEA ones, has been the development of a durable basis for the acquisition and exercize of political power. While there are problems in nearly all of the Asian states, more progress has been made in some countries than in others.

In Thailand, for example, a democratic system of government has been slowly gaining ground despite the periodic setbacks it has suffered. Over time, alternative systems such as military and technocratic rule have become much less acceptable, although some may still view them as interim possibilities in situations of crisis. The present king is a key element in the political equation and his support is crucial for the legitimacy of the political system. Economic performance in this situation is critical for the survival of specific governments, but not for the system itself. Good performance, however, can contribute to the long-term consolidation of the system, while persistent poor performance is likely to undermine support for it and to make alternative systems more attractive. In Thailand, thus, the economic crisis has so far not affected the political system in a significant way. In fact, the severity of the economic crisis conferred greater moral authority on the incoming Chuan government and has enabled it to initiate several policies that are likely to translate into severe economic pain for a large segment of the Thai population. As long as these policies are perceived to be in the interest of the body politic and provided that they deliver in the not too distant future, then the economic crisis should not affect the legitimacy of the present government.

The new Korean President, Kim Dae Jung, transformed his election into a broader mandate for reform. South Korean conglomerates (chaebols), at first set back by the shock of events, will resist any major restructuring that threatens their power. The Korean unions are growing restive as the economic effects of unemployment and bankruptcies follow financial turmoil. Their first demonstrations may help President Kim to overcome his opposition, but before long the public will hold the new president responsible if there is no upturn in the economy. Democracy has given these countries a new beginning, but it will not, as Europe experienced in the 1930s, ensure the vital mixture of leadership, sound policies and public support that is needed.

In Singapore, the political consequences of the economic crisis have thus far been minimal. Although economic performance is a key factor, political legitimization in the island city-state of Singapore is closely related to the goal of survival, and the PAP claim that only a one-party dominant system can ensure the survival and prosperity of Singapore. The regional economic crisis, the relatively good performance of Singapore's economy in the midst of a sea of trouble, and rising tensions with neighbouring Malaysia and Indonesia, have re-sensitized the Singaporeans to their vulnerabilities, strengthening the hand of the PAP government and enhancing its capacity to undertake tough policy measures. Prolonged tensions with its neighbours and a deterioration in economic conditions may, in the long run, raise questions about the PAP style of governance and the system advocated by it. But this is not an immediate concern.

Unlike Singapore, Malaysia has suffered a severe downturn in its economy and the recent events which led to the dismissal of Anwar Ibrahim by Prime Minister Mahatir have fostered political protests and mass demonstrations. Nevertheless, it is still too soon to talk about a lack of political legitimacy in Malaysia. The Mahatir government has had wide latitude in responding to the economic crisis. Should Mahatir's radical policies fail to deliver, however, it is likely that he and his policies will be largely discredited, and the current calls for change in party leadership will start to resound more loudly.

Unlike Thailand, Singapore and Malaysia, the economic crisis has brought about dramatic political turmoil and change in Indonesia. The economic crisis precipitated and fed on the political crisis. Notwithstanding Suharto's various manoeuvres, his autocratic regime had already suffered considerable erosion in legitimacy well before May 1998. The economic crisis and the pain caused by his policies – both old and new – and the loss of trust in Suharto resulted in a political backlash that eventually forced him out of office. Suharto's departure has triggered a broad and far-reaching transition. Indonesia's future depends heavily on the army, and, specifically on whether the army will accept that new actors on the stage may play significant roles. Also important are the army's fears that protests will threaten national cohesion, and its own ability to remain united. Meanwhile, Habibie, the President who took over, is apparently unable to initiate credible and effective policies to stabilize the political and economic situations – even if he has made some unprecedented and courageous steps, introducing new reform laws and announcing his willingness to contemplate independence for East Timor. Poverty, however, is spreading rapidly, and the food shortages are becoming too harsh a reality to ignore. Twenty years of development have been wiped out in a single year, amidst widespread ethnic violence.

The caveat from Indonesia is – to put it very simply and somewhat superficially – that economic development in the absence of political change can rapidly be undercut. Unfortunately, some countries – Vietnam, Myanmar and North Korea – are likely to draw very different political lessons from Indonesia's turmoil. From their perspectives, the strategy is to maintain strong central control backed by intimidating military force.

'Diversification' is thus both a premise and a consequence of the economic crisis. As already seen, the factors inhibiting change are in general very evident, but they have taken on very different specific forms in the various countries. Equally obvious, in the first year of the Asian crisis management, is the conflict that exists between economic necessities and the objective of social stability. This has been underestimated by the IMF in its approach to the programmes implemented in some of the Asian countries, and in particular in Indonesia. All in all, quick-fix solutions appear to be very difficult.

7.2 From a 'confident' nationalism to an 'unconfident' nationalism

The interdependence of economic dynamics and security dynamics is the factor that will naturally determine the prospects for stability in the area (Cossa and Khanna, 1997). This will occur in a framework that is dominated, politically, by a complex mix of these nations' strengths and weaknesses. When this factor is linked to security issues, two relatively contradictory characteristics emerge:

1. The first characteristic is the dominant weight of the state in the recently decolonized societies, which are undergoing a phase of complex economic modernization (Alagappa, 1997). This helps to explain the crucial political value that is given to national integrity and sovereignty. Conversely, it also explains the difficulty in reaching binding regional accords in sectors, such as security, that are the essence of national sovereignty. At least in the medium-term, the competitive moves of nations with unsettled territorial claims will continue to characterize the regional situation. This is highly visible, for instance, in the case of the Taiwan–China tensions. Here, the ingredients are on the one side the historic objective of 'reunification of the fatherland' for mainland China, a country where nationalism is the ideology that has clearly supplanted Maoist communism, and on the other side, the neo-independence temptations in Taiwan, which are buoyed up by that country's successes in economic modernization and by the political democratization process. (It is not by chance that one of the consequences of the Asian economic crisis was penalization of the 'pro-independence' forces in Taiwan.)

   The 'absolute' value of the nation-state, and the role of nationalism in Asian regional dynamics have important international implications. It is not surprising that a country like Malaysia reacted to the Asian crisis by placing the blame primarily on Western interventions (speculative investments, IMF prescriptions, the US designs for an opening up of the Asian markets). China, too, drew some 'defensive' lessons from the 1997–98 financial crisis. In particular, China has adopted a more cautious position on its prospects for WTO membership. As a result, the Asian crisis will make the future of processes such as the global financial and trade liberalization more complex.

2. This does not mean at all – as seen before – that these states are solid or strong (meaning by 'strong' those states in which national

communities are consolidated and integrated, the political elites are legitimated and there are institutional mechanisms in place for the transfer of power). In actual fact, only a small number of the Asian states (Japan, and to a much lesser extent Taiwan, South Korea and Thailand) could be classified as relatively 'mature' states – considering the political transition processes that are still under way. The other countries in this area have domestic problems (such as separatist movements, scant legitimisation of political power, personalism, and so on) that make them weak states, and at least in part, states with an authoritarian internal structure. (This authoritarianism that can be more or less 'soft', to use Robert Scalapino's well-known classification.) The financial shock, by undermining the old mechanisms linked to economic growth that legitimated the ruling elites, has made these problems more acute. A telling case is that of Indonesia, where the economic crisis developed into a crisis of the regime – and which has also resulted in the resurgence of violence against the Chinese ethnic minority.

The problem of a weak central state applies to China, too, but in a different way. How to govern the centrifugal forces that have been generated by economic reform has become one of the decisive variables in that country's internal politics. In conclusion, the financial and economic shock resulted in a loss of legitimacy for a part of the Asian ruling classes, with a rapid succession of domestic crises and changes in government, which may have been more successful (as in the case of South Korea or Thailand) or less so (as in Indonesia). This means that in many cases a factor was lost, a factor which had long been considered as an essential ingredient for the success of the Asian model, namely an adequate level of domestic stability. The credibility of the 'Asian way' (neo-authoritarianism cum market) and the great ideological battle that had been waged in past years in support of 'Asian values' took a severe beating.

The implications of these developments for security scenarios are of two, apparently inconsistent, different types. On one side, the domestic dimension of security will continue to have a major role in the Asian conception of national security. Focusing on their own domestic problems, the weaker states of the area will have little energy and few resources to spare in a bid to become significant regional actors, or to make international projections of any relevance. In some respects, the financial crisis has accentuated this inward-looking tendency of the Asian regimes. Not by chance, the operational response to the crisis in the summer of 1997 was left in practice to the US and to the IMF, as the feebleness of any regional responses became evident. A typical example was the failure of the idea to create an Asian stability fund that was ventilated in the autumn of 1997. At a national level – together with radical projects for economic adjustment – defensive trends are emerging, along with the search for safety nets. For instance, Beijing seems to have shelved the old projects for the full convertibility of its currency (since the non-convertibility of the RMB was the main factor that protected China from the financial shock), and Hong Kong has decided to intervene directly on the equity market (with a massive buying of shares to discourage speculative attacks). Also, the Prime Minister of Malaysia, Mahatir, has reinstated currency exchange controls and brutally ousted the leadership of the liberalizing stream in Malaysian economic policy.

On the other hand, it will not be easy to mark out clearly the borders between internal and external security. There will be a growing trend on the part of relatively weak leaderships to release pressure externally or to compensate internal tension with an assertive foreign policy. In other words, the nationalist card may be played for internal reasons. This is exactly the card that Indonesia (through the conflict with ethnic Chinese) and Malaysia (with the forced repatriation of foreign workers) are playing in different ways. Finally, the strengths and weaknesses of nation states will hinder the development of regional institutions, just as the economic integration process in the area will be slowed down by the economic crisis. The 1997 financial shock caught ASEAN off-guard, and the bankruptcy of Indonesia deprived the Association of SEA nations of its key country. APEC, to which the US belongs, was hardly more successful, as its ability to draw up regional measures was severely hampered by cross vetoes (for instance, between Taiwan and China).

One of the important political implications of the economic crisis, has thus been the way it revealed in full the current weaknesses of the regional institutions, which had appeared instead to be expanding in the early nineties. In the security field, the only forum that has so far seen the light – the Asean Regional Forum (ARF), created in 1994 – is little more than a talking shop: with its obvious flaws and potential virtues that were highlighted in the management of the difficult territorial disputes in the South China Sea (where there has recently been a build-up in tension between China and Vietnam). The absence of any real regional security organizations means that the balance of power between the main regional players remains absolutely central to the area. This balance of power – following the decline of the former Soviet Union as an Asian power – is dominated by the relative pull in weight in the US–Japan–China 'triangle'.

7.3 China: a stabilizing factor or the next country at risk?

It may be exaggerated to say that the crisis 'rewarded' China: since the 1997 financial shock spared China, mainly thanks to the non-convertibility of the RMB on capital accounts and the size of China's currency reserves. The Asian crisis, nonetheless, holds deep problems for the Chinese economy as well. However, it is certainly true that Beijing has been able to exploit the crisis politically. The Chinese decision not to devalue the currency (though many analysts continue to predict a slight devaluation in 1999) was presented as a gesture of regional 'responsibility'. The upshot is that while in 1996, following the tension in the Strait of Taiwan, China was seen as a potential threat to regional security, in 1998 China is instead considered as an essential pillar of Asian stability. Perceptions have been reversed.

One of the important consequences of the end of bi-polarism, from the Chinese standpoint, has been the growing importance of the regional dimension in that country's foreign policy. More specifically, there is a widespread belief that the ascent of China as a global power will reflect first and foremost its central role in the Asian chessboard (Kim, 1997). True, there had been a considerable degree of ambiguity in China's Asian policy strategy in the early nineties. A dual trend seemed to have emerged. On the one hand, growing importance was given to regional economic integration, while on the other hand, Chinese national claims were re-asserted, also through a number of military initiatives (clashes with Vietnam over the possession of the Paracels and Spratly Islands; the dispute with Manila over the possession of Mischief Reef; intimidations in 1996 in the Strait of Taiwan). Détente diplomacy and assertive national policy options went hand in hand.

It is hard to fathom what sort of Asian power will finally emerge. There are two very different theories on this. According to the first, economic growth in China, together with the main features of its political system (which could by now be defined as a variant of Asian neo-authoritarianism) and its tradition of Asian centrality, will necessarily translate into the search for a not especially benevolent regional hegemony. A completely different and more reassuring line of thought tends to scale back China's ambitions, emphasizing the fact that for the next decade, at least, China will be absorbed by the problem of its economic growth, and will not yet have the necessary military capability for a policy based on foreign projections. According to this argument, Beijing's options will in any case be strongly oriented by its economic interdependence constraint. To increase these constraints through a strategy of incremental integration of China is, therefore, the comprehensive security strategy to be adopted *vis-à-vis* Beijing (and it is the vision put forward in the policy paper on relations with China approved by the EU in 1995). ASEAN countries are in line with this approach, and they are attempting a difficult balancing act. On the one hand, they wish to maintain a US military presence in the area (Malaysia, alone, has supported an Asia-first line, calling resolutely for the creation of a regional bloc, which would be not only economic, but also political). On the other hand, ASEAN countries aim at dampening tension with Beijing and gradually integrating China into regional and international accords. Clinton's visit to Beijing – wearing his strategic partnership badge – shows that the difficult debate on policy toward China that has been carried forward in the last five years within the Clinton administration has reached similar conclusions.

The Chinese response to the Asian crisis has done a lot to bolster this evolution in foreign perception, as Beijing exercized an objective function of stabilization – by keeping its currency stable, and by deciding for the first time to participate in International Monetary Fund assistance programmes. It could, however, be argued that China's diplomatic rise is still mainly a reflection of the decline of the other Asian actors: Japan, first, and then ASEAN as a whole. On the crucial issues, Beijing has done little more than use its power of interdiction. This is especially true in the case of Taiwan, which, following the return of Hong Kong under the sovereignty of the People's Republic, is the unresolved national issue. Chinese leadership was in general successful, after the tensions in 1996, in its attempt to block Taipei's diplomatic bid to win international recognition. China countered Taiwan's attempt to exploit its stable economic performance in 1997–98 politically. Briefly, the two sides played a very similar trump card. They both tried to use the financial crisis to strengthen their political and diplomatic status. This hand was won by China, as can be presumed from the anxiety that Clinton's visit to Beijing generated in Taiwan. On the other hand, the financial crisis increased the economic incentives for a bilateral détente between Taipei and Beijing, and the indirect dialogue that had been frozen since 1996 showed some signs of thawing.

On another sensitive front – Korea – the Chinese can be said to have played generically a function of mediation. The key point to be emphasized here is that the end of the old division does not fit in with the geopolitical interests of Beijing. Moreover, the financial crisis has made it much more difficult to envisage a reunification, owing to the huge costs that a German-style scenario would entail for the South Korean economy, which is now clearly in difficulty. China has no desire to witness the rise of a new regional power, such as a unified Korea could become, at least in theory, in East Asia. But also a traumatic implosion of the North Korean regime, with conflict reverberating externally, does not fit with China's interest, as China has been traditionally close to Pyongyang, but is increasingly keen to develop economic relations with Seoul. A reorganized and well-controlled status quo (involving for instance the implementation of the 1994 Accord on the North Korean renunciation of nuclear weapons) would be the lesser evil from the Chinese standpoint. Meanwhile, the North Korean decision to carry out a missile test in the Pacific Ocean[1] sparked a deep crisis with Japan, that has decided to put on hold its participation in KEDO, the Korean Energy Development Program.

Most likely, China's response to the Indonesian crisis is of greater significance. With a gesture that did much to build China's new 'détente style' image, China decided both to support the IMF-promoted bail-out programme and to reassure Djakarta that it would not interfere in the Indonesian internal crisis, despite the wave of violence against Chinese minorities. Considering the precedent in the mid-sixties, this was obviously a very sensitive issue to handle, which Beijing has managed to minimize to date. It is also true that the crisis in Indonesia – the main country in the area, that in many ways was at the origin of the creation of the ASEAN in 1967 – has gone a long way towards weakening that organization. This has made new room for China, in which it may wield its influence in the future (Dibb *et al.*, 1998).

In a nutshell, Beijing was successful in containing the crisis, and in exploiting the situation to its advantage, more than in proposing regional solutions which were *de facto* delegated to the US. For the time being, the Chinese leadership has a clear focus on, and it is largely absorbed by, its domestic priorities. Unfortunately, it cannot be taken for granted that Deng's successors will be able to carry forward the two crucial reforms that are pending. The first being the reform of the financial system (in the Chinese case the bad loans problem is at least equal to that of the other Asian countries, which have already been hit by the crisis), and the second being the reform of state-held companies (which carries social risks, mainly due to increasing unemployment). In the meantime, China has drawn a number of 'defensive' lessons from the Asian crisis. One of the most important of these lessons, owing to its global impact, concerns the prospects for a speedy entry of Beijing into WTO. The brake has certainly been put on this prospect and it is an option that deserves deep consideration. According to authoritative opinion, if China were to opt for a speedy and 'premature' liberalization of its financial markets, it would trigger an internal recession, which would in turn involve the other economies in the area. The US trade negotiators are therefore invited to adopt a more flexible and gradual approach – a position that is not far-removed from the European approach to the issue of China's membership in the WTO (Lardy, 1998).

7.4 Shifts in the Asian triangle

As suggested above, the Asian crisis has brought the central role played by the US into the limelight. China seems to be willing to accept this state of affairs, both in the economic and financial spheres. There is a proviso, though: that Washington keep closely to a one-China policy, that the prestige of Beijing as a power on the rise be explicitly recognized and that dialogue be sufficiently on a par – also concerning the controversial issues, such as human rights. These results were basically obtained during the visit by Clinton to Beijing. The interim outcome of the Chinese leadership's internal debate on international policy options seems to be that China has a much better chance of obtaining a regional and global status through a co-operative relationship with Washington, rather than through adversarial confrontation. This is an old 'lesson' in Chinese diplomacy (from Chou Enlai in early seventies to Deng in the late eighties), which had appeared to be forgotten in the post-Tiananmen chill. The fact is that all of this is likely to be true as long as China is still a virtual, rather than a real great power, and as long as China's priorities are clearly linked to economic development. What is much less clear is the Chinese perception of the future role of the US in Asia; or better, how this perception will evolve with the evolution of China – either in the case of economic success (when Beijing will be in a better position to aspire to regional hegemony) or in the case of a failure of the economic reform process (when a critical internal situation could send ripples of instability outwards).

In broader terms, the Asian economic crisis has put all three of the sides of the US–China–Japan triangle in motion. For Tokyo, the trend since the beginning of the nineties has been one of a steady decline, in the economic and in political spheres. Japan, however, is still considered to be the major player in Asia owing to its economic position and its regional influence, backed as it is by the strong security commitment of the US. This remains true, but the financial crisis has undoubtedly weakened Japan's image. It would be an exaggeration to say that the centre of gravity of the triangle has shifted, from the prioritary Washington-Tokyo relationship, toward China. Security-wise, the US has confirmed and strengthened its defensive alliance with Tokyo in 1997–98, according to guidelines (such as the active contribution of Japanese forces to regional crisis management), which Beijing strongly criticized. The US–Japan security relationship is reassuring to many of the smaller countries in the area, which see the American presence not only as a guarantee against the emergence of China, but also as bulwark against a possible resurgence of nationalism in Japan. However, in June 1998 the way in which China practically constrained the US to intervene in support of the yen (by emphasizing the risk of a forced devaluation of the Chinese currency) will certainly be remembered as a jolt in the sensitive balance of the three sides of the triangle. More generally, the Japanese economic crisis has in no way reinforced that country's relations with Washington, which hoped for more rapid and radical reforms and a greater opening of the Japanese markets. The issue of the huge American trade deficit *vis-à-vis* Tokyo (and its influence on the US internal debate on Asian policy) will continue to point to, and in a certain sense, to gauge the level of difficulty in bilateral relations.

A strong ambivalence continues to be the hallmark of relations between China and Japan.[2] In a certain sense, this is the 'unfinished' side of the Asian triangle. During 1997–98, Beijing was outspoken in its criticism of Tokyo – as were the US and most of the Asian countries – for not having done enough to react to the economic crisis. At the same time, China certainly is not looking forward to Tokyo regaining a strong regional position and taking on growing responsibilities in the political and military arenas (as it had seemed to be doing in the early nineties). Both of these points explain the frosty Chinese reaction in the autumn of 1997 to Japan's tentative proposal for an Asian response to the financial crisis, as an alternative to the dominant role assumed by the IMF.

At least part of the international prestige which China has earned, is in fact due to the loss of prestige by Japan. In other words, China's diplomatic rise is the other side of the coin to Japan's relative decline. This is not, however, a guarantee of stability. A case could be made for the fact that a higher level of stability in the area, and the future strengthening of Asian regionalism, would instead require a real understanding between China and Japan, backed by a US guarantee. This would mean, however, that the two countries would have to overcome their mutual distrust, and also achieve a higher degree of economic integration. Also, it would require the US to have the perception that this state of affairs does not harm its interests.

The scenarios of the Asian 'triangle' are in reality much more uncertain. They will be largely determined by the respective economic performance of the two main Asian actors and by the extent to which the US, taking into account all of the internal factors that condition US international options, will remain effectively committed in the region. Another crucial variable is the future evolution of the Chinese political system.

The forecasts of Asian experts on the balance of power in the next century thus continue to oscillate between widely diverging hypotheses (such as a gradual decline of the US presence in the Pacific and the emergence of a Chinese hegemony; the maintenance of the US military supremacy in the area and a re-launching of US–Japan relations to contain China; and a China–Japan rapprochement as an anti-American function – possibly with Russian external support and so on).

7.5 The decline of Russia

For now, Europe seems to have no major role to play. And as the Asian crisis has shown once again, Europe can contribute economically (as was the case with substantial contributions to the multilateral bailout programmes for Thailand and South Korea), but without counting politically. Also Russia, overwhelmed as it is by its domestic economic and political crisis, appears to be very marginal in the Asian scenario. But if Moscow were to emerge from its dramatic domestic situation, then a future re-launching of relations between a China clearly on the rise and a Russia that is striving to hold its own on a slippery slope would be feasible, owing to at least two factors. The first is that the two countries no longer perceive each other as a security threat. The growth in the sale of former Soviet armaments to China is perhaps the clearest sign of the changes that have taken place from this point of view (according to ACDA,1995 China is now the main buyer of Russian weapons).[3] This change in perception was followed by a settlement in the historical border dispute, which was achieved through a negotiation process lasting several years. The result was the 1997 Accord, which governs the 4000 km border, from Mongolia to Tumen, near the Sea of

Japan. The second of these factors is that the ideological clashes of the past have been clearly left behind, while a 'realpolitik' vision of these countries' common interests appears to be prevailing. The interim outcome of the Russian crisis could even be that the two leaderships could adopt a closer approach to the problems in the reform of their respective economies.

Externally, the relations between these two countries will strongly condition the balance of power in Central Asia. For the time being, there is a common interest in stabilizing the area – and this objective was embodied in the 1996–97 *ad hoc* agreements between China, Russia and the former Soviet Central Asian Republics. From the Chinese stand-point, the issue at stake is to keep control over Xinjiang (a north-western province with a strong Muslim minority and considerable oil reserves), as well as over its northern borders, which have traditionally been unstable and insecure. The Russian priority is to continue to hold sway in the former Soviet Republics of Central Asia and not lose out in the new 'great game' that has opened in Central Asia, an area of vital strategic importance due to its huge energy resources and geo-political position.[4] This does not mean that this convergence of interests is nec-essarily going to last in the long-term. Historically, the great Central Asian game has divided rather than united the two countries. And there is also no doubt that Kazakhstan sees the expansion of relations with China, especially in the oil sector, as a way to win autonomy from Moscow (and to 'anchor' itself to the Asian growth area). For now, however, collaboration is prevailing and may even be stepped up by the launching of new joint ventures in the energy sector (such as laying a gas pipeline from Siberia to the eastern shores of China, to supply not only China itself, where a growing energy deficit is expected, but also Japan and South Korea).

Moreover, there is an obvious mutual interest for Moscow and Beijing to use their developing bilateral relations to condition the US, or to counteract what is perceived by both countries as the drift towards US hegemony in the post cold war years. In essence, while relations with Washington are crucial and prioritary, both for Moscow and for Beijing, both countries have a strong interest in offsetting the predominant weight of the US in international affairs and in vital strategic areas. A typical example is the *de facto* alignment of China and Russia against the US strategy in the Persian Gulf. Another example is the support given by China to Moscow's initial stance against NATO enlargement. While this case does not involve any direct interests of Beijing, the value that is attributed to the mutual relationship to contain what are perceived as the unipolar trends of the international system are highly significant.

The consolidation of Russia–China relations must, however, be seen against the backdrop of a gradual decline of Russia in the Pacific Asian region, especially when compared to Russian's importance in the sixties and seventies, when it could rely on a system of alliances, from India to Vietnam – and when Russia had a huge military presence, which was later scaled back. Though, and once again providing that Russia emerges from its domestic crisis, Moscow's attraction to the Asian shore is likely to increase (as confirmed, incidentally, by its overtures to Japan).

7.6 Conclusions

In conclusion, a rising China, a declining Japan, a marginal Russia and a central US, along with weak regional institutions, are the main factors in the security scenario that has emerged from the Asian financial crisis, alongside the other factors that were mentioned at the beginning of this chapter (the legitimization in part of the authoritarian regimes, internal political crises, growing ethnic problems and unconfident nationalism). In the relations between each of the major Asian actors, their interest in co-operation as well as the reasons for friction evolve in a fluid situation. For this reason, none of the sides of the so-called Asian triangle foreshadow conventional alliances. In the long run, the relative weight of Tokyo and Beijing, and their mutual relations, will play an essential role in determining the future of regional stability. Moreover, according to some analyses, a protracted crisis in the ASEAN countries could give rise to a sort of North–South fracture in regional development,[5] with all of its security implications (for instance: a greater assertiveness of China in it's territorial claims).

In the short term, however, the priority that individual countries must give their domestic economic problems means that the US has a decisive role in the management of regional problems. As was seen above, even the rising power – China – at present has only a limited capability to exert its influence. All taken, the response to the financial crisis has confirmed this outlook, with impracticable Asian solutions losing much of their credibility due to the Japanese crisis. Clearly the conclusion of this – the overexposure of the US – carries a number of risks. If the economic recovery plans were to fail, then national counter-shocks would be rendered all the more likely by the ruling elites, which have experienced the decline of Asian values and the solutions proposed by the IMF, as a sort of brutal delegitimization. If one of the US objectives (as claimed by many critics, not only Asian) had been to 'force' the opening of Asian markets, the results until now have been decidedly disappointing. This suggests that the current central role of the US in the Asian scene may in the future run up against problems of no small consequence. And a situation such as the one described above – with fragile regional institutions and without powers that can exercize a leadership role (at least for the time being) – is by definition an unstable situation, where it is not difficult to imagine that new conflicts and tensions may emerge.

All of this has important implications for Europe. From 1994 onwards, with the approval of its new Asian strategy policy paper, the EU has made an obvious effort to get back into the playing field, an effort which included the launching of the ASEM process. The impact of the Asian financial crisis may lead to a diminished European interest for an area that is no longer considered as the engine of the world economy. But this would be a serious mistake. In the positive scenario, East Asian countries will succeed in relaunching their global competitiveness, thanks to a set of structural reforms. In the more negative scenario, namely a protracted recessionary phase, the Asian crisis will inevitably spill over and severely affect the old continent.

The idea that the Asian crisis cannot simply be 'isolated' is a reasoning that holds true in security matters as well (it is enough to consider the energy issues or the role of China and North Korea as suppliers of ballistic missiles to Middle Eastern countries). More in general, the overall trend of multilateral accords in crucial sectors of international relations (from non-proliferation to the next round of trade liberalizations) will depend to a large extent on the solutions that will be found to the receding Asian miracle. And the same reasoning applies to the future of the institutions: from the reform of the UN Security Council (with the, at least temporary, weakening of the Japanese candidacy), to the future of the WTO (and in this case with at least a temporary slowdown in the Chinese membership process). This is reason enough to understand that the Asian crisis – on its own, and together with the Russian crisis – should be seen not only as an underlying risk, but also as an underlying stimulus to reconsider the instruments and rules for the governance of post-bipolar international relations. In this perspective – the future of multilateralism – Europe has a strong interest in returning to the great game of Asian politics, and may be able to do so effectively once the euro has proven its ability to function as an international reserve currency.

It is not by chance that China has announced its intention to convert part of its huge US\$ financial reserves[6] – once the euro works effectively. Equally interesting is the Japanese attempt to play a kind of euro card so as to keep the yen 'in' the multilateral dialogue over the financial architecture 'on', and the currency exchange crisis 'down'. From this point of view, the euro is bound to create new links between Europe and Asia that will influence the emerging debate on the restructuring of international financial institutions. The issue, both for the EU and the Asian actors, is to utilize this new 'asset' in a co-operative way with the US, to make it possible that it makes a real contribution to a more stable international financial system. In a scenario of growing Asian–European financial links, however, the traditional 'indifference' of the Europeans towards Asian security issues will become harder to maintain.

Notes

1. According to American sources it was a failed test for the launch of a satellite with a three-stage missile (*International Herald Tribune*, 16 September 1998).
2. As clearly shown by the failure of the visit to Tokyo, in November 1998, of the Chinese Premier: this visit had been considered as 'historical' but it ended in a reiteration of the two countries' misunderstandings on the past heritage.
3. ACDA, World Military Expenditures 1995, pp. 153–7.
4. On this and other points in the China–Russia rapprochement, see Menon (1997).
5. See, in this sense, the statements of the Prime Minister of Singapore at the Vancouver Summit of APEC, reported by Michael Richardson, 'China, an Asian "Tiger" that Kept its Claws', *International Herald Tribune*, 29–30 November 1997.
6. As a result of the European trip of Premier Obuchi, in January 1999, Tokyo has signed joint statements on the issue of the stability of currency exchanges with France and Germany, and a document in the same direction with Italy.

References

ACDA, 'World Military Expenditures', 1995.

Alagappa, M., 'Systemic Change, Security and Governance in the Asia-Pacific Region', in Chan Heng Chee (ed.), *The New Asia-Pacific Order* (Singapore: ISEAS, 1997).

Brittan, L., 'A Long Term Policy for China – Europe Relations', COM (95) 279 final (Brussels: 5 July 1995).

Buzan, B. and G. Segal, 'Rethinking East Asian Security', *Survival*, Vol. 36, No. 2, (summer 1994).

Cossa, R.A. and J. Khanna, 'East Asia: economic interdependence and regional security', *International Affairs*, No. 2, (April 1997).

Dibb, P., D.D. Hale and Peter Prince, 'The Strategic Implications of Asia's Economic Crisis', *Survival*, 2, (summer 1998).

Dole, B., 'Shaping America's Global Future', *Foreign Policy*, No.98 (spring 1995).

Kim, S.S., 'China as a Great Power', *Current History*, September (1997).

Lardy, N., 'China and the Asian Contagion', *Foreign Affairs*, No. 4, (June–July 1998).

Menon, R., 'The Strategic Convergence between Russia and China', *Survival*, No. 2, (summer 1997).

Scalapino, R.A., 'Northeast Asia – Prospects for Cooperation', *The Pacific Review*, No. 2 (1992)

Simon, S.W., 'Realism and neoliberalism: international relations theory and Southeast Asian security', *The Pacific Review*, No. 1 (1995).

Sutter, R., *China in World Affairs: US Policy Choices*, (Washington D.C.: Congressional Research Service, January 1995).

United States Security Strategy for the East-Asia Pacific Region, Department of Defence, Office of International Security Affairs, (February 1995).

Valencia, M.J., 'China and the South China Sea Disputes', *Adelphi Paper*, No. 298.

Whiting, A.S., *China Eyes Japan*, (Berkeley: University of California Press, 1989).

8
Coping with the Dragon: Western Relations with China

Filippo Andreatta

8.1 Introduction

The issue of the West's relations with China is becoming increasingly central to the post cold war world. Sometimes, this importance is overrated due to the psychological interdependence of the CNN age, which attributes global importance to local events. For example, during the financial turmoil in the summer of 1998, it seemed at one time that global stability depended on China's ability to avoid devaluation of the yuan, while in fact China's share of world trade accounts for merely two per cent of the total. Similarly, the common fallacy of futurologists, which project current trends indefinitely in the future, has raised the issue of China becoming the largest economy in the world in the space of the next two decades, even if current growth rates are unsustainable in the medium run. The larger and more developed it will become, the more difficult it will be to make it grow at double-digit rates. Measured in constant dollars, China's GDP is today only about a third smaller than Italy's, while its per capita GDP is about four times smaller than Korea's.

Nevertheless, it is beyond doubt that Asia's relative importance has grown in recent years and that the trend is likely to continue. Even without going as far as predicting the dawn of a Pacific Century, the industrialization of EA could rapidly transform the region into the most important economic centre in the world economy. Asia is in fact recovering the rank it enjoyed until the Napoleonic Wars, when the industrial revolution allowed the countries of Europe, which were much less populated, to increase exponentially their productivity. Now that the industrial revolution has finally taken off in Asia as well, the sheer force of its numbers is again making its weight felt around the globe.

This long-term trend is unlikely to be interrupted by the Asian crisis, although it will be considerably slowed down by it. As the previous period of stunning growth was not due to any peculiar cultural characteristic of the EA countries nor to peculiar Asian values, but by the mobilization of vast reserves of factors of production, so the current crisis is also not the product of any inherent inability to develop a modern economy, but by the difficulty of sustaining growth with qualitative improvements once the simple introduction into the economy of quantitative additions has slowed down (Krugman, 1994). From now on, Asian growth will demand an increasingly efficient allocation of capital and information, which requires a long and constant effort. What is therefore likely to happen is that Asian convergence with the standards of living of the developed world will continue, although the kind of growth which will allow this process will prob ably be increasingly similar to the one experienced in the developed world itself.

Furthermore, on the political side, EA will be likely to increase its weight as it witnesses the presence of all the most likely candidates to become the 'other' superpower alongside the US in the next century: China, Japan and Russia (Betts, 1993/94). Not only will Asia be more central to the global balance, but also its actual political configuration could actually favour the emergence of a great power controlling a vital share of resources. Even if it is unlikely that a full hegemonic challenge will emerge, because the presence and eventual reaction of multiple local powers should inhibit it and because political relations are today encouraging, it still is nevertheless more probable that a key political conflict will in the future develop in Asia than elsewhere. It is for this reason that the future of Western policy toward China is so crucial, as the maintenance of a constructive relationship should decisively contribute to global stability. This chapter will analyze this issue in three stages. First, the general conditions of the EA sub-system will be compared with those of Europe, where systemic stability is generally considered exceptionally high, with the aim of demonstrating the political volatility that still persists in the region. Second, a closer look to the record of Western (especially US) relations with the future major power in the region – China – will put contemporary issues into perspective. Third, three scenarios will be proposed which cover the range of opinions on the future role of China, assessing their strengths and weaknesses as well as their potential policy implications. It will be argued that a prudent and modest policy of international engagement is probably the wisest choice in the present circumstances.

8.2 The relative instability of the Asian international system

The end of the cold war has been greeted with enthusiasm in most quarters, as the spectre of a global bipolar and nuclearized confrontation disappeared. The end of the cold war has indeed opened an era of unprecedented international stability in Europe where, despite local conflicts in the Balkans, the prospects of a major war are probably more remote now than at any time in the past hundred years. While the causes of this situation are complex and probably multiple, analysts have advanced a number of crucial processes, which can be grouped into four main categories: the configuration of great powers and the military balance between them; the degree of political and economic homogeneity among the states in the region; cultural and historical factors; and the presence of international institutions. Each of these factors is currently present in Europe, contributing to the establishment and maintenance of international stability. In other regions however, some of these factors may be missing, as is testified by the local instability which has followed the end of the cold war in certain regions. In the Asian case, as also Aaron Friedberg has suggested, the impact of all of the four factors is smaller than in Europe, contributing to a relatively more unstable situation (Friedberg, 1993/94).

First, although there is by no means a consensus in the literature, proponents of bipolarity point to the simplicity of a two-power world and to the tendency of a more complex system to become unstable (Waltz, 1993; Mearsheimer, 1990). States in a multipolar setting may find it difficult to identify a major threat, given the simultaneous presence of various powers. Even when a threat is correctly identified, there may be problems in organizing an effective response. On the one hand, states could 'pass the buck' of containment onto others hoping that they share the benefits of collective action without paying the burdens. On the other hand, states may 'chain gang' by over-reacting to a local threat out of fear of upsetting their allies, which are necessary for their other purposes. In either case, bipolar systems would not exhibit the same syndrome. Threats are clearer because there is only one other superpower and enforcement is also clearer because there is no other superpower to turn to (Andreatta, 1997). As for the contemporary situation, the effects of multipolarity in Europe are tamed by the strong identity of views between the US and Western Europe and by their good relationship with Moscow. More than a truly multipolar system, Europe today resembles a unipolar configuration in which there are compromises within a single coalition rather than a set of competing alliance blocs. By contrast, the system in Asia is more genuinely multipolar as the alignments between the great powers in the region are more fluid and flexible.

In general terms, the end of the cold war has reduced tension in the centre of the system (including Europe) by reducing the probability of general war. However, the end of bipolar competition has also severed the link between the central balance and the various regional balances. While during the cold war each superpower would not allow its counterpart to achieve advantages even in peripheral areas, which could then be used against it elsewhere, in a more diffused environment regional balances are less crucial. In turn, this provides both the incentive (because superpowers no longer lend easily their protection) and the opportunity (because superpowers no longer restrain and control their clients tightly) for regional powers to develop independent strategies, which may include a higher profile.

The military relationship between the great powers is more volatile in Asia. In Europe, the dimension and quality of the nuclear arsenals is a guarantee for a stable balance in which no atomic power can hope to win a general war (Jervis, 1989). In Asia, the smaller dimension and the backward quality of some of the arsenals may in fact be destabilizing as small and vulnerable forces provide an incentive for their beholder to launch them early before they are pre-empted, and for its opponent to knock them off the board before they are used (Sagan and Waltz, 1995). Furthermore, the nuclear tests by India and Pakistan in the summer of 1998 threaten to undermine the non-proliferation efforts in Asia, while the Chinese arsenal has grown to more than 400 warheads at a time when the other atomic powers are reducing theirs. Also on the conventional side, Western predominance is much clearer, not because the technological lead is greater, but because the higher stakes involve a higher readiness to use force in Europe, while the sheer size of some of the Asian powers such as China and India would make a full-scale intervention prohibitive. Finally, EA has contravened the trend in the reduction of armaments which has followed the cold war elsewhere. Military acquisitions in the region have steadily increased throughout the 1990s and include power projection capabilities such as rapid reaction forces, missiles and strike aircraft (Ball, 1993/94).

Second, another set of variables which has been advanced to explain the current era of stability in Europe concerns the domestic structure of states. The democratic peace proposition maintains that democracies do not fight each other – there has in fact hardly been a war between two such states in history – because representative governments inhibit expansionism whose costs are to be born by the electorate, which is more concerned with welfare than warfare; because democracies tend to employ the same legal and non-violent mechanisms for resolving international conflict that they employ in domestic politics; and because democracies which rest on popular sovereignty would undermine their own legitimacy by doubting the good will of a state based on a similar principle (Doyle, 1983; Russett, 1993). Even without going as far as Francis Fukuyama in predicting the end of history because of the universal establishment of liberal democracy, there is indeed in Europe a Western security community which is gradually expanding its separate peace to the East (Fukuyama, 1989). By contrast, political heterogeneity in Asia is still stark, including established parliamentary democracies (Japan and India), communist dictatorships (China, Vietnam), military dictatorships (Myanmar), 'failed' states (Cambodia, Afghanistan, Tajikistan), theocracies (Iran), authoritarian leaderships (Singapore, Indonesia), and states in 'democratic transition' (Taiwan, Korea and Russia). This variety is compounded by wide wealth differentials both within and between countries, which has been exacerbated by the recent economic crisis and which could contribute to political tension.

Third, other political factors include cultural and historical legacies. Europe has indeed been divided by bloody wars and deep divisions. However, Europe has also experienced throughout the centuries a sense of community – the ideas of 'Christianity', 'Ius Gentium' and 'Concert' – which has facilitated the current solution of historical grievances and the process of European integration (Mueller, 1989). Asia has not witnessed anything similar, with relatively large and self-contained subsystems: China, SEA, India, Japan which would come into contact (such as China and Indochina) when the imperial ambitions of one would bring it to dominate another. This has left on the agenda a complicated set of rivalries. For example, the four great 'Asian' powers (China, Japan, the US and Russia) have fought almost continuous conflicts over the last half century, each with changing alignments. Japan invaded China and fought Russia and America in World War II; Japan and the US were allied against the SU and China at the height of the cold war; in the 1970s, China changed camp and aligned itself against the SU. In other words, each great power has been in conflict with each of the other at least once, while the only alignment which has not happened this century has been that between Japan and Russia.

There is also no shortage of territorial disputes and criss-crossing claims, which were not uncommon in Europe in the past but have today mostly disappeared. For example, Japan is in dispute with Korea over the Takeshima Rocks, with Russia over the Kurile Islands, with China over the Senkaku Islands. China also disputes Taiwan with the republican regime in Taipei, the Paracel Islands and the demarcation line in the Gulf of Tonkin with Vietnam, and the Spratly Islands in the South China Sea with Vietnam, Brunei, Malaysia, Taiwan and the Philippines.

Finally, one of the suggested reasons for stability in Europe is the presence of a tight web of international institutions (Keohane, 1989; Keohane and Martin, 1995; Kupchan, 1995). Institutions can facilitate co-operation by providing neutral focal points for bargaining, by altering expectations of reiteration and reciprocity and by establishing rules which restrain anti-functional behaviour. The European institutional network is crosscutting and self-reinforcing and concerns most issue areas. On the contrary, there is in Asia no alphabet soup of EU, NATO, WEU, OSCE or the Council of Europe. Asian countries mostly belong to global organizations such as the UN and the WTO, but have fewer regional fora for the resolution of specific issues and search for homogeneity in smaller numbers. ASEAN and APEC are still underdeveloped compared to their European counterparts and are mainly concerned with discussion rather than decisionmaking.

On all four counts, Asia is deficient with respect to Europe, providing therefore a less secure international environment. This does not mean that Asia is 'ripe for rivalry' or that a major war or a 'coming conflict' will erupt in the near future. However, the lack of a stable balance, the fluidity of diplomatic alignments, the political and economic heterogeneity, the presence of historical grievances and territorial claims, and the lack of institutionalized co-operation necessarily affect the foreign policies of states in the region, forcing them to take their own protection from eventual dangers and their security dilemmas more seriously. Although this will not result in certain conflict, it will determine an environment in which diplomacy will be cautious and – at times – tense and in which co-operation will be precarious.[1]

8.3 Western relations with China

It is against this relatively insecure and volatile background that relations with China must be placed. China has in fact experienced over the last century the imperial penetration of its empire, the invasion and occupation by Japan, and the paranoia of a communist regime fearful for its survival and on a civil war footing until the end of the Cultural Revolution. It is therefore not surprising that Beijing finds it difficult to trust counterparts from a position of weakness and seeks a policy to enhance its security and prestige. After all, China is one of the great powers which has found herself using force most often this century: with Japan in the Manchurian War, the Sino–Japanese War and World War II, with the US and the UN in the Korean War, with India in 1961, with the SU in 1968 and with Vietnam in 1978 and 1986.

Relations with the West in particular have gone through three stages since the revolution. Initially, the tension of the cold war and the American delusion for the 'loss of China' have brought Sino–Western relations to a Nadir. When General MacArthur's troops, after the Inchon landing, were approaching the Yalu river, the Communist Party perceived a vital danger as Western armies were approaching China's borders for the first time. The ensuing intervention of Chinese 'volunteers' in the Korean War soured relations for two decades and even saw Beijing competing with Moscow as the most intractable enemy in Washington's eyes.

Following the American withdrawal from Vietnam and the Sino–Soviet rift culminated in armed exchanges on the Ussuri river, China was ready for Nixon's overtures and Kissinger's triangular diplomacy, as Moscow had replaced Washington in Chinese eyes as the most compelling threat. The 1973 Shanghai Communiqué opened a new stage in Sino–Western diplomacy and allowed for the establishment of a strategic relationship. 'Normalization' was intensified with Deng Xiaoping's rehabilitation and the beginning of economic reforms in 1979. Relations improved further as China's modernization required access to developed markets as well as an inflow of Western capital and technology (Foot, 1995).

The third and current era began with the Tiananmen Square massacre of democratic activists in the early summer of 1989. The emotional reaction in the West and the ensuing sanctions drastically altered perceptions and attitudes. However – in truth – the event was mainly a catalyst for deeper processes which had been under way for some time.[2] On the one hand, at the international level, the decline of the SU had removed the common threat which held China and the West in the same camp. Moreover, not only China was less needed by the West (and vice versa) but also other local powers needed the West less. In other words, the idea of a regional (and especially Japanese) higher profile was more probable and, due to geographic proximity and historical animosity, a worrisome prospect in China. On the other hand, at the domestic level, the Tiananmen uprising had delivered the conviction of the domestic vulnerability of the communist leadership. Together with the subsequent example of the disintegration of communist rule in Russia and Eastern Europe, this process led the government in Beijing to reinforce its strategy of economic modernization without political reform, even at the cost of friction with the outside world. Sino–Western relations, in short, were altered from the comforting certainty of the eighties strategic and economic partnership to a more ambiguous era in which elements of conflict and co-operation coexisted, as is revealed even by a cursory analysis of the main recent issues. In particular, it seems that a separation of the economic and security spheres has occurred, in which the first realm exhibits more potential for constructive negotiation than the second.

On the economic front, the most important question remains China's accession to the WTO. Initial political problems in this field linked to the reaction to the use of force against democratic protesters have gradually given way to problems of a more technical nature, such as Chinese tariffs (which have been halved from 40 per cent in 1992 to 20 per cent) or the laws on intellectual property. It is politically significant that such a crucial issue has maintained a low profile in order to insulate it from more visible quarrels. More generally, economic relations have been very good. Foreign investment in China was restarted merely a few months after the Tiananmen episode and has accelerated following China's change of its constitution in a more liberal sense in 1992. Chinese behaviour during the latest financial turmoil has also been responsible, with a gallant and probably successful defence of the renminbi. However, the annual review of China's most-favoured-nation (MFN) (now normal-trade-relations) status by the US Congress routinely are punctuated by calls of linkage to Chinese domestic policies on human rights, but are also routinely dismissed by the majority in congress. There are also some clouds in the distance linked to the growing Chinese trade surplus (explained by protectionists as wage, social and environmental dumping) and to some projections indicating China's prominence early in the next century. Despite the fact that these allegations and predictions are exaggerated, the narrower the gap will become between China and the developed economies and the fiercer the competition that Chinese exports will provide, they are likely to intensify.

On the political front, China has begun co-operation on a number of institutionalized discussions on peacekeeping and arms control, which it had traditionally shunned. Beijing has for the first time in the nineties contributed to UN efforts around the world and is being constructive especially on Cambodia (where it has abandoned its long-standing support for the Khmer Rouge) and it has joined the non-proliferation regimes for nuclear weapons and for missiles. The arms build up mentioned earlier is a cause for concern, but it has not yet produced a force capable of challenging Western prominence, even in the immediate seas around China (Gallagher, 1994). Nevertheless, China has also allegedly transferred crucial technology for non-conventional weapons to Pakistan and Iran. Furthermore, it has engaged in a series of diplomatic–military stand-offs in the region, leading some analysts to identify a novel 'expansionist' course in its policy.

In the spring of 1996 China undertook vast military manoeuvres on the shore in front of Taiwan and launched missiles off its coast, triggering a US response – the dispatch of two carrier groups in the straits of Taiwan – leading China to back down. In line with its policy of 'one China, two systems' bolstered by the success of the transition of Hong Kong, Beijing was trying to reinforce its claim for reunification. The Chinese gesture was also an attempt to influence the coming Taiwanese elections and to discourage it from seeking independence, after that island's president had been granted a private trip to the US, which could vaguely hint at some sort of recognition. Although Beijing moves are somewhat understandable because of Taipei's growing military confidence and the rising fortunes of its pro-independence opposition, the readiness to use force threatening Taiwan as well as the freedom of the seas in the East China Sea is an indication of its newly found resolve in front of what it perceives are its vital interests.

An even more intriguing signal is represented by China's affirmation of its claim to the Spratly Islands in the South China Sea, also including the use of its navy and air force. Unlike Taiwan, the Spratlys' strategic and historical value is negligible, as they are mostly underwater. Furthermore, China's claim is, given their distance from the coast, much more doubtful than in the case of Taiwan, for which Beijing has won wide recognition of its 'one China, two systems' policy. The only value of the Spratlys is an alleged reserve of oil, for which China is increasingly thirsty due to its industrialization, as well as their capability to help to control the Straits of Malacca, which would be completely unacceptable to the other powers in the region.

8.4 Three scenarios

This ambiguous policy is probably due in large part to the systemic volatility described earlier, which forces the key players in the region to play a cautious game. However, how the uncertainty of the environment will precisely affect its interaction with Chinese intentions remains an open question which is impossible to answer at the moment. In this context, it is possible to advance three scenarios which point to different assumptions about Beijing's motivation, highlight the relative importance of different factors, and suggest different prescriptions for Western policy. Each of the scenarios – which I will term democratic, liberal and realist – has also different supporters in Western academic and policy circles and it is therefore still unclear which one of them will influence Western policy in the future. Naturally, these scenarios are ideal-types and many people would probably find that their views are only partially represented by any one of them. Nevertheless, it is useful to describe these views in their most coherent forms, so as to better identify their relative strengths and weaknesses.

8.4.1 Democratic

This scenario is based on the Kantian democratic peace proposition mentioned earlier, which maintains that peace can be achieved only between two democracies. Not only there has been no war between democracies, but also when they have found themselves engaged in war they have fought on the same side. However, when a democracy confronts a non-democracy, the same factors of ideological solidarity and homogeneous domestic organization which cause the democratic separate peace, pull relations in the opposite direction. While wars between non-democracies are more frequent than those between democracies, the most conflictual pairs tend therefore to be those between democracies and non-democracies. This view considers the present relations between the West and China to be potentially unstable because of the dictatorial nature of the regime in Beijing.

The main thrust of policy would thus be aimed at obtaining a change in regime in China, facilitating economic liberalization and political democratization. Only revolutionary change could drastically alter foreign policy and it would thus be necessary to engage in an ideological crusade. Positive evidence in this respect would be the establishment of the so-called grassroot democracy at the village level, while negative signals would be represented by the routine repression of dissidents. As was suggested by British free trade imperialists like John Stuart Mill in the nineteenth century, foreign policy instruments such as the negotiations for China's accession to the WTO or the yearly renewal of the MFN status should be conditional on implementation of certain domestic reforms in China – for example a more liberal stance on human rights – as is often argued by many members of parliament in Western countries, especially after the Tiananmen massacre. Since there is a certain deterministic view of the conflict of interest between the West and the present Chinese communist leadership, there is also no fear of antagonizing Beijing, because only a democratic China could be easily accommodated in the present international system.

8.4.2 Liberal

This scenario is less optimistic about the possibility of attaining a radical reform in China, but is more optimistic about the chance of reaching a reasonable relationship even with the present leadership. Peaceful coexistence would be possible quite irrespective of the domestic organization of states, but could instead be based upon compatible foreign policy interests and a web of international institutions and relations. Political homogeneity may be a bonus, but could not be imposed from the outside and only indirect incentives – such as the advantages of free trade – could favour domestic reform by strengthening those modernizing groups which could then liberalize the country. Relations with China could therefore be constructive, even and especially if Chinese power grows, if its interests are accommodated and its stake in the maintenance of the status quo is augmented. China's responsible stance in the Asian crisis, its efforts to join the non-proliferation regime and its reforms of domestic economic legislation are all achievements to be rewarded and encouraged.

It follows that international agreements with Beijing should be pursued for their own merits and should not be linked to China's domestic behaviour, because the taumaturgic effects of interdependence would otherwise be lost, as was the stance of pure free traders like Cobden to the free trade imperialists. China should therefore be 'engaged' and 'reassured' so as to avoid its alienation and enhance its constructive participation to the international community, both in the trade area with its accession to the WTO and in the security sphere with its active participation to the arms control regimes. As Robert Ross has argued in the columns of *Foreign Affairs*, articulating what the majority of Western executives implement: 'Engagement, not isolation, is the appropriate policy' (Ross, 1997 p. 43).

8.4.3 Realist

The realist scenario is based on the idea that international relations are dangerous and that only a balance of power can check the evil consequences of power politics under anarchy. Not only democratic domestic structures, but also liberal international agreements are quite irrelevant for states under the constraints of international politics. In the absence of a world government capable of protecting them, states are forced to take care of their own survival, including the expansion of their capabilities when the opportunity arises. The only reliable means to avoid these expansionist impulses is to counterbalance them with power. The recent accumulation of power by China is therefore destabilizing, because it will produce a more aggressive policy unless it is appropriately contained by the West and its allies. Far from giving it greater stake into the status quo, China's greater economic strength would therefore be soon translated into a greater ability to pursue antagonistic policies, as demonstrated by the Taiwan and Spratly episodes.

The prescriptions are therefore those of monitoring increases in Chinese relative capabilities closely and to respond to them either with rearmament or with an alliance policy aimed at establishing a *cordon sanitaire* around China, including Japan, Korea, Taiwan and the ASEAN countries. Only deterrence could contain China. International agreements in the trade or security areas should be concluded only when they do not jeopardize the relative position of the West by disproportionately favouring Beijing. Eventual rapproachments by China should instead be seen as suspicious as foreign policy change is reversible and domestic change irrelevant if China increases its power in the longer term. In the words of Bernstein and Munro, which echo the worries of pessimists in the West: 'China's sheer size and inherent strength, its conception of itself as a centre of global civilisation, and its eagerness to redeem centuries of humiliating weakness are propelling it toward Asian hegemony' (Bernstein and Munro, 1997b pp. 19; Segal, 1996).

Each of these scenarios can find corroborating evidence in contemporary Chinese policy: China's recent relaxation of its stance on human rights, its responsible behaviour during the financial crisis, its assertive position over Taiwan or the Spratly Islands. This ambiguity is due to the fact that China is itself in transition and that the EA international environment is still one of the most volatile in the globe. Its goals of economic reform probably require a stable international system and collaboration in this sense with the West. However, the uncertainties of the system may also trigger a temptation to solve its security dilemmas by itself, even at the expense of a more multilateral approach. After all, China could very well face dangers – such as Japanese or Indian rearmament or Taiwan's declaration of independence – which could significantly damage what it deems are its vital interests.

Nevertheless, until ambiguity persists, the safest route is probably the liberal one, at least by default. China's significance within an increasingly important Asia is probably too high to dismiss attempts to socialize it in the international community. Both the democratic and the realist views risk to antagonize China, producing a self-fulfilling prophecy instead, as China would be likely to respond to an increase in its perceived vulnerability. Moreover, as far as the democratic scenario is concerned, the prospects of inducing democratization from the outside are probably illusory, as centuries of despotism and the domestic success of the Tiananmen episode in stemming the tide of reform demonstrate. Even if begun, the initial stage of regime transition may also be destabilizing in its own right, as the old system could crumble before the new one is established (Mansfield and Snyder, 1995). Finally, as a huge entity which has never experienced forms of limited government, China would probably find it difficult to smoothly transit to liberal democracy without the consent of the only structures which today pull the country together. On the other hand, the realist worry of China's expansion is still so distant given current technological differentials and it would probably generate such indigenous reactions on the Asian rimland that it could well be contained even at a later stage. In this light, the isolation of China at this stage is not only a way to miss an opportunity to enhance regional and global stability, but it is probably an unwise choice as well.

Notes

1. The anomaly of the EA situation is also demonstrated by the peculiar nature of certain arrangements in China, Korea and Japan. The prospects of 'normalization' – in the form of Chinese or Korean unification, American withdrawal or Japanese rearmament – are not necessarily seen by all quarters as reassuring.
2. While the emotional reaction to the Tiananmen episode may have lasted longer and still endure, the official diplomatic reaction was quite short lived, as the Western need for Chinese acquiescence in the UN to approve the Gulf War removed all types of sanctions by the end of 1990.

References

Andreatta, F., 'Configurazione polare e stabilità del sistema internazionale, sistemi bipolari e multipolari a confronto' (Polarity and stability of the international system: A comparison between bipolar and multipolar systems), *Quaderni di Scienza della Politica*, Vol. 4, No. 2 (1997).

Ball, D., 'Arms and Affluence, Military Acquisitions in the Asia-Pacific Region', *International Security*, Vol. 18, No. 3, Winter (1993/94).

Bernstein R. and R. Munro, 'The Coming Conflict with America', *Foreign Affairs*, Vol. 76 (1997a).

Bernstein R. and R. Munro, *The Coming Conflict with China*, (Random House, 1997b).

Bernstein R.L. and R. Dicker, 'Human Rights First In China', *Foreign Policy*, No. 94, Spring (1994).

Betts, R.K., 'Wealth, Power, and Instability, East Asia and the United States after the Cold War', *International Security*, Vol. 18, No. 3, Winter (1993/94).

Dibb P. *et al.*, 'The Strategic Implications of Asia's Economic Crisis', *Survival*, Summer (1998).

Doyle, M.W., 'Kant, Liberal Legacies and Foreign Affairs', Parts 1 & 2, *Philosophy and Public Affairs*, Vol. 12, (1983).

Doyle, M.W., 'Liberalism and World Politics', *American Political Science Review*, Vol. 80, December (1986).

Foot, R., *The Practice of Power*, (Oxford: Clarendon, 1995).

Freeman, C., 'Sino-American Relations, Back to Basics', *Foreign Policy*, No. 104, Autumn (1996/97).

Friedberg, A.L., 'Ripe for Rivalry, Prospects for Peace in a Multipolar Asia', *International Security*, Vol. 18, No. 3, Winter (1993/94).

Fukuyama, Francis, 'The End of History', *The National Interest*, No. 16, Summer (1989).

Fukuyama, F., *The End of History and the Last Man*, (New York: Hamish Hamilton, 1992).

Gallagher, M., 'China's Illusory Threat to the South China Sea', *International Security*, Vol. 19, Summer (1994).

Jervis, R., *The Meaning of the Nuclear Revolution, Statecraft and the Prospect of Armageddon*, (Ithaca: Cornell University Press, 1989).

Jervis, R., 'The Future of World Politics, Will It Resemble the Past?', *International Security*, Vol. 16, No. 3, Winter (1991/92).

Johnston, A.I., 'China's New "Old Thinking", The Concept of Limited Deterrence', *International Security*, Vol. 20, No. 3, Winter (1995/96).

Keohane, R.O., *International Institutions and State Power*, (Boulder: Westview Press, 1989).

Keohane, R.O. and L. Martin, 'The Promise of Institutionalist Theory', *International Security*, Vol. 20, No. 1 (1995).

Keohane, R.O., J.S. Nye and S. Hoffmann (eds), *After the Cold War, International Institutions and State Strategies in Europe*, (Cambridge: Harvard University Press, 1993).

Krugman, P., 'The Myth of Asia's Miracle', *Foreign Affairs*, Vol. 73 (1994).

Kupchan, C.A., 'Concerts, Collective Security and the Future of Europe', *International Security*, Vol. 16, No. 1, Summer (1991).

Kupchan, C.A., 'The Promise of Collective Security', *International Security*, Vol. 20, No. 1, Summer (1995).

Lampton, D., 'China', *Foreign Policy*, No. 110, Spring (1998).

Lilley, J., 'Freedom Through Trade In China', *Foreign Policy*, No. 94, Spring (1994).

Mansfield E.D. and J. Snyder, 'Democratization and War', *Foreign Affairs*, Vol. 74, May/June (1995).

Mearsheimer, J.J., 'Back to the Future, Instability in Europe after the Cold War', *International Security*, (1990).

Mueller, J. *Retreat from Doomsday, The Obsolescence of Major War*, (New York, Basic Books, 1989).

Mueller, J., 'A New Concert of Europe', *Foreign Policy*, No. 77, Winter (1989–90).

Ross, R., 'Enter the Dragon, China and the WTO', *Foreign Policy*, No. 104, Autumn (1996).

Ross, R. 'Beijing as a Conservative Power', *Foreign Affairs*, Vol. 76, March (1997).

Russett, B., *Grasping the Democratic Peace, Principles for a Post-Cold War World*, (Princeton: Princeton University Press, 1993).

Sagan S.D. and K.N. Waltz, *The Spread of Nuclear Weapons, A Debate*, (New York: W.W. Norton, 1995).

Segal, G., 'East Asia and the "Constrainment" of China', *International Security*, 20, Spring (1996).

Waltz, K.N., 'The Stability of a Bipolar World', *Daedalus*, Vol. 93, (1964).

Waltz, K.N., 'The Emerging Structure of International Politics', *International Security*, Vol. 18 (1993).

Zoellick, R.B., 'China, What Engagement Should Mean', *National Interest*, Winter (1996/97).

9
The Wobbly Triangle: Europe, Asia and the US after the Asian Crisis

Vinod K. Aggarwal

Discussion of the potential conflict among three actors – Japan, Europe, and the US – has been a popular topic among academics, policymakers, and popular commentators.[1] More recently, China has replaced Japan in this role. Less pessimistically, there have also been co-operative efforts among different regions – or what I term transregional arrangements. These include the formation of the APEC forum that ties North America to Asia, ASEM, TABD, FTAA linking North and South America, and EU-Mercosur agreement. Thus, at least in theory, the three poles in the global economy might be able to stabilize and lead the world economy together, particularly if co-operative arrangements develop among major regions. The recent Asian crisis, however, has thrown this three-legged stool into a wobbly crisis, and speculation that Asia is now 'finished' because of mismanagement, gross corruption, poor state planning and the like, rule the day. Yet reports of Asia's demise recall what a healthy Mark Twain cabled in 1897 upon reading his obituary: 'The reports of my death are greatly exaggerated.'

This chapter analyzes the changing strategic relationship among Europe, Asia and the US, with a focus on institutional forms of economic co-operation in trade and the financial arenas. Section 9.1 of the chapter provides an analytical framework to the global economy that links governance structures and economic interactions, and the driving factors that account for their development and change. Section 9.2 of the chapter provides a stylized empirical discussion of how these regions' economic relationships and institutional arrangements have varied prior to the Asian crisis and discusses the three major trends in organizing the global economy (globalism, regionalism and sectoralism). Section 9.3 examines scenarios for possible new economic and institutional patterns after the Asian crisis.

9.1 A framework to analyze the global economy

To systematically examine the global economy, we first consider the relationship between economic interactions and various types of governance structures, and then briefly the factors that influence changes in governance structures and interactions. In addition, we consider how various types of international institutions might be reconciled with each other.

Starting with the right part of Figure 9.1, I distinguish between two aspects of institutions: meta-regimes and regimes[2]. Meta-regimes represent the principles and norms underlying international arrangements or overarching purpose of the international institution. International regimes refer specifically to rules and procedures. International regimes can be examined in terms of several characteristics, their strength, nature, and scope.

International regimes, whether multilateral or bilateral, are developed to regulate the actions of states. National actions can include unilateral actions or ad hoc bilateral or multilateral accords. These measures in turn affect the types and levels of interactions that we observe in particular issue areas. Examples of such interactions, which generally result

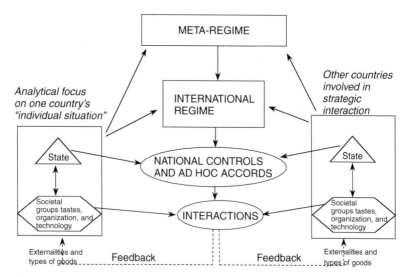

Figure 9.1 The institutional bargaining problem

from non-governmental activities by private actors, include trade, investment, or short-term capital flows[3].

The left hand portion of Figure 9.1 shows that governance structures and interactions arise from the strategic interplay of countries, based in turn on the interplay of societal interests and the state in each country. Interactions, or economic flows of various sorts, are affected by changing technology, tastes and modes of organization. In turn, changes in interactions will influence state and societal actors. The most common response for states in such situations is to respond to societal pressure through some type of unilateral action or bilateral arrangements. The former can include such things as the imposition of quotas or tariffs. The latter include the negotiation of voluntary export restraints (VERs) or other types of market sharing between states.

Governance efforts generally do not, however, end at the level of unilateral or bilateral actions. The imposition of unilateral controls and the conclusion of bilateral arrangements will often create some type of externality or affect the provision of goods, leading states to respond by negotiating with others that are affected. This may result in the formation of an international regime and meta-regime.

Traditionally, the supply side focus has been on the presence of a hegemon – that is, a single major power in the international system as essential to foster the development of institutions.[4] These states are able to provide both positive and negative incentives for other states to adhere to regimes. On the demand side, three factors appear to be important: the influence of 'institutional nesting'; a desire to control the behaviour of other countries; and information and organizational costs. With respect to the first issue, institutional nesting, states will often be concerned about how new and old institutions will fit together. In addition, countries might prefer regimes as compared to bilateral arrangements because of their potential for exerting indirect control over other countries' actions. If a country finds it costly to use power directly to influence the actions of others it might prefer a rule-based arrangement to control their behaviour. Regimes can also be seen as a device by which decisionmakers control domestic pressure groups.[5] Therefore, regimes may help to reduce organizational and information costs.

The supply of meta-regimes is influenced by the development of consensual knowledge among experts on developments in different issue areas.[6] The analogue to the demand for regimes in the meta-regime case is the goals of decisionmakers, who respond to pressure groups in various countries.

Finally, actors must decide on how the institutions they adapt or create will be reconciled with existing arrangements. Will there be institutional conflict among these various accords, will one institution be dominant, or will there be some division of labour? I have addressed this question on institutional reconciliation at length elsewhere.[7] To briefly summarize the analysis, I refer to achieving reconciliation among institutions as 'nesting' of broader and narrower institutions in hierarchical fashion. Another means of achieving harmony among institutions is through an institutional division of labour, or 'parallel' linkages. To sum up: this section has provided us with an approach to examine institutions and changes in the global economy. The elements we have focused on include the characterization and relationship between governance structures and interactions, some theoretical ideas on their evolution and discussion of the reconciliation of new and old institutions.

9.2 The evolution of the global economy: trade interactions and institutional trends

Next we trace developments in trade trends, and trade and financial institutions. The objective is to simply note the types of trends we have seen in the post World War II period to gauge the likely impact of the Asian economic crisis that began in 1997.

9.2.1 Trade interactions among the major players

What types of trends have we seen in trading patterns among the major powers? Figure 9.2 provides an overview of these patterns. Turning first to the US, exports from the fifties to 1990 to Asia have dramatically increased in percentage terms while it's exports to South and Central America have steadily fallen. Exports to Mexico began to increase in the eighties. American exports to the EEC rose from the fifties into 1980, but some of this is due to the addition of countries to EEC/EC. Between 1990 and 1997 the picture has changed with East Asia (including the Pacific Rim, Japan, China, Australia, and New Zealand) remaining the most important US trading partner while exports to the EU have fallen off somewhat, as trade shifts have taken place to Mexico and South America as a result of trade liberalization and economic recovery in the region.

Japanese exports have been primarily oriented toward the US and Pacific Rim from the fifties to the seventies, with a host of other countries making up the rest of its trade. With the addition of countries

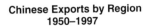

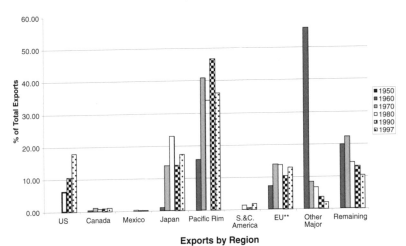

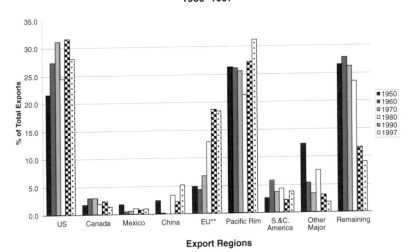

Figure 9.2 Country exports by region

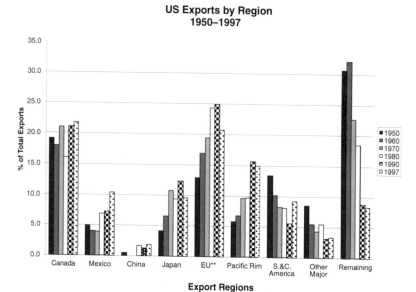

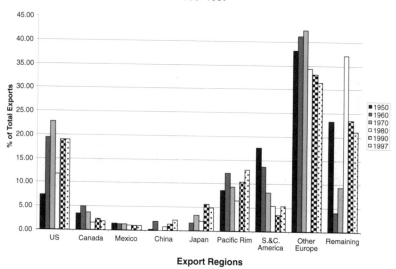

Figure 9.2   (Continued)

Source: Direction of Trade Statistics Yearbook (71. 61)
UN Statistic Office Yearbook of International Trade (1950–52)

Note: trade data for China not available for 1950
**EU includes the following countries:
1950: Belgium, France, Germany, Italy, Luxembourg, Netherlands
1960: Belgium, France, Germany, Italy, Luxembourg, Netherlands
1970: Belgium, France, Germany, Italy, Luxembourg, Netherlands
1980: Belgium, Denmark, France, Germany, Ireland, Italy, Luxembourg, Netherlands, United Kingdom
1990: Belgium, Denmark, France, Germany, Greece, Ireland, Italy, Luxembourg,
Netherlands, Portugal, Spain, United Kingdom
1997: Austria, Belgium, Denmark, Finland, France, Germany, Greece, Ireland,
Italy, Luxembourg, Netherlands, Portugal, Spain, Sweden, United Kingdom

Pacific Rim includes the following countries (where data is available):
Australia, Brunei, Hong Kong, Indonesia, Republic of Korea, Malaysia, New
Zealand, Papua New Guinea, The Philippines, Singapore, Taiwan, Thailand,
Vietnam

South/Central America includes the following countries (where data are available):
Argentina, the Bahamas, Brazil, Chile, Colombia, Costa Rica, Dominican Repub-
lic, Ecuador, El Salvador, Guatemala, Honduras, Jamaica, Mexico, Netherlands
Antilles, Panama, Paraguay, Peru, Trinidad and Tobago, Venezuela

Others include the following countries (major export markets apart from those
listed):

For Japan	1950	Pakistan, South Africa, Burma
	1960	Burma, Liberia, Nigeria
	1970	India, Iran, South Africa
	1980	Iraq, Saudi Arabia, USSR
	1990	Saudi Arabia, Switzerland, USSR
	1997	Saudi Arabia, Switzerland, United Arab Emirates
For US	1950	India, South Africa, United Kingdom
	1960	Cuba, India, Switzerland
	1970	India, Israel, Switzerland
	1980	Saudi Arabia, South Africa, Switzerland
	1990	Saudi Arabia, South Africa, Switzerland
	1997	Saudi Arabia, South Africa, Switzerland
For EU		Intra-EU trade
For China	1960	Czechoslovakia, East Germany, USSR
	1970	Romania, Sri Lanka, Tanzania
	1980	Iran, Nigeria, Romania
	1990	North Korea, USSR, Zaire
	1997	India, Pakistan, Russia

to the EC, Japanese exports to this region increased in the seventies and continued to increase until 1990. Since 1990, however, the Pacific Rim and China have become Japan's dominant trading partners, with the US in second place, and the EU trailing behind at about 18.5 per cent. Chinese exports have shown a clear shift to the US market and to the Pacific Rim from a previous East Bloc orientation. The rise in exports to the US from 1980 to the present is clearly the most striking trend.

Exports shares for the EEC (excluding trade among the member countries) from the fifties to 1960 rose dramatically to the US while steadily falling to Latin America. As new member states came to make up the EC, the relative share of exports to the US initially declined but then returned to the 1960–70 level by 1990. In addition, EU exports began to increase to the Pacific Rim more generally, while exports to Latin America have not changed much.

9.2.2 Institutional changes in trade

Although GATT has served as the key institution to manage trade on a multilateral basis since 1948, it has faced repeated challenges. When the International Trade Organisation (ITO) failed after opposition in the US from a coalition of protectionists and free traders, the Executive branch in the US quickly took up the GATT as the key liberalising instrument. What followed were several rounds of negotiations in the forties and fifties, with the most significant post World War II trading round beginning with the Kennedy Round negotiations (1962–67). This round focused primarily on significant reductions in tariffs and took a stab at non-tariff barriers (NTBs) but these NTBs were not addressed in any comprehensive manner until the Tokyo Round (1973–79). Following a failed effort to start a new round of multilateral negotiations in 1982, the Uruguay Round of negotiations began in 1986. After repeated delays, negotiations involving older issues as well as new ones, such as intellectual property, services and trade related investment measures, found their way into the WTO. This organization, now putting trade on a more equal, institutionalized footing with the Bretton Woods institutions, became operative in 1995.

Despite the dominance of GATT in the trade arena, we have also seen the parallel development of sectoralism and regionalism. With respect to sectoralism, since the fifties, and accelerating in the eighties, be it in textiles, steel, electronics, cars, footwear, or semiconductors, we have seen market sharing arrangements. At the same time, a new trend in promoting sector by sector liberalization has begun, an issue that we will take up in Section 9.3. The second key deviation from the multi-lateral process has been the developments of regional accords. Beginning in the fifties, we have seen, among others, the formation of the European Economic Community (EEC), EFTA, LAFTA and ASEAN. During the nineties, growing regionalism has arisen with Mercosur, NAFTA, and the ASEAN commitment to form the ASEAN Free Trade Agreement (AFTA). Each of these institutions has developed its own meta-regime and set of regime rules and procedures.

In addition to these geographically circumscribed regional arrangements, new transregional arrangements or summits have come into place. These include links between North America and Asia (APEC), the EU and US, and the EU and East Asia (ASEM). In addition, we have seen growing links between the US and Latin America and EU links to this region as well. See Section 9.3 for discussion of current developments in and among regional groupings after the Asian crisis.

In the Asia–Pacific, APEC has been in existence since 1989 – although it became a relatively significant forum only in 1993, when heads of states met in Seattle, giving the Uruguay Round of negotiations a strong boost. Since then, with the Bogor declaration, issued in November 1994 in Indonesia, APEC members set a target for achieving open trade for developed nations by 2010 and developing nations by 2020. As I have shown elsewhere,[8] considering all of APEC's norms together (although APEC is a regional accord) in its present relatively embryonic state it is more oriented toward openness than the WTO itself. APEC leaders met in November 1995 in Osaka, Japan to hammer out details of how to reach the free-trade goal. They also met in Manila in 1996 and then in 1997 in Vancouver, a meeting that was dominated by financial issues. Despite some progress, most would agree that trade liberalization, with the exception of sectorally based agreements, has not proceeded smoothly.

A second transregional arrangement has been created in response to APEC. The ASEM process began in 1996 in Bangkok, bringing together the 15 members of the EU, the seven ASEAN members, and China, Japan and South Korea. While created as an effort to create links between a dynamic East Asia and a relatively slow growing Europe, the recent 1998 meeting in London has taken place under very different economic circumstances. As we shall see below, European financial aid for the region and questions about ASEM's direction face some of the same problems as APEC.

The third major link, between the US and EU, has been even less institutionalized than ASEM, although obviously bilateral discussions and collaboration between the US and EU member states have been ongoing. Following the NAFTA discussions, the notion of a TAFTA was vetted by both academics and policymakers. Despite regular transatlantic Summits between the EU and US, little progress has been made on the creation of a TAFTA. However, paralleling organizations of business people in the Asia-Pacific, TABD was created in 1995 as an annual conference to promote investment and eliminate trade barriers between the US and the EU.

Within the Americas, an effort to link arrangements in North and South America has proceeded with the Free Trade of the Americas Agreement. This arrangement is linked to the NAFTA agreement, which in turn is connected to an earlier suggestion for open hemispheric trade known as the Enterprise for the Americas Initiative (EAI) that President Bush proposed in June 1990. Building on the EAI and NAFTA agreement, the US, pressed by Latin American countries to develop an APEC-type arrangement, organized a Summit of the Americas in Miami in December 1994 involving 34 countries. The participants agreed to work toward a free-trade agreement for the Western Hemisphere by the year 2005. This accord attempts to link five existing regional trade bodies (NAFTA, Central American Common Market (CACM), CARICOM (Caribbean), Andean Pact, and Mercosur) into a Free Trade Area of the Americas Agreement.

The final transnational arrangement we focus on is Mercosur. The four members of Mercosur – Argentina, Brazil, Paraguay, and Uruguay – signed an agreement with the EU on 15 December 1995 to set up a free trade area by the year 2005. The timing of this agreement, and the rapidity with which the EU proceeded to negotiate the agreement with Mercosur, was tied closely to the December 1994 Summit of the Americas initiative. At the same time, Mercosur officially became a customs union in January 1995, giving additional impetus to a unified negotiating stance.

To summarize this discussion, the trading order of the fifties to the early nineties, has been structured in the manner depicted in Figure 9.3. In the old trading order, GATT has been the dominant institution at the global multilateral level. Even though the GATT multilateral system has been challenged by the trend toward sectoralism and regionalism, it has at least until the last few years, been able to indirectly or directly encompass these arrangements. With respect to regionalism among countries, these arrangements have been explicitly permitted under Article 24 of the GATT, which allowed the formation of free trade areas and customs unions. And although sectoralism has posed a greater

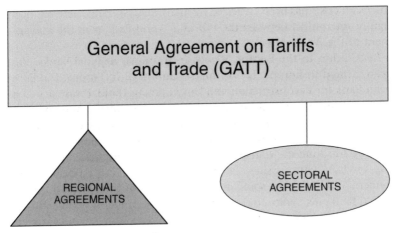

Figure 9.3 The old trading order

challenge, the Multifiber Arrangement in textiles and apparel trade, the most important exception, was explicitly incorporated as a part of the GATT system.

9.2.3 Institutional trends in finance

The Bretton Woods system created the IMF and the International Bank for Reconstruction and Development (World Bank) in 1944. Older institutions, such as the Bank for International Settlements (BIS) continued, with a focus on co-ordination of activities by central bankers. With the new Bretton Woods institutions, the objective was to provide both a short-term and long-term approach to lending, with the IMF taking care of the former in connection with the gold–dollar exchange rate system, and the World Bank initially focusing on reconstruction and then later shifting its focus to lending for development projects. Following the collapse of the fixed exchange rate system in 1971, the IMF continued to function in a modified fashion, with lending to stabilize economies rather than to simply ensure the management of exchange rates at a particular parity.

The debt crisis of the eighties gave the IMF a new boost. It became the key institutional player in the management of debt rescheduling efforts throughout the eighties, albeit with limited success. The 1989 Brady Plan, a debt reduction effort promulgated by the US and supported by other creditor governments, and the Mexican crisis of 1994–95, saw the IMF again playing a key role. The IMF's recent role in the Asian crisis has been criticized by many analysts, and there has been significant conflict between the IMF and World Bank over the management of the Asian crisis.

In addition to the Bretton Woods institutions, regional banks have been created in Europe, Latin America and Asia. In Europe, the European Bank for Reconstruction and Development (EBRD) was created in 1990 to foster the transition of East European countries and countries of the former Soviet Union towards open market-oriented economies.[9] To avoid conflict with the World Bank, the EBRD sought to focus on lending for domestic transportation and telecommunications, emphasize environmental issues and to form close links to private sector lenders. While there is some degree of nesting of the EBRD within the World Bank, it's ability to develop a distinctive mission tied to the link between democracy and market reforms, as well as encouraging the further integration of Europe, gives it more of a parallel relationship to the World Bank based on a division of labour.

The IDB was established in 1959 with the purpose of accelerating the process of economic and social development in Latin America. The Bank promotes the investment of public and private capital, the utilization of its own capital for financing the development of member countries, the encouragement of private investment in projects and the provision of technical assistance for the preparation, financing and implementation of development plans and projects.

The ADB was founded in 1966 to promote social and economic progress in the Asia–Pacific. The initial activities of the ADB were limited to raising money from donor countries to finance infrastructure projects in poorer member countries with provisions for repayment guarantees from their governments. Yet the effectiveness of ADB's pure financial role began to deteriorate in the seventies. With the Asian economies 'taking off' in rapid succession, global and emerging private Asian financial institutions became capable and willing to raise funds (often also with a government guarantee) on terms as attractive as ADB loans.

In summary, we have examined trends in the global economy with respect to trade and financial institutions and trading patterns. The Asia–Pacific has clearly emerged as a key actor from a trade perspective. At an institutional level, we have seen a multiplicity of trade and financial institutions that have emerged which potentially challenge the GATT/WTO and IMF/World Bank. Still, at least until recently, regional and sectoral institutions have for the most part been adequately reconciled with global arrangements.

9.3 Scenarios to examine the impact of the Asian crisis

This section presents scenarios for the evolution of the global economic system after the Asian crisis. We focus on two questions: what kinds of trade and financial trends are we likely to see following the Asian crisis? and, how are current institutional arrangements likely to change in response to these trends, both with respect to their characteristics and to their relationships to each other?

9.3.1 Economic trends

We can begin with trade by examining exports from the three key different regions to one another that we are focusing on in this chapter in Table 9.1. As we can see from this figure, the most likely pattern in trade is a sharp increase in exports from EA to the US, EU and elsewhere. At the same time, as EU and US exports fall to the region, firms will likely make efforts to replace these markets with greater exports to each other's markets. They will also shift their focus to markets in Latin America, other parts of Asia less affected by the crisis and Eastern Europe. Some of the areas in which exports from Asia and falling imports are likely to become a political issue are steel, automobiles, aircraft, chemicals and a host of other products. The question of burden sharing of imports

Table 9.1 Export patterns pre- and post-Asian crisis (per cent of total exports)

Exports from one region to another %	1997	Expected trend
EU to US	19	up
EU to East Asia	2.25 (China)	down
	4.9 (Japan)	
	13.0 (Pacific Rim)	
US to EU	20.8	up
US to East Asia	1.9 (China)	down
	9.55 (Japan)	
	14.9 (Pacific Rim)	
East Asia to US	17.9 (China)	up
	28.1 (Japan)	
	18.3 (Pacific Rim)	
East Asia to EU	13.0 (China)	up
	18.5 (Japan)	
	14.7 (Pacific Rim)	

Note: EU percentage of total exports is extra-EU trade. Pacific Rim excludes Taiwan and Vietnam.

Table 9.2 Gross private long-term debt flows to developing Asia (current $ billions)

1996	1997	Jan.–June 97	July–Dec. 97	Jan.–June 98	July–Sept. 98
71.51	74.69	41.75	32.94	12.79	6.64

Source: World Bank (1998), p. 25.

from EA thus has increasingly come to the fore and become a critical issue in various institutional fora.

Moreover, with respect to financial trends, there has obviously been a significant drop off in capital flows to EA, which played a significant role in exacerbating the crisis. With respect to gross private-source capital flows to developing EA and the Pacific, Table 9.2 illustrates the sharp drop.

As can be seen, the fall-off in gross capital flows (accompanied by short term outflows from EA as well), accelerated in the latter half of 1997 and was near collapse by the end of 1998. This flow, which includes foreign direct investment, portfolio equity, bond issues and commercial bank lending, has created a severe credit crunch in EA.

In terms of the relative exposure of the EU and the US in the Asian crisis, while the data is difficult to obtain in view of the many different types of financial instruments, European banks are much more heavily exposed in Asia than their American counterparts. One estimate is that of $381 billion lent to Asian banks and firms, some 47 per cent was by the EU as opposed to 9.7 per cent by the US.[10] In terms of exposure to direct foreign investment in 1993, the EU accounted for 12.9 per cent of the stock of foreign investment in developing EA, while Japan had a 21 per cent share and the US had a 14.1 per cent share.[11]

9.3.2 Institutional trends: an overview

The Asian crisis is clearly having an effect on both trade and financial institutions. With respect to trade institutions, we can illustrate some possible futures, driven by the Asian crisis and its effect on domestic pressure groups as well as changing views of the effect of globalization. Focusing for the moment on the trading system, possibilities are illustrated in Figure 9.4.

First, globalism could continue to dominate. The WTO, the successor of GATT, could increasingly become the sole forum for trade negotiations, and existing sectoral and regional arrangements could begin to

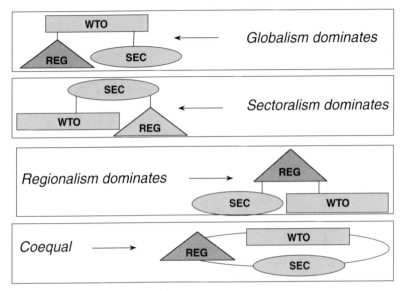

Figure 9.4   Which trading order?

wither. A second possibility is that the trading system will be dominated by sector specific regimes for steel, electronics, aircraft and other products. In this scenario, we would have managed markets by sector, and the WTO and regional arrangements would decline in importance. Third, we could have a world where the global economy breaks up into three or more regions. A fourth possibility is that all three forms of organization will continue to coexist and that no form of organization will be dominant. In this scenario, trade negotiations, both to liberalize and to protect markets, might take place in all three fora.

To examine likely futures, Table 9.3 summarizes both the likely changes in trade institutions and broader relationships among them. Because many of the 'trade' groupings have begun to deal with financial issues, for ease of presentation, we consider financial institutions in Table 9.3 as well and discuss their role after the Asian crisis in Section 9.3.4 below.

9.3.3 Institutional change and trade after the Asian crisis

With respect to sectoral trading arrangements, until the Asian crisis it appeared that the phasing out of VERs and other sectoral arrangements such as the MFA (as called for in the Uruguay Round negotiations), was

Table 9.3   Post-Asian crisis institutional trends in trade and finance

Organization type		pre-Asian crisis	post-Asian crisis
Sectoral arrangements (e.g. VERs, MFA, ITA)		APEC based negotiations and phasing out of VERs under the WTO	WTO based sectoral negotiations and unilateral restrictions on imports
Regional trade arrangements	EU	Deeper integration	Continued but problems with widening
	NAFTA	U.S. interest in Mexico	Stronger focus on Latin America
Regional financial arrangements	ASEAN	Efforts to develop common market	Slowing of integration efforts
	ADB	Regional lending efforts and project aid	Greater focus on playing a role in the Asian crisis
	IDB	Regional lending	Need to react to spillover from Asian crisis on Latin America
	EBRD	Regional lending	Need to react to spillover from Asian crisis on Russia
	APEC	Movement toward APEC as forum for sectoral liberalization and more general regional liberalization	Stalled trade negotiation efforts as financial issues take precedence over trade; debate over Asian Monetary Fund
	ASEM	European interest in countering U.S. push	Slowing effort in EU-East Asian cooperation

		Transatlantic business dialogue	
Transregional arrangements	US-EU		Increased pressure to undertake further sectoral liberalization in this forum and formalize arrangements
	FTAA	Efforts to move forward blocked by lack of fast track authority in U.S.	Asian crisis spillover and lack of fast track stalls FTAA and shifts focus to financial issues
	EU-Mercosur	Movement toward an accord stalled by agricultural issues	Financial crisis and agricultural issue slow progress
Global	WTO	WTO and China; new negotiations with Millenium Round of WTO	No rush on China accession; delay in new round
	IMF	Conditional short term lending with standard economic policy packages	Need to react to criticism of conditionality policies in the Asian crisis
	World Bank	Project lending and infrastructure development	Active role as a participant in Asian crisis resolution and effort to distinguish its policy proposals from IMF
Nesting or Parallel: regional within WTO and Bretton Woods institutions		Efforts to reconcile regional and sectoral accords	Growing debate over nesting regional and sectoral accords

on track. However, with the dramatic fall of exports to Asia in several product areas and an influx of imports from these countries as they attempt to service their debt, protectionist pressures are now on the rise. The escalating protectionist tensions have centred on the question of whether the US or Europe will absorb the global repercussions of the Asian crisis. The sectors of escalating protectionist sentiments between the US and the EU range from steel, air transport and cars, to bananas and beef. In air transport, massive layoffs by Boeing following sales losses in Asia have led House Minority Leader Richard Gephardt to suggest that the US should file a complaint with the WTO for the continuing subsidies in research and development that have enabled Airbus to unfairly price its aircraft.[12] And in steel, a massive influx of cheap steel imports from Asia, Brazil, Eastern Europe and Russia, driven by the appreciation of dollar against currencies of major steel-producers and by the low demand in Asia, has prompted anti-dumping charges in the US and EU.[13]

Other sectoral efforts have been taking place in an effort to liberalize trade, rather than restrict it. These arrangements, including the information technology agreements, the telecommunications accord, and the agreement on financial services, negotiated under the auspices of the WTO as a holdover of unresolved issues from the Uruguay Round. But at the same time, APEC has played an active role in setting the agenda on these issues, at least until recently, and is an issue we take up below.

Turning to regional trading arrangements, we do not expect to see significant changes as a result of the Asian crisis in the EU and NAFTA. For example, the EU effort at monetary integration has been proceeding apace. On the other hand, it might become more difficult for the EU to widen, despite current commitments to do so, because of growing protectionist pressures from industries affected by the crisis. In North America, NAFTA is continuing to guide trade in the region, and does not appear to be affected by the crisis. Among ASEAN countries, by contrast, we expect the movement to liberalize trade through AFTA to stall. This topic is taken up in the chapter by Benedetta Trivellato.

Shifting our focus to transregional arrangements, in the last couple of years, APEC members have played an important role in promoting sectoral liberalization. In an effort to push negotiations forward in information technology, APEC members agreed to an APEC wide liberalization programme in this area in Manila in 1996, and then pressed to have it become a multilateral agreement at the WTO December 1996

Singapore Ministerial meeting. The agreement calls for the phasing out of tariffs on several categories of equipment. This effort can be seen as using sectoralism regionally to pursue sectoral liberalization globally.

The US chose this path with enthusiasm, using this model to promote liberalization in a variety of other sectors. In Vancouver in 1997, ministers agreed to consider nine additional sectors: chemicals, energy-related equipment and services, environmental goods and services, forest products, medical equipment, telecommunications equipment, fish and fish products, toys, and gems and jewellery. The US led a movement to make the nine-sector liberalization a package in order to discourage countries from picking and choosing sectors based on domestic concerns. But at Kuala Lumpur at the 6th Leaders' Summit in November 1998, Japan, supported by other Asian countries who were concerned about moving forward with liberalization in their weakened economic state, refused to liberalize fishing and forestry products. This development threw the US strategy of using APEC as the vanguard for sectoral liberalization into disarray, forcing the participants to send the whole package to the WTO for negotiation. Thus, for the moment, as a result in large part of the Asian crisis, APEC's role in trade liberalization has stalled.

Unlike the APEC forum, the 25 member ASEM was originally designed to explicitly balance Asian and European co-operation in the areas of politics, security, society and economics. At the end of its inaugural summit launch at Bangkok in 1996, the 15 EU and ten Asian states agreed that ASEM need not be institutionalized. At the April 1998 London summit, the emphasis shifted dramatically with respect to issues. With the Asian crisis now at the top of the agenda, other issues on the agenda were sidelined. With an even weaker meta-regime than APEC's, the issue of its purpose continues to bedevil negotiations. Despite the adoption of a TFAP to lower non-tariff barriers between Asian and European countries, trade liberalization has taken a back seat to the financial crisis (discussed below). ASEM's current intangible institutional structure is hardly conducive to liberalization on the scale and scope of APEC, let alone the EU. Thus, contrary to what might be expected a priori, a weakening APEC has not led to a strengthening of the ASEM relationship.

Despite ongoing agricultural conflicts, the TABD has been closely involved in developing closer business relations between the EU and the US. It has helped set the agenda for the talks that led to the 1997 signing of a series of Mutual Recognition Agreements on conformity assessment. This has led to promising co-operative arrangement proposals on standards and regulatory policy in a wide range of sectors, with recent discussions centring on facilitating Internet commerce through further policy harmonization. On 11 March 1998, the TABD also provided a forum to gather support for the official Transatlantic Marketplace initiative, which later led to the Transatlantic Economic Partnership (TEP) initiative. Under this plan, the elimination of numerous technical barriers to trade, the harmonization of regulations, government procurement issues and intellectual property are now under active discussion. Yet politically salient issues are likely to be conducted in more politically driven networks such as the Transatlantic Policy Network, involving members of the European Parliament and the US Congress.

In terms of the effect of the Asian crisis, one might also have expected closer co-operation between the US and EU as a result of the weakening of the third leg of the global economy. Instead, we have seen a sharp negative spillover from the crisis on their relations. At the November 1998 TABD conference, in response to various American criticisms, the harmonization agenda fell by the wayside as EU officials used the forum to argue that the EU was doing as much as the US to absorb increased Asian imports. With US officials insisting that '[t]he US cannot be the importer of only resort'[14] and warning of pressures for protectionism, the EU responded by issuing a string of statistics on the role that it had played in the crisis. This data did not do much to convince the participants, instead setting off additional acrimony between the US and EU. Thus, as in other transregional fora, the Asian crisis has served to undermine institutional progress.

The Asian crisis has also shifted the focus of FTAA discussions as the US remains unable to move forward without fast track authority. The spillover of the crisis to Brazil and other countries in Latin America has shifted attention to financial issues. Ironically, the financial aid effort mounted through the IMF by the US has helped to counter warming relations between the EU and Mercosur. The result has been to increase the level of conflict over agricultural issues as part of EU–Mercosur free trade discussions, as the need to move closer among these groups has diminished with US financial support for Brazil.

Finally, with respect to the WTO, the prospect for a new round has been potentially endangered by the financial crisis as Asian participants must cope with their immediate short-term financial problems. On one key issue, the accession of China, the crisis has had an interesting dual effect: on the one hand, the US is pleased that the Chinese have held the line on devaluation of the yuan, preventing another round of crises; on the other hand, the continued success of the Chinese in exporting to the US market, compounded by the rise in imports from the Pacific Rim, has made its accession a more complicated issue. Thus, for the moment, a considerable further delay on Chinese accession appears to be the net result.

9.3.4 Institutional changes and finance after the Asian crisis

With respect to the Asian crisis and the subsequent financial bail out, many of the institutions in the Asia–Pacific have attempted to play an active role, but in an effort to maintain its dominance the IMF continues to resist. Beginning with its first key Asian programme after the crisis began, a total package of $17 billion to Thailand in August 1997, the IMF, supported by the US, attempted to deter any rival institutions from taking a significant role. With the US failing to participate financially in the Thai rescue package, the Japanese took the lead in September 1997 with a proposal for an Asian Monetary Fund (AMF), to be backed by $100 billion that they had lined up in commitments in the region. But the IMF and US attempted almost immediately to quash this initiative, with the Treasury leading the charge.[15] The US viewed such a fund as undercutting the conditionality imposed by the IMF. In addition, it expressed concern about the relationship that any such fund would have to the IMF. Three positions quickly emerged: the Japanese argued for some division of labour and parallel linkage between the two funds, with an AMF playing a role in crisis prevention as well. A second view, expressed by Malaysian Prime Minister Mahathir, was to have an AMF that would be independent of the IMF, thus creating a clear institutional rivalry. The third view, the IMF and American position, was that any Asian fund should be fully nested within the purview of the IMF.

The success of the US and the IMF in forestalling creation of a rival financial institution was embodied in the November 1997 Vancouver APEC summit meeting leaders' endorsement of the so-called Manila framework, agreed to by APEC financial ministers shortly before the start of the summit. The Manila framework called for the IMF to take the lead in providing emergency loans to Thailand, Indonesia and South Korea, with APEC member nations taking only a secondary role, if necessary, to supplement IMF resources on a standby basis without any formal commitment of funds. Thus, with the APEC action providing the seal of the US–IMF backed plan, the AMF idea was put on hold. During

1998, two additional formal meetings and an ad hoc one were held under the auspices of the Manila framework. Little of major significance in changing the handling of the Asian crisis took place at these meetings, but prior to the last meeting held in Kuala Lumpur, the Japanese again raised the issue of an AMF. But the US again resisted this idea. It succeeded in watering down the effort to a $10 billion fund for Asian economies, calling for creation of a new $5 billion joint initiative of the US, Japan, the World Bank and the ADB with the US contributing an additional $5 billion. Still, the Japanese continue to press forward with the notion of a separate AMF, and Finance Minister Kiichi Miyazawa this time called for regional funds in Latin America and East Europe as well. It remains to be seen if this idea will make headway, but in the current context US and IMF opposition seems certain.

Efforts by APEC to play a more significant role in crisis resolution have also been paralleled by ASEM. At their April 1998 summit in London, members agreed to create an ASEM Trust Fund. The fund, managed and administered by the World Bank, is designed to soften the impact of the crisis on Asian economies. Through October 1998, the Trust fund has raised $47 million from European members. Although a start, this effort remains extremely modest in view of the scope of the crisis. Indeed, the ASEM Trust Fund has been criticized by Germany and Japan as duplication of IMF and World Bank efforts.

Meanwhile, the Asian crisis has intensified the ongoing debate over the ADB's organizational mission: on the one hand, a sharp rise in demand for its loans has rekindled contentions over resource distribution; on the other hand, the ADB's role appears irrelevant in the midst of heavy IMF and US intervention. Total lending rose from $5.54 billion in 1996 to $9.41 billion in 1997, but has fallen to an estimated $5.98 billion in 1998, of which programme-based lending rose to 44 per cent of total loans approved this year from its historic 15 per cent.[16] The ADB's shift in priority toward regional banking reform, anti-corruption policies, and other aspects of the multilateral organizations' bailout packages has generated concern that the expansion of ADB's institutional scope in the aftermath of the Asian crisis will lead to overlap with multilateral institutions.

9.3.5 Reconciling institutions

What has been the impact of the Asian crisis on the reconciliation of institutions? As we have seen, the trading system is facing challenges from sectoral and regional arrangements. Yet ironically, the lack of progress in APEC as a result of the Asian crisis, the shift in agenda in ASEM toward financial issues, and the absence of movement in the FTAA as a result of the lack of fast track and Latin American problems, has served to strengthen the WTO as a forum for trade negotiations. As relatively un-institutionalized transregional arrangements find it difficult to move forward on trade issues, we can expect trade liberalization efforts to shift to the WTO. At the same time, however, the Asian crisis poses dangers of the revival of protectionism as Asian countries attempt to export their way back to financial health. Thus, the global effort to liberalize trade now confronts the strong unilateral temptation to block imports.

In the financial arena, the IMF has managed to retain its dominance in financial restructuring efforts. More than ever, however, the fund faces increasing criticism in its handling of the Asian crisis from voices across a wide variety of the political spectrum. Even the World Bank has turned to open criticism of the IMF, arguing that the policy of exchange rate stability at all costs through high interest policies has served to undermine the functioning of Asian economies and undermined weakened but healthy firms. In addition, as we have seen, calls for alternative approaches, including an Asian fund, continue to be made, and Japan has not desisted from backing such a programme, despite its own weakened state. Thus, the ability of the IMF to sustain a smooth nesting of subregional arrangements and possible new accords faces a growing challenge.

9.4 Conclusion

This chapter has focused on the relationship of the major regions in the global economy – the US, Asia and Europe – in the context of the Asian crisis and from an institutional perspective. The first section of the chapter presented a way of linking governance structures with economic interactions, and discussed causal arguments on the evolution of meta-regimes and international regimes. The question of how these international institutions fit with one another is a crucial issue: I suggested that institutional reconciliation can take place through two means, by parallel linkage (a division of labour) or in nested fashion (with efforts to promote compatibility in hierarchical manner).

The second section of the chapter traced the evolution of trade and financial institutions in the post World War II era until the onset of the

Asian crisis, as well as considering trade trends among the major regions. At the trade level, we have seen the oft-remarked importance of the Asian economies, in this case with a focus on the growing importance of these countries as both a source of imports and a market for the exports of major regions. With respect to institutions, we have seen the GATT continually challenged by both sectoral and regional accords, but at least until recently, it has been able to ensure that they were nested within its purview. The financial system has seen the clear dominance of the IMF and World Bank: together, these institutions have occupied nearly all the institutional space in finance, and regional banks have clearly been subordinated to the activities of these institutions.

So what might we expect to see after the Asian crisis? Section 9.3 first examined current trade trends, arguing that they pose a critical challenge for the liberal trading system. As in previous eras of high debt, the question of burden sharing that arises as countries are forced to fully pay their debt, primarily through exports, raises the question of the link between trade and finance. With financial flows dramatically falling to the region, the only alternative for these countries, barring willingness of creditors to engage in debt writedowns, is for these countries to focus on running balance of payments surpluses. From an institutional perspective, we have seen that this effort has undermined the ability of transregional arrangements such as APEC, ASEM and TABD/TPM to mediate trade liberalization efforts. Ironically, then, the immediate pressure to cope with financial problems has enhanced the position of the WTO. Yet at the same time, this development raises the spectre of unilateral trade restrictions that will undermine rule-based agreements in trade, as developed countries' governments respond to falling exports and rising imports from developing debtors.

Although institutions in trade and finance have remained robust in the face of the Asian crisis and regional institutions have thus far not undermined global ones, the broader issue of institutional reconciliation between trade and financial institutions has yet to be addressed. As in previous financial crises, the relationship between free trade and free flows of capital has become a topic of dispute. In the present crisis, the question of burden sharing between the real sector of the economy and financial institutions remains to be settled. Until additional efforts are made to find some means of truly increasing collaboration between the Bretton Woods institutions and the WTO, financial crises and protectionist backlashes will continue to haunt the global economy.

Notes

1. I would like to thank Kun-Chin Lin, Trevor Nakagawa, Moonhawk Kim, Khim Lee, Grace Wong and Deanna Wu for their research assistance and comments on this chapter.
2. See Aggarwal (1985). Zacher (1987) and (1996) uses the distinction developed in this work in his analysis of regimes.
3. In security matters, we could examine weapons flows, the movement of fissionable materials, and so on.
4. Kindleberger (1973), Gilpin (1975), and Krasner (1976). Keohane (1984) provide a valuable critique and discussion of hegemonic stability theory.
5. See Aggarwal (1985) for this discussion of 'control'.
6. See Haas (1980).
7. See Aggarwal (1998).
8. Aggarwal (1994).
9. See Weber (1994) for a discussion of the creation of the EBRD.
10. *Los Angeles Times*, 9 August 1998.
11. EC/UNCTAD (1996), p. 29.
12. *Journal of Commerce*, 12 November 1998, p. A1.
13. *Journal of Commerce*, 11 June 1998, p. 3A.
14. Vice President Albert Gore, *The Washington Post*, 7 November 1998.
15. See *Financial Times*, 14 November 1997, for details on the proposal.
16. *Financial Times*, 22 December 1998, p. 5.

References

Aggarwal, V. *Liberal Protectionism: The International Politics of Organized Textile Trade* (Berkeley and London: University of California Press, 1985).

Aggarwal, V. 'Comparing Regional Cooperation Efforts in Asia-Pacific and North America', in A. Mack and J. Ravenhill, *Pacific Cooperation: Building Economic and Security Regimes in the Asia Pacific Region* (Sydney: Allen and Unwin, 1994).

Aggarwal V. (ed.) *Institutional Designs for a Complex World: Bargaining, Linkages, and Nesting* (Ithaca: Cornell University Press, 1998).

Aggarwal, V., R. Keohane and D. Yoffie, 'The Dynamics of Negotiated Protectionism', *American Political Science Review*, Vol. 81, No. 2 (June 1987).

EC/UNCTAD, *Investing in Asia's Dynamism: European Union Direct Investment in Asia* (Luxembourg: EC/UNCTAD, 1996).

Gilpin, R. *U.S. Power and the Multinational Corporation* (New York: Basic Books, 1975).

Haas, Ernst, 'Why Collaborate? Issue-linkage and international regimes', *World Politics*, Vol. 32, No. 3, pp. 357–405, (1980).

Keohane, R. *After Hegemony: Cooperation and Discord in the World Economy* (Princeton: Princeton University Press, 1984).

Kindleberger, C.P. *The World in Depression, 1929–1939* (Berkeley: University of California Press, 1973).

Krasner, S.D. 'State Power and the Structure of International Trade' *World Politics*, Vol. 28, No. 3 (April 1976).

Weber, S. 'Origins of the European Bank for Reconstruction and Development', *International Organization*, 48 Winter (1994).

World Bank, *Global Economic Prospects and the Developing Countries: Beyond Financial Crisis, 1998/99* (Washington, D.C.: World Bank, 1998).

Zacher, M. 'Trade Gaps, Analytical Gaps: Regime Analysis and International Commodity Trade Regulation' *International Organization*, Vol. 41, No. 2, Spring (1987).

Zacher M. with B. Sutton, *Governing Global Networks: International Regimes for Transportation and Communications* (Cambridge: Cambridge University Press, 1996).

10
Conclusions

A The Economics of the Asian Crises: Roles and Myths

Fabrizio Galimberti

After the Asian Crises: the plural 'crises' in the title of this book is particularly appropriate. In fact, the unfolding of the crisis in Asia has exposed a complex mosaic of causes and effects, harking back to many unresolved issues of Asian development. An attempt is made here to untangle the different strands and to highlight those features of the Asian crisis or crises that can be useful in trying to project a future course of economic and social development. In so doing, I try to regroup these issues under three headings of convenience: quantities, qualities, and remedies.

Quantities

The issue of 'quantity' can be briefly disposed of. In a seminal article,[1] Paul Krugman, drawing on earlier work by Alwin Young of Boston University and Harry Lau of Stanford, gave his considerable intellectual weight to a new interpretation of the Asian economic miracle. This miracle – decade after decade of rapid expansion – had not been driven by a catch-up in efficiency, spurts of productivity or by the magic of 'enlightened intervention' by a benevolent state hell-bent on economic growth. No, the miracle had been obtained the old way: by applying big doses of labour and capital. Growth was input-driven, not efficiency-driven. The high savings rate of the Asian masses, honed by centuries of frugality, and the apparently inexhaustible supply of a labour force flushed out of the massive underemployment in the countryside, had provided the building blocks for a glorious period of growth.

Krugman's analysis had a disturbing implication: as the supply of inputs could not keep the same pace in the future (the labour force reserves – hidden or open – are finite quantities, and the propensity to

199

invest could not be maintained at a very high level for too long, because after all the masses cannot be fed and clothed with capital goods), the Asian 'miracle' was bound to slow down. In the event, this is what happened, even if the word 'slowdown' is not the most adequate for the sudden crumbling of 1997–98 (and beyond?).

But did the downturn occur because of a slowdown in the availability of inputs? No, the causes were quite different, and Paul Krugman honestly admitted as much (I was 80 per cent wrong, but the others were 150 per cent wrong, he characteristically conceded). Krugman's analysis still stands as an interpretation of the past and as an indication for slow structural change in the future. But it would be wrong to say that in the years to come Asian growth will be constrained by scarcities in the availability of labour and capital. Quite apart from the slack that has unfortunately arisen from the recession itself and even without a recession, growth in Asia could have gone on for a long time: the saving rate would diminish, but only slowly (in Japan, where per capita income is well above the rest of Asia, the overall saving rate was still over 30 per cent), the educational system is good and considerable reserves of manpower still exist, both in the countryside and among women. Quantities of labour and capital will not be a limiting factor in the future.

Qualities

The economic problem of Asia is a problem with qualities, not quantities. But a qualification is required. Like a glass half-full or half-empty, Asian virtues and vices are not unequivocal. In fact, much of Asia's problems stem from the virtues of yesteryear turning sour and becoming a hindrance to expansion along the new developmental roads mapped by the pressures of social change and technology. The first hint may be found in the problems of Atlantic economies. It has become part of received wisdom to say that growth in Western advanced economies needs more flexibility in labour and product markets. Sand has been turned into chips and chips have changed the way the economy operates. Hardware and software have empowered the individual, have lowered the break-even point for many lines of business, have created new jobs and whole new sectors: resources must be permitted to flow from declining to rising areas – both sectoral and geographical. The new 'division of labour' – both within and without nations – demands it; and the progress of technology – computers, telecommunications, transports – allows such redistribution of resources to happen. This, it was said, is by now received wisdom in Western policymaking. But, if this analysis and these prescriptions are correct, what are the implications for Eastern policymaking?

The few last decades have seen impressive economic growth in Asia. So impressive, in fact, that the Asian model has been studied as a new paradigm for growth. And the 'Asian values' – a mixture of discipline, hard work, capacity to fall into line and strive for the common good, leavened by wise government guidance – have been hailed as almost an alternative way to organize an economic system, a 'third way', beyond the market economy and the command economy. Now, the other side of the coin has been uncovered. The 'Asian values', as described, turned out to be 'fair weather' values. They could provide dynamism and impetus, but only as long as growth was there to bear fruits and mask tensions. Government guidance could – and did – degenerate into cronyism and sometimes nepotism and corruption. But in a more profound sense the Asian model was called into question. This model was based on a mould of social cohesion – either spontaneous or enforced by the uneven distribution of power which bred submissiveness – and, as long as growth was proceeding *à la* Krugman, by the brute force of heavy doses of capital and labour, discipline and easily available factors of production could carry the day: expansion was assured.

Two deep currents, however – the pressures of technology and democracy – were undermining that model. Growth needed an organization of society which gave more emphasis to the power of the individual. The fragments of collectivism present in many Asian societies – for example, the lifetime employment system in Japan, the government meddling into the allocation of bank credit in many countries – had suddenly outlived their usefulness; they had become an obstacle to the reallocation of resources which was needed given the changes in the path of economic growth. The restructuring of the world economy under the pressures of a technological and managerial revolution – a phase of 'creative destruction', a 'deep breath' of capitalist development, to use two expressions by Joseph Schumpeter – had caught the Asian economies with the wrong foot forward. And when the accident happened, in mid 1997 – Thailand and other countries had been running too fast, current deficits had developed and reckless lending had created lots of bad debts – a hiccup quickly developed into a pneumonia.

That 'growth accident' could have turned into a simple correction. But it became a fully-fledged crisis because it exposed a deeper malaise in the quality of Asian development. The 'spontaneous collectivism' of Asian attitudes had sinned by commission and by omission.

By commission, because the unholy alliance between the banks and the state had produced a financial system incapable of performing the basic function of the intermediaries: to allocate savings to the best uses. This failure of market signals had been slowly building up, until the misdirection of the resources – too much speculative construction, too many loans to favoured big companies, too much investment in the financial system itself – became so evident that sparked off a proper confidence crisis.

By omission, because the emphasis on social and family ties had prevented the emergence of a modern safety net. The share of social expenditure in GDP is not necessarily an adequate indicator of a 'caring' government. After all, the best safety net is the one provided by a good job. If a country succeeds in expanding employment and giving access to adequate insurance against the risks of old age and illness, a low share of social expenditure is a measure of success and not of ruthlessness. But it is equally true that the adequacy of a safety net must be judged when the times are lean. In the decades of roaring growth the absence of an adequate system of income support had gone unnoticed: there was no need for it. Not only: the combination of low tax rates and a minimal welfare system had received much acclaim, leading to large-scale inflows of capital, anxious to be invested in such a 'promising' environment. But, when the 'accident waiting to happen' did indeed happen, the absence of a safety net became a liability, compounding the turbulence, and making the disturbance spill over from the economic to the social and political scene. It was an illusion to think that rapid urbanization could be reversed, that the newly impoverished urban masses could go back to the countryside if the economy spun into a recession. Maybe the saddest and meanest policy measure of the Asian crisis was the one taken by the Indonesian government when the economy went into a tailspin: the government reduced train ticket prices for the trip from Jakarta to the countryside, and increased them for the reverse journey.

The Asian economies, in summary, were not brought down by the usual trappings of an unsustainable spurt of growth: developing external imbalances, wage pressures, asset price bubbles, and so on. These could have been dealt with by the usual remedies: restrictive policies and international financial support. Asian economies were brought down by a systemic crisis: by the realization – slowly building up at first, flaring up thereafter – that the 'Asian model' had some fundamental flaws and was unable to cope with a world economy which prized individual entrepreneurship and required freely circulating capital, but demanded at the same time that the unfettered mobility of capital be tempered by robust national financial structures.

Japan: a special (?) case

Is Japan a special case in this broad canvas of Asian economic woes? It is useful to dwell both on the similarities and the differences between Japan and its Asian brethren. And the similarities are more striking than the differences. The main difference is in the external position. Japan enjoys (probably is not the right word) a huge external surplus. An annual flow of over US$ 100 billion keeps adding to a stock of reserves which is already the highest in the world. But the main similarity is in the 'hidden collectivism' of Japan's economic make-up. From the lifetime employment system, which is now crumbling under the weight of the recession, to the 'thin' welfare system (which is not, as in Indonesia, tolerating outright poverty, but which nevertheless snuffs out the propensity to consume because its own thinness breeds worries about the future), from the bloated financial system to the cross-shareholdings which prop up – in an embrace which could be deadly – lenders and borrowers, from the inefficient tertiary sector (Asian countries embraced openness in external trade of goods, but kept services sheltered from the forces of competition) to an ineffectual institutional make-up (politics and parliament) which lacked transparency and accountability.

To all this, Japan adds a dubious distinction. Right now, the Japanese economy reminds one of that wonderful description, by P.G. Wodehouse, of a noisy slurping by an illmannered guest: 'The way he eats soup' wrote Wodehouse 'alters one's whole conception of man as Natures's last word.' Similarly, the way the Japanese economy (mis)behaves alters one whole's conception of the inherent superiority of the market economy. Japan is supposed to be a market economy; and economics has long held that the economic cycle is not doomed, at the lower turning point, to fall into a recessionary spiral; there are self-stabilizing forces which lead an economy to rebound; and even if these fail, policymaking has in its weaponry the ways and means to stimulate an economy that refuses to recuperate on its own. Alas, all this does not seem to apply in today's Japan. Consumers and producers are lethargic: the propensity to spend is languishing and no amount of stimulation – monetary and fiscal – seems to be able to induce them to part with their income or their savings. And Japan seems to be digging itself ever deeper into a morass of disequilibria: ineffective fiscal stimuli are adding to the public deficit, the weight of public debt is soaring and demography is meanwhile conspiring to create, through the rapid ageing of society, a financial nightmare for future budget planners.

It is too easy to see in Japan's quandary a textbook illustration of the 'liquidity trap'. Much more is at stake than the theoretical inability of monetary policy to push on a string. It is the Japanese mindset – a hesitancy to strike on your own and refuse conformity – that is ill-suited to face a restructuring of the economy away from the export sector and towards goods and services intended for domestic demand. It is the preoccupations for a future with too many pensioners and not enough earners which is forcing a people of savers to save even more. It is the imperfect grafting of parliamentary democracy on to an old feudal system and a 'client–server' relation between politics and big business which is stalling decisionmaking in a web of reciprocal interdictions.

The remedies

Remedies, of course, are more easily formulated than implemented. And all the more so when the problems do not reside in 'what we do' but in 'what we are'. The healing of the Asian economies will take a long time, and we can see today two possible roads towards that healing process. The first road is what we can call the 'learning by doing' process, or, in a less learned way, the 'scalded cat' approach. The crisis has been a painful reminder that something did not work in the way those economies operated. In a few cases, the reminder has been so painful – financially and socially – that governments have been toppled and a ruling class been replaced. Change has not been for the sake of change: change has occurred because it was felt that a new approach was needed, that the practices of cronyism in the allocation of economic favours could only lead to an unhealthy economy. Hopefully, the new governments will abide by market values, enhance openness and favour liberalization, especially in financial markets, which also need better prudential supervision. And what has been called the 'risk-averting mindset' might slowly change: the new generations belong already to a different mould.

In Asia the stabilization of the currencies at lower values has set the stage for a massive adjustment of the current balances of the area. The governments of the worst hit countries will have to tread a razor-thin line between the transfer of resource in favour of the export sector and the assistance to displaced workers and to the many millions that have suffered a relapse into poverty. The relatively good fiscal position at the onset of the crisis could facilitate this re-orientation of resources.

In countries like China or India the challenge is different again. In a sense, they compound the threat of the Asian crisis with the problems of the 'transition economies' (from a command or a pre-capitalistic economy to a market economy). In the two most populous countries in the world strong economic growth is much more than desirable: they are the 'bicycle economies', that are condemned to run as the only way to avoid falling. In China, for example, the restructuring of the state firms, replete with redundant labour, would create so much unemployment that strong growth elsewhere becomes the only viable policy option. But all of Asia is condemned to grow again. And the years to come will see the unfolding of an historical clash: between a 'sentence to grow' on one side, and a complex and tiresome process of political reform, cultural change and financial restructuring on the other side.

Note

1. P. Krugman, 'The Myth of Asia's Miracle', *Foreign Affairs*, (November 1994).

B After the Asian Crises: Open Issues

Maria Weber

For years East Asia succeeded in converting high growth rates into improvements in welfare. 'The miracle was real and tangible: the region reduced the number of people living in poverty by half in the last twenty years'.[1] Two years on, the level of devastation in the aftermath of the Asian crisis is high, with tens of millions of people likely to be pushed below the poverty line. The crisis has assumed systemic proportions in Indonesia, Malaysia, Thailand and South Korea, where many banks and firms have been forced into insolvency. However the economic contraction is aggravating social vulnerabilities.[2] The effects of the crisis are acute in Indonesia and severe in Thailand, Korea and Malaysia. In these countries, there is a real risk of ethnic and religious conflicts breaking out. Muslim attacks on the Christian community in Indonesia may only be the beginning of a 'clash of civilizations' in a part of the world in which economic growth had for years assured the peaceful cohabitation of different ethnic groups and religions. A further danger is political instability. Although apparently strong the regimes of these countries are in actual fact weak. There is a lack of democracy and politics often only means corruption. Political institutions are too young to assure political stability. The declining role of some charismatic leaders may accelerate a process of political instability not only in these countries but elsewhere in the region.

Furthermore, the economic crisis has exposed the current weakness of the regional institutions. The ASEAN, one of the most important and long-standing regional associations, has been unable to propose a solution to bail out this region. It's response to the crisis, including both immediate crisis management of unstable financial markets and its policy for longer-term adjustment and economy restructuring seemed cumbersome, inefficient and inadequate. This raises some questions about the role of regional co-operation frameworks, and of ASEAN in particular, as it has been played out in the recent past, and as it could be in the future.

The absence of real regional security organizations implies that a balance of power between the main players in the region remains absolutely crucial. This equilibrium appears to be determined by the shifting relationships between China, Japan and the US, after the decline, for the time being at least, of the former SU as an Asian power. As Marta Dassù underlines, the most intriguing factor is represented by China. China has obtained some immediate benefits from the Asian crisis in as much as it has offered the Chinese leadership a great opportunity to reinforce its regional role and to stake its claim as one of the terms of reference in the international system being shaped from the great disorder following the end of the cold war. The most probable scenario, as Maria Weber and Renzo Cavalieri write, is that of greater integration of China with the rest of the world and a substantial Chinese hegemony within the Asian region, also thanks to the network of *overseas Chinese*. A powerful China could upset the already complex equilibrium between Japan, China and SEA. For many decades the US tried to contain China, worrying about the risk of a communist expansion in the area. On the other hand, China's significance within an increasingly important Asia is probably too great to dismiss its attempts to socialize within the international community, as Filippo Andreatta writes.

Other countries are going through a process of reappraisal of their international and security role. The most important is Japan, who is cautiously attempting to raise international profile by seeking a permanent seat in the UN Security Council. Japan is undergoing a confusing process of domestic political change, which may slow down the pace of its foreign policy change. As Corrado Molteni writes, Japan is striving to develop particularly strong ties with ASEAN, providing a clear indication of its strategic priorities and goals in the region.

Central and South Asia have remained on the periphery of the crisis. Paolo Panico and Gianni Vaggi analyze SA (India, Pakistan and Bangladesh), where economic growth in the last 20 years has been lower than that in the rest of Asia. These economies are still relatively closed to foreign trade and are struggling to increase their share of world trade. The hostilities between India and her two neighbours, Pakistan and Bangladesh, make the risk of war in SA possible, and this is a handicap for the future success of this region. The Asian crisis does not seem to have had any particular impact on Central Asia. As Piacentini and

Pastori underline, the approach to this region differs significantly from the approach to other Asian regions. Central Asia is still feeling the shockwaves of the collapse of the SU and the consequent power-vacuum.

Another important issue for the future of Asia is the environment. Maria Julia Trombetta points out that environmental problems play a growing role in Asia; they could threaten regional stability and compromise further economic development. Competition for renewable resources, flows of refugees and losses in agricultural productivity due to environmental degradation, could add new dimensions to the social crisis or could increase the likelihood of violent conflicts. On the other hand awareness of environmental problems and the perception of ecological interdependence could improve regional co-operation and boost confidence building. Environmental problems differ widely from region to region, as do their security and trade implications. In NEA environmental dumping and 'pollution havens' are a probable scenario, not only between industrialized and developing countries but also within the latter, especially in Russia and along the Chinese borders. In SA latent conflicts, especially between India and Pakistan or between India and Bangladesh, could be exasperated by environmental change, competition for fresh water or flows of refugees, while in CA, in spite of the seriousness of the problems, which already threaten health and productivity, environmental issues take second place and conflicts are frozen.

Benedetta Trivellato underlines that the crisis has left SEA with two choices. One is to introduce more measures to secure a stable internal economic environment and reduce the risk coming from external sources. The other possibility is to proceed on the road to integration and co-operation, ensuring that closer and faster integration is further developed in the framework of an open multilateral trading system. The second choice would be the better one: an open market can secure outside support for ASEAN, which is important to maintain sustainable growth.

Regional institutions could have played an important role in the recovery of Asia, but their capability to react to the crisis was weak. ASEAN could not produce an effective response to the crisis: the consensual decisionmaking process blocked many decisions. ASEAN countries have always been against deeper integration and more formalized institutions. For the future, ASEAN will improve its efficacy by introducing some changes in its decisionmaking structure, possibly drawing from other experiences, like those of the EU. The other main sub-regional institution for mutual co-operation in Asia is the SAARC, established in 1985 between India, Pakistan, Bangladesh, Sri Lanka, Bhutan, Nepal and the Maldives. With regard to trade and security, the two main dimensions of the world's major international associations of this kind, SAARC cannot by any means be considered a significant regional player. As far as security is concerned, India has open borders with Nepal but disputes still exist with all the major partners of SAARC (Pakistan, Bangladesh and Sri Lanka). This actually prevents the effective functioning of the SAARC.

Vinod Aggarwal underlines the fact that while trade and finance institutions have remained stable despite the Asian crisis and, so far, regional institutions have not undermined global ones, the broader issue of reconciliation between trade and financial institutions remains to be addressed. As in previous financial crises, the relationship between free trade and free flows of capital has become a topic of dispute. In the present crisis, the question of burden-sharing between the real economy and financial institutions remains to be settled. Until additional efforts are made to find some means of truly increasing collaboration between the Bretton Woods institutions and the WTO, financial crises and protectionist backlashes will continue to haunt the global economy.

Globalization does not represent the key either to order and stability or to freedom and democracy. The prevailing international balance of interests appears such that we can speak, at the dawn of the third millennium, in terms of a gradual evolution towards new social and political structures, which in turn are an expression of a rational balance of power and of economic interests heralding a new order and a new future.

Notes

1. World Bank, *East Asia. The Road to Recovery*, Washington D.C., p. 2 (1998).
2. World Bank, *Social Consequences of the East Asian Financial Crisis*, Washington D.C. (1998).

Index

Afghanistan, xix, 15, 70, 74, 77–81, 91, 98, 162
APEC, xxii, 65, 131, 146, 163, 173, 181–2, 190, 191, 193, 195
ASEAN, xvii, xix, xx, 3, 4, 44, 65, 66, 96, 114, 131, 146, 148, 149, 154, 163, 169, 181, 190, 206, 207, 208
ASEM, xxii, 155, 181, 191, 194, 195, 196

Bangladesh, xix, xx, 96, 97, 112, 113, 132, 207, 208, 209
Bank system, reform of
  in China, 4, 5, 6
  in Japan, 30, 31–5, 36–9

Cambodia, xix, 50, 59, 62, 65, 129, 136, 162, 166
Central Asia, xvi, xvii, xix, xxi, 70–92, 133–6
  actors, main, 70–3; *see also* Kazakhstan; Kyrgyzstan; Tajikistan; Turkmenistan; Uzbekistan
  actors, peripheral, 73–81; *see also* Afghanistan; Iran; Pakistan; Russia
  economic issues, 82–92
  environmental issues, 133–6
  geopolitical and security issues, 70–82
  independence of Central Asia Republics, questions raised by, 70–3
  and China, 89–90
  and Russia, 73–7, 79, 82–6
  and West, 87–8
China, xvi, xvii, xviii, xxi, 3–26, 43–4, 64–5, 80–2, 84, 89–90, 125–8, 139–41, 144–56, 158–72, 161–70, 173, 176, 180–1, 185, 192, 205, 206–7

Autonomous Regions: institutional issues, 7, 9–13; minorities protection, 13–17; *see also* Tibet; Xinjiang
  centre-periphery relationships, 7–21
  economic performance, 3–5
  environmental issues, 125–8
  reunification issue *see* Taiwan
  security issues, 147–52 *compare* international security
  Special Administrative Regions *see* Hong Kong
  State owned enterprises (SOEs) reform of, 4, 6, 7, 24
  Western relations with C., 128–51, 158–72
  and Japan, 150–2
  and US, 163–70
  and WTO, 144, 150, 155, 192
  see also: bank system; ethnic issues; international system; regionalism
CIS *see* Russia
crises
  financial/economic dimension, xvi, 4, 5, 22, 23, 28, 30, 33–41, 43–5, 50–61, 75, 81–2, 96, 98, 101, 104, 106, 109, 111, 119, 127, 129–31, 139–40, 142–5, 148–51, 154, 159, 162, 168, 169, 173, 176, 184, 186–7, 190–6, 202, 204, 206, 207, 208; break-up/evolution, 50–2
  effect on global economy, 185–95
  environmental, 119–36
  security implication of, 139–40, 147–55
  social-political dimension, 50–61, 140–7

democracy, 7, 19, 20–4, 54, 81, 102, 114, 142, 162, 167, 170, 184, 201, 204
drug traffic, 77, 79–80, 112

economic issues, *see under individual countries or regions*; *see also* global economy
environment, 119–38
  and economic globalization, 121
  and NEA, 124–9
  and SEA, 129–32
  and security, 120
  see also under CA; China; Japan; SA
ethnic issues, 8, 13, 14, 52, 71, 72, 76, 80, 81, 89, 102, 145, 146, 149
  ethnic Chinese, 52, 145, 146, 149
  ethnic Slavic, 71, 76, 86
  minorities, 8, 13, 14, 71, 74, 77
Europe *see* European Union
European Union, xviii, xx, 41, 75, 98, 113, 114, 132, 136, 148, 155, 156, 163, 173, 179, 180–1, 185, 186, 190–2, 208

global economy, 173–96
  after the Asian crisis, 185–95
  institutional evolution/trends: in finance, 183–4, 193–5; in trade, 180–3, 186, 187–95
  governance structure, 174–9
  trade interaction, 176, 180
globalization, 70, 74, 82, 119–21, 123–5, 173–4, 176, 184, 186–7, 190, 192, 195, 196

Hong Kong, xvi, xvii, xxiii, 3, 5, 8, 9, 16, 17–20, 23, 24, 25, 60, 146, 148, 166, 179
human rights, 10, 65, 150, 165, 168, 169

IMF, xviii, 44–6, 51–3, 56, 61–2, 75, 88, 106, 143, 144, 146, 149, 151, 183–4, 192–6
India, xix, xx, 78–81, 96–114, 132, 154, 161, 162, 164, 179, 205, 207, 208, 209
Indochina, 59–61, 162 *see also* Cambodia; Laos; Myanmar; Vietnam
Indonesia, xvi, xvii, xviii, 4, 50–6, 59, 64, 67, 129, 130, 131, 141–3,
145, 146, 149, 162, 178, 181, 193, 206
East Timor, 143
international disputes *see under* international security
international institution
  transregional arrangements, 173, 181, 190, 192, 195, 196
  and environment, 121–3
  see also global economy; regimes
international security
  international disputes, 23, 24, 25, 64, 113, 114, 124, 140, 146, 147, 152, 162, 163, 166, 169, 209; Mischief Rief, 147; the Kurile Islands, 124, 163; the Paracel Islands, 147, 163; the Senkaku Islands, 124, 163; the Spratly Islands, 24, 25, 64, 147, 163, 166, 169; Tekeskima Rocks, 163
  nuclear proliferation, 80, 140, 155, 161, 166, 168
  nuclear tests, xvi, xx, 96, 109, 149, 161
  UN Security Council, role of, 155
  and Asian Crises, *see under* crises
international system
  Asian balance of power, 140, 146–7, 152–3, 161, 163, 168
  Asian international system/the Asian triangle, 150–2
  East Asia sub-system, 160–3
  regional hegemony, 159, 175; China, 22, 23, 147, 150, 152, 155, 169; India, 112–14; Russia, 152–4; US, 155
Iran, xix, 70, 74, 76–9, 90, 91, 162, 166, 178
Islam, 8, 14, 15, 25, 54, 56, 73–4, 77–81, 89, 90
  taliban regime, 15, 79–81
  Islamic law, 81

Japan, xvi, xvii, xviii, xxi, 3, 25–6, 28–44, 56, 62–5, 101–2, 128–9, 139–40, 148–52, 154, 156, 159, 162, 164, 169, 173, 179–81,

Japan – *continued*
 184–6, 191, 193–5, 200–1, 203–4,
 207
 crisis of the banking sector,
 30–5
 structural reforms, 36–43
 environmental issues, 128–9
 international role of J., 43–4

Kazakhstan, xix, 70, 72, 82–5, 87–91,
 135, 153
 see also under Central Asia
Koreas
 North K., xvi, 98, 123, 124, 143,
 155, 178
 South K., xvii, xviii, 3, 4, 28, 44–6,
 60, 65, 82, 96, 99–102, 109,
 112, 124, 140, 141, 145, 152–3,
 158, 162, 163, 169, 178, 181,
 193, 206
 unification of, xxi, 148, 149
Kyrgyzstan, xix, 70, 80, 80–91, 133
 see also under Central Asia

Laos, xix, 50, 59–61, 63, 67, 130

Malaysia, xvi, xviii, xix, 24, 50–7, 59,
 64, 67–8, 114, 129, 131, 142–6,
 148, 163, 179, 206
Myanmar, xix, 50, 59–67, 127, 143,
 162

nuclear tests, *see under* international
 security
nuclear proliferation, *see under*
 international security
North Korea, *see under* Koreas

Pakistan, xvi, xix, xx, 70, 74, 76–81,
 91, 96, 97–8, 112, 113, 132, 161,
 166, 179, 207, 208
Philippine, xvi, xix, 59

regime
 international, 121, 175, 181
 meta-regime, 175, 181, 191
regionalism, xxi, 9, 65, 151, 173,
 180–2
 China, 9

SEA, 65, 151
 see also Global economy
Russia, xvi, xix, xx, 25, 70, 73–5,
 78–9, 82–6, 90–2, 98, 107,
 111, 112, 124, 126, 135, 136,
 152–4, 159, 162–5, 179, 190, 208
 security issues, *see* environment
 and security; international
 security

Singapore, xvi, xvii, xix, xx, 23, 50,
 57, 58, 60, 63, 67, 114, 131, 141,
 142, 143
South Asia, xvi, xvii, xix, xx, 96–114,
 132, 207
 economic issues, 96–114
 environmental issues, 132
 see also under India; Pakistan
South Korea, *see under* Koreas
Soviet Union, *see* Russia

Taiwan, xvii, xxi, 3, 4, 8, 9, 18–20,
 23–6, 102, 144–8, 162, 163, 166,
 169, 179, 185
 see also under Central Asia
Tajikistan, xix, 15, 70, 76–9, 82, 83,
 85, 87, 133, 134, 162
 see also under Central Asia
Thailand, xvi, xvii, xviii, 4, 50–1, 59,
 63–4, 67, 100, 109, 129–31,
 141–5, 152, 179, 193, 201, 206
Tibet, xvii, 8–9, 13, 15–17
 see also China
Turkmenistan, xix, 25, 70, 77, 78, 83,
 85, 87, 90, 133–5
 see also under Central Asia

United States, 22, 23, 30, 40–4, 59,
 65, 76, 81, 82, 88, 98, 109, 110,
 114, 121, 122, 127, 128,
 144–56, 159–66, 173, 179, 195,
 207
Uzbekistan, xix, 70, 72, 77, 79, 82–9,
 133–4
 see also under Central Asia

Vietnam, xix, 24, 50, 59–63, 67, 114,
 129–30, 143, 146–7, 154, 162,
 163, 164, 179, 185

World Bank, 22, 61, 75, 98, 99, 103, 106, 110, 127, 130, 183, 184, 186, 194–6
World Trade Organization
GATT, 122, 180, 182, 183, 184
WTO, xxi, xxii, 22, 23, 24, 121, 144, 150, 155, 163, 165, 167, 168, 181, 184–7, 190–2, 195–6

Xinjiang, xvii, 8, 9, 13, 14–16, 25, 89, 153
see also China